Sovereignty

Sovereignty

ORGANIZED HYPOCRISY

Stephen D. Krasner

PRINCETON UNIVERSITY PRESS

PRINCETON, NEW JERSEY

Copyright © 1999 by Princeton University Press
Published by Princeton University Press, 41 William Street,
Princeton, New Jersey 08540
In the United Kingdom: Princeton University Press,
Chichester, West Sussex

All Rights Reserved.
Krasner, Stephen D., 1942–

Sovereignty: organized hypocrisy/Stephen D. Krasner.
p.   cm.
Includes bibliographical references and index.
ISBN 0–691–00702–0 (cl.: alk. paper). — ISBN 0–691–00711–X (pbk.: alk. paper)
1. Sovereignty.   I. Title.
KZ4041.K73   1999

320.1'5—dc21   99-12204 CIP

This book has been composed in Galliard

The paper used in this publication meets the minimum requirements
of ANSI/NISO Z39.48-1992 (R1997) (*Permanence of Paper*)

http://pup.princeton.edu

Printed in the United States of America

10 9 8 7 6 5 4 3 2 1

10 9 8 7 6 5 4 3 2
(pbk).

FOR DANIEL AND RACHEL

Who do change

Contents

Acknowledgments

WHEN I began this study I was under no illusions about how recalcitrant the whole question of sovereignty might be to systematic and persuasive analysis. My expectations were borne out. This project went through many iterations and has benefited from the generous comments of many scholars, often at seminars from which I could not always reconstruct the remarks of specific individuals, some of whom I have no doubt failed to recognize. My friend and colleague Peter Katzenstein read through the entire manuscript and provided not only astute observations about the general theoretical presentation but also specific advice about organization and presentation. Hendryk Spruyt also was kind enough to peruse the entire project and to provide many helpful suggestions. It is a cliché, and conveniently vague, to acknowledge standing on the shoulders of giants, but what is more true is the extent to which we, as scholars, depend upon the stimulation provided by our immediate colleagues even in this age of electronic communication. The idea of using the concept of organized hypocrisy was suggested to me by John Meyer after I had struggled for many years to find an appropriate conceptualization for what seemed to me the defining characteristic of Westphalian sovereignty—the existence of durable principles and norms, which were also frequently compromised. Masahiko Aoki saved me from what would have been an embarrassing conceptual blunder.

The following people were kind enough to comment on earlier, many many, earlier versions of this project: David Abernethy, Delia Boylan, Bruce Bueno de Mesquita, Ellen Comisso, Lynn Eden, Tanisha Fazal, John Ferejohn, Martha Finnemore, Geoffrey Garrett, Judith Goldstein, Philip Genschel, Ronald Jepperson, Robert Keohane, Joseph Lepgold, Lisa Martin, Rose McDermott, James Morrow, Michael Oksenberg, Francisco Ramirez, Condoleezza Rice, Philip Roeder, Philippe Schmitter, Heiner Schulz, Beth Simmons, James Smith, Duncan Snidal, Georg Sorensen, Ole Waever, and Monika Wohlfeld.

This project was begun during a year when I was a Fellow at the Center for Advanced Study in the Behavioral Sciences, which was supported by the National Science Foundation, grant no. BNS-8700864. Walter Falcon, the director of the Institute for International Studies at Stanford until 1998 where I am a Senior Fellow, has been unfailing in his support.

Tanisha Fazal, Daniel Froats, Erica Gould, Heiner Schulz, James Smith, and Chris Way provided invaluable research assistance.

Sovereignty

CHAPTER 1

Sovereignty and Its Discontents

SOME ANALYSTS have argued that sovereignty is being eroded by one aspect of the contemporary international system, globalization, and others that it is being sustained, even in states whose governments have only the most limited resources, by another aspect of the system, the mutual recognition and shared expectations generated by international society. Some have pointed out that the scope of state authority has increased over time, and others that the ability of the state to exercise effective control is eroding. Some have suggested that new norms, such as universal human rights, represent a fundamental break with the past, while others see these values as merely a manifestation of the preferences of the powerful. Some students of international politics take sovereignty as an analytic assumption, others as a description of the practice of actors, and still others as a generative grammar.[1]

This muddle in part reflects the fact that the term "sovereignty" has been used in different ways, and in part it reveals the failure to recognize that the norms and rules of any international institutional system, including the sovereign state system, will have limited influence and always be subject to challenge because of logical contradictions (nonintervention versus promoting democracy, for instance), the absence of any institutional arrangement for authoritatively resolving conflicts (the definition of an international system), power asymmetries among principal actors, notably states, and the differing incentives confronting individual rulers. In the international environment actions will not tightly conform with any given set of norms regardless of which set is chosen. The justification for challenging specific norms may change over time but the challenge will be persistent.

The term sovereignty has been used in four different ways—international legal sovereignty, Westphalian sovereignty, domestic sovereignty, and interdependence sovereignty. International legal sovereignty refers to the practices associated with mutual recognition, usually between territorial entities that have formal juridical independence. Westphalian sover-

---

[1] Contrast Cerny 1990, 86–87, with Rosenau 1990, 13. For typical statements about the erosion of sovereignty see Group of Lisbon 1995, 9; Fowler and Bunck 1995, 137–38, Gottlieb 1993. For the importance of international society, see Bull 1977; Jackson 1990.

eignty refers to political organization based on the exclusion of external actors from authority structures within a given territory. Domestic sovereignty refers to the formal organization of political authority within the state and the ability of public authorities to exercise effective control within the borders of their own polity. Finally, interdependence sovereignty refers to the ability of public authorities to regulate the flow of information, ideas, goods, people, pollutants, or capital across the borders of their state.

International legal sovereignty and Westphalian sovereignty involve issues of authority and legitimacy, but not control. They both have distinct rules or logics of appropriateness. The rule for international legal sovereignty is that recognition is extended to territorial entities that have formal juridical independence. The rule for Westphalian sovereignty is the exclusion of external actors, whether de facto or de jure, from the territory of a state. Domestic sovereignty involves both authority and control, both the specification of legitimate authority within a polity and the extent to which that authority can be effectively exercised. Interdependence sovereignty is exclusively concerned with control and not authority, with the capacity of a state to regulate movements across its borders.[2]

The various kinds of sovereignty do not necessarily covary. A state can have one but not the other. The exercise of one kind of sovereignty—for instance, international legal sovereignty—can undermine another kind of sovereignty, such as Westphalian sovereignty, if the rulers of a state enter into an agreement that recognizes external authority structures, as has been the case for the members of the European Union. A state such as Taiwan can have Westphalian sovereignty, but not international legal sovereignty. A state can have international legal sovereignty, be recognized by other states, but have only the most limited domestic sovereignty either in the sense of an established structure of authority or the ability of its rulers to exercise control over what is going on within their own territory. In the 1990s some failed states in Africa, such as Somalia, served as unfortunate examples. A state can have international legal, Westphalian, and established domestic authority structures and still have very limited ability to regulate cross-border flows and their consequent domestic impacts, a situation that many contemporary observers conceive of as a result of globalization.

This study focuses primarily on Westphalian sovereignty and, to a lesser extent, on international legal sovereignty. Domestic authority and control and the regulation of transborder movements are examined only insofar

---

[2] See Thomson 1995 for a lucid elaboration of the contrast between authority and control. The distinction between a logic of appropriateness and a logic of consequences is developed by March and Olsen 1998 and March 1994.

as they impinge on questions associated with recognition and the exclusion of external actors from domestic authority structures.

This study does not attempt to explain the evolution or development of the international system over the millennia. I offer no explanation for the displacement of other institutional forms, such as the Holy Roman Empire, the Chinese tributary system, or the Hanseatic League by an international system in which states are the most prevalent organizational unit.[3] Rather, this study is an effort to understand what sovereign statehood has meant in actual practice with regard to international legal and Westphalian sovereignty.

All political and social environments are characterized by two logics of actions, what James March and Johan Olsen have called logics of expected consequences and logics of appropriateness. Logics of consequences see political action and outcomes, including institutions, as the product of rational calculating behavior designed to maximize a given set of unexplained preferences. Classical game theory and neoclassical economics are well-known examples. Logics of appropriateness understand political action as a product of rules, roles, and identities that stipulate appropriate behavior in given situations. The question is not how can I maximize my self-interest but rather, given who or what I am, how should I act in this particular circumstance. Various sociological approaches offer examples.[4]

These two logics are not mutually incompatible but their importance varies across environments. If a logic of appropriateness is unambiguous and the consequences of alternative courses of action unclear, the behavior of actors (primarily rulers for this study) is likely to be determined by their roles. If actors find themselves in a situation in which they have multiple and contradictory roles and rules, or no rules at all, but the results of different courses of action are obvious, a logic of consequences will prevail.[5] In a well-established domestic polity a logic of appropriateness will weigh heavily, although within the confines imposed by specific roles (president, general, senator, voter) actors will also calculate the course of action that will maximize their interests. Even in very well settled situations, such as Swedish local governments, which Nils Brunsson uses to motivate his study of what he has ingeniously termed the organization of hypocrisy, actors never fully conform with the logic of appropriateness associated with their specific roles; they also engage in purely instrumental behavior generated by a logic of expected consequences.[6]

---

[3] See Tilly 1990a, Spruyt 1994, and Strang 1991 for general discussions of the evolution of institutional forms in the European and later global international system over the last millennium.

[4] March and Olsen 1989, 24–26; March 1994, 57–58; March and Olsen 1998.

[5] March and Olsen 1998.

[6] Brunsson 1989

The basic contention of this study is that the international system is an environment in which the logics of consequences dominate the logics of appropriateness. Actors embody multiple roles, such as head of state, diplomatic representative, government leader, party organizer, ethnic representative, revolutionary avatar, or religious prophet, that imply conflicting rules for action. International rules can be contradictory—nonintervention as opposed to the protection of human rights, for example—and there is no authority structure to adjudicate such controversies. In most cases domestic roles will be more compelling than international ones, because domestic rather than international logics of appropriateness are most likely to dominate the self-conceptualization of any political leader. Moreover, the international system is characterized by power asymmetries. Stronger actors can, in some cases, conquer weaker ones, eliminating the existence of a particular state, although not necessarily challenging the general principles associated with Westphalian or international legal sovereignty. Conquest simply changes borders. But rulers might also choose to reconfigure domestic authority structures in other states, accepting their juridical independence but compromising their de facto autonomy, a policy that does violate Westphalian sovereignty. Stronger states can pick and choose among different rules selecting the one that best suits their instrumental objectives, as the European powers did during the era of colonialism when they "resuscitated pre-Westphalian forms of divided sovereignty" such as protectorates and subordinate states.[7] In the international environment roles and rules are not irrelevant. Rulers do have to give reasons for their actions, but their audiences are usually domestic. Norms in the international system will be less constraining than would be the case in other political settings because of conflicting logics of appropriateness, the absence of mechanisms for deciding among competing rules, and power asymmetries among states.

The prevailing approaches to international politics in the United States, neorealism and neoliberalism, properly deploy a logic of consequences, although their ontology, states conceived of as unified rational autonomous actors, is not suitable for understanding some elements of sovereignty, especially the extent to which the domestic autonomy of states has been compromised. Various efforts to employ a logic of appropriateness, reflected most prominently in the English school and more recent constructivist treatments, understate the importance of power and interest and overemphasize the impact of international, as opposed to domestic, roles and rules.

Both international legal sovereignty and Westphalian sovereignty can be defined by clear rules or logics of appropriateness: recognize juridically

[7] Strang 1996, 24.

independent territorial entities; exclude external authority structures from the territory of the state. Yet both of these logics have been violated, more frequently for Westphalian sovereignty than international legal sovereignty, because logics of consequences can be so compelling in the international environment. Rulers have found that it is in their interest to break the rules. Violations of international legal sovereignty have taken place through mutual agreement, since recognition depends on the voluntary acceptance of other states. Violations of Westphalian sovereignty have occurred through both voluntary agreements and the use of coercion.

The starting point for this study, the ontological givens, are rulers, specific policy makers, usually but not always the executive head of state. Rulers, not states—and not the international system—make choices about policies, rules, and institutions. Whether international legal sovereignty and Westphalian sovereignty are honored depends on the decisions of rulers. There is no hierarchical structure to prevent rulers from violating the logics of appropriateness associated with mutual recognition or the exclusion of external authority. Rulers can recognize another state or not; they can recognize entities that lack juridical independence or territory. They can intervene in the internal affairs of other states or voluntarily compromise the autonomy of their own polity.

Any actor-oriented approach must start with simple assumptions about the underlying preferences of actors. These preferences must be applicable to all actors across space and time. If the preferences, the underlying interests of actors, are problematic, then the preferences become something to be explained rather than something that can do the explaining. The assumption of this study is that rulers want to stay in power and, being in power, they want to promote the security, prosperity, and values of their constituents. The ways in which they accomplish these objectives will vary from one state to another. Some rulers need to cultivate their military; others seek a majority of votes. Some will enhance their position by embracing universal human rights; others succeed by endorsing exclusionary nationalism. Some are highly dependent on external actors for their financial support; others rely almost exclusively on domestic sources.

International legal sovereignty has been almost universally desired by rulers, including rulers who have lacked juridical independence and even a territory. Recognition provides benefits and does not impose costs. Recognition facilitates treaty making, establishes diplomatic immunity, and offers a shield against legal actions taken in other states. International legal sovereignty can indicate to domestic actors that a particular ruler is more likely to remain in power if only because that ruler can more easily secure external resources.

The basic rule of international legal sovereignty, that mutual recognition be extended among formally independent territorial entities, has never been universally honored. The fact that rulers want recognition does not mean that they will always get it. Nonrecognition has been used as an instrument of policy. Rulers with territory and juridical and de facto autonomy, such as the Chinese Communist regime from 1949 to the 1970s, have not been recognized. At the same time rulers have recognized entities lacking in formal juridical autonomy—Byelorussia and the Ukraine were members of the United Nations. Even entities without territory have been recognized. The Iranian mullahs had a better chance of staying in power in 1979 by violating diplomatic immunity (a long-standing rule associated with international legal sovereignty) than by honoring it. These departures from the standard norm have not, however, generated alternative logics of appropriateness.

While almost all states in the international system have enjoyed international recognition (even if other kinds of entities are sometimes recognized as well), many fewer states have enjoyed Westphalian sovereignty. Rulers have frequently departed from the principle that external actors should be excluded from authority structures within the territory of their own or other states. Westphalian sovereignty can be violated through both intervention and invitation. More powerful states have engaged in intervention, coercing public authorities in weaker states to accept externally dictated authority structures. Rulers have also issued invitations, voluntary policies that compromise the autonomy of their own polity, such as signing human rights accords that establish supranational judicial structures, or entering into international loan agreements that give the lender the right not just to be paid back but also to influence domestic policies and institutions. The norm of autonomy, the core of Westphalian sovereignty, has been challenged by alternatives including human rights, minority rights, fiscal responsibility, and the maintenance of international stability. Moreover, in the international system principled claims have sometimes merely been a rationalization for exploiting the opportunities presented by power asymmetries.

The logic of appropriateness of Westphalian sovereignty, the exclusion of external actors from internal authority arrangements, has been widely recognized but also frequently violated. The multiple pressures on rulers have led to a decoupling between the norm of autonomy and actual practice. Talk and action do not coincide. Rulers might consistently pledge their commitment to nonintervention but at the same time attempt to alter the domestic institutional structures of other states, and justify this practice by alternative norms such as human rights or opposition to capitalism. Rulers must speak to and secure the support of different constituencies making inconsistent demands.[8] Nationalist groups agitate for an end to external influence; the International Monetary Fund (IMF) insists on a legitimated role in domestic policy formation. Rulers might talk non-intervention to the former, while accepting the conditionality terms of the latter. For rulers making choices in an anarchic environment in which there are many demands, multiple norms, power asymmetries, and no authoritative decision-making structures, adhering to Westphalian sovereignty might, or might not, maximize their utility.

Outcomes in the international system are determined by rulers whose violation of, or adherence to, international principles or rules is based on calculations of material and ideational interests, not taken-for-granted practices derived from some overarching institutional structures or deeply embedded generative grammars. Organized hypocrisy is the normal state of affairs.

Violations of the basic rule of Westphalian sovereignty have occurred more frequently than violations of the basic rule of international legal sovereignty and have been more explicitly justified by alternative principles. Departures from the logic of appropriateness associated with international legal sovereignty have often been unproblematic because they involve agreements among rulers that are mutually beneficial; everyone is better off and no one needs to be convinced. In contrast, coercive violations of the logic of appropriateness associated with Westphalian sovereignty can leave some actors worse off; justifications in the form of alternative principles or rules have been offered, sometimes to convince targets and sometimes to insure support from domestic constituents in those states engaged in coercion.

FOUR MEANINGS OF SOVEREIGNTY

The term sovereignty has been commonly used in at least four different ways: domestic sovereignty, referring to the organization of public authority within a state and to the level of effective control exercised by those holding authority; interdependence sovereignty, referring to the ability of public authorities to control transborder movements; international legal sovereignty, referring to the mutual recognition of states or other entities; and Westphalian sovereignty, referring to the exclusion of external actors from domestic authority configurations. These four meanings of sovereignty are not logically coupled, nor have they covaried in practice.

---

[8] Brunsson (1989, 27–31), notes that political organizations are inevitably confronted with multiple constituencies.

Embedded in these four usages of the term is a fundamental distinction between authority and control. Authority involves a mutually recognized right for an actor to engage in specific kinds of activities. If authority is effective, force or compulsion would never have to be exercised. Authority would be coterminous with control. But control can be achieved simply through the use of brute force with no mutual recognition of authority at all. In practice, the boundary between control and authority can by hazy. A loss of control over a period of time could lead to a loss of authority. The effective exercise of control, or the acceptance of a rule for purely instrumental reasons, could generate new systems of authority. If a practice works, individuals might come to regard it as normatively binding, not just instrumentally efficacious; conversely, if a mutually accepted rule fails to control behavior, its authority might be rejected over time.[9] In many social and political situations both a logic of consequences, in which control is the key issue, and a logic of appropriateness, associated with authority, can both affect the behavior of actors.[10]

Westphalian sovereignty and international legal sovereignty exclusively refer to issues of authority: does the state have the right to exclude external actors, and is a state recognized as having the authority to engage in international agreements? Interdependence sovereignty exclusively refers to control: can a state control movements across its own borders? Domestic sovereignty is used in ways that refer to both authority and control: what authority structures are recognized within a state, and how effective is their level of control? A loss of interdependence sovereignty (control over transborder flows) would almost certainly imply a loss of domestic sovereignty in the sense of domestic control but would not necessarily imply that the state had lost domestic authority.[11]

---

[9] Sugden (1989) in his discussion of evolutionary game theory suggests that a rule that is initially accepted for purely consequential reasons can come to be normatively binding, authoritative, over time, because it works and is generally accepted.

[10] For further discussions of the distinction between authority and control with reference to sovereignty, see Wendt and Friedheim 1996, 246, 251; Onuf 1991, 430; Wendt 1992, 412–13; Shue, 1997, 348.

[11] Similar distinctions are developed by Thomson (1995) who emphasizes the critical difference between control on the one hand, which may be threatened by what is called here a loss of interdependence sovereignty, and authority on the other. Daniel Deudney has also noted the different ways in which the term sovereignty has been used and confounded. Deudney defines sovereignty as the ultimate source of authority in the polity. "This meaning of sovereignty," he goes on to point out, "is often conflated with the related questions of authority, which refers to the exercise of legitimate power (what is here termed an aspect of domestic sovereignty), autonomy, which refers to the independence of a polity vis-à-vis other polities (which is here referred to as Westphalian sovereignty), and recognized autonomy, which involves the rights, roles, and responsibilities of membership in a society of states

Domestic Sovereignty

The intellectual history of the term sovereignty is most closely associated with domestic sovereignty. How is public authority organized within the state? How effectively is it exercised? Bodin and Hobbes, the two most important early theorists of sovereignty, were both driven by a desire to provide an intellectual rationale for the legitimacy of some one final source of authority within the state. Both were anxious to weaken support for the religious wars that tore France and Britain apart by demonstrating that revolt against the sovereign could never be legitimate.[12] Strayer, in his study of the early state, suggests that "For those who were skeptical about the divine right of monarchs there was the theory that the state was absolutely necessary for human welfare, and that the concentration of power which we call sovereignty was essential for the existence of the state."[13] F. H. Hinsley writes, "at the beginning, at any rate, the idea of sovereignty was the idea that there is a final and absolute political authority in the political community; and everything that needs to be added to complete the definition is added if this statement is continued in the following words: 'and no final and absolute authority exists elsewhere,' ".[14] Later theorists from Locke, to Mill, to Marx, to Dahl have challenged the notion that there has to be some one final source of authority, but the work of all of these writers is concerned primarily with the organization of authority within the state.

Polities can be organized in many different ways without raising any issues for either international legal or Westphalian sovereignty. Authority may be concentrated in the hands of one individual, as Bodin and Hobbes advocated, or divided among different institutions, as is the case in the United States. There can be federal or unitary structures. The one point at which the organization of domestic authority could affect international legal sovereignty occurs in the case of confederations in which the individual units of the state have some ability to conduct external relations.[15]

(which is called in this study international legal sovereignty)" (1995, 198). Although Cerny does not explicitly use the term sovereignty, he also makes a set of distinctions that recognize the difference between internal and external autonomy. Internally states can be strong or weak. Externally they can be dependent or autonomous. A state that is internally weak and externally dependent is classified by Cerny (1990, 101) as penetrated.

[12] Skinner 1978, 287.

[13] Strayer 1970, 108.

[14] Hinsley 1986, 25–26.

[15] This was the case, for instance, for Bavaria, which retained the right to independent foreign representation, although largely for honorary purposes, after German unification in 1870. Oppenheim 1992, 247; Brierly 1963, 127–28.

The effectiveness of political authorities within their own borders may also vary without empirically or logically influencing international legal or Westphalian sovereignty. Whether operating in a parliamentary or presidential, monarchical or republican, or authoritarian or democratic polity, political leaders might, or might not, be able to control developments within their own territory. They might, or might not, be able to maintain order, collect taxes, regulate pornography, repress drug use, prevent abortion, minimize corruption, or control crime. A state with very limited effective domestic control could still have complete international legal sovereignty. It could still be recognized as a juridical equal by other states, and its representatives could still exercise their full voting rights in international organizations. The Westphalian sovereignty of an ineffective state would not necessarily be compromised. Domestic leaders might continue to exclude external actors, especially if these actors were not much interested in local developments. Domestic sovereignty, the organization and effectiveness of political authority, is the single most important question for political analysis, but the organization of authority within a state and the level of control enjoyed by the state are not necessarily related to international legal or Westphalian sovereignty.

Interdependence Sovereignty

In contemporary discourse it has become commonplace for observers to note that state sovereignty is being eroded by globalization. Such analysts are concerned fundamentally with questions of control, not authority.[16] The inability to regulate the flow of goods, persons, pollutants, diseases, and ideas across territorial boundaries has been described as a loss of sovereignty.[17] In his classic study, *The Economics of Interdependence*, Richard Cooper argued that in a world of large open capital markets smaller states would not be able to control their own monetary policy because they could not control the transborder movements of capital. James Rosenau suggests in *Turbulence in World Politics* that the basic nature of the international system is changing. The scope of activities over which states can effectively exercise control is declining. New issues have emerged such as "atmospheric pollution, terrorism, the drug trade, currency crises, and AIDs," which are a product of interdependence or new technologies and which are transnational rather than national. States cannot provide solutions to these and other issues.[18]

[16] Thomson 1995, 216.
[17] Mathews 1997; Wriston 1997.
[18] Rosenau 1990, 13.

While a loss of interdependence sovereignty does not necessarily imply anything about domestic sovereignty understood as the organization of authoritative decision making, it does undermine domestic sovereignty comprehended simply as control. If a state cannot regulate what passes across its borders, it will not be able to control what happens within them.

It is nowhere near as self-evident as many observers have suggested that the international environment at the end of the twentieth century has reached unprecedented levels of openness that are placing new and unique strains on states. By some measures international capital markets were more open before the First World War than they are now.[19] The importance of international trade has followed a similar trajectory, growing during the last half of the nineteenth century, then falling from the first to the fifth decades of the twentieth century, then growing after 1950 to unprecedented levels for most but not all states.[20] International labor movements were more open in the nineteenth century than they are now.[21] Some areas have become more deeply enmeshed in the international environment, especially East Asia; others, notably most of Africa, remain much more isolated. Regardless of the conclusions that are reached about changes in international flows, there have still been considerable variations in national political responses. Increases in transnational flows have not made states impotent with regard to pursuing national policy agendas; increasing transnational flows have not necessarily undermined state control. Indeed, the level of government spending for developed countries has increased along with various measures of globalization since 1950.[22]

Interdependence sovereignty, or the lack thereof, is not practically or logically related to international legal or Westphalian sovereignty. A state can be recognized as a juridical equal by other states and still be unable to control movements across its own borders. Unregulated transborder movements do not imply that a state is subject to external structures of authority, which would be a violation of Westphalian sovereignty. Rulers can lose control of transborder flows and still be recognized and be able to exclude external actors.

In practice, however, a loss of interdependence sovereignty might lead rulers to compromise their Westphalian sovereignty. Indeed, neoliberal institutionalism suggests that technological changes, which have reduced the costs of transportation and communication, have led to a loss of interdependence sovereignty, which, in turn, has prompted states to enter into

---

[19] Obstfeld and Taylor 1997.
[20] Thomson and Krasner 1989.
[21] J. Williamson 1996, 16, 18, table 2.1.
[22] Garrett 1998.

agreements (an exercise of international legal sovereignty) to create international institutions, some of which have compromised their Westphalian sovereignty by establishing external authority structures.[23]

Thus the first two meanings of sovereignty, interdependence sovereignty and domestic sovereignty, are logically distinct from the basic concerns of this study—international legal sovereignty and Westphalian sovereignty. The structure of domestic political authority and the extent of control over activities within and across territorial boundaries are not necessarily related to international recognition or the exclusion of external actors, although behaviorally the erosion of domestic or interdependence sovereignty can lead rulers to compromise their Westphalian sovereignty.

International Legal Sovereignty

The third meaning of sovereignty, international legal sovereignty, has been concerned with establishing the status of a political entity in the international system. Is a state recognized by other states? Is it accepted as a juridical equal? Are its representatives entitled to diplomatic immunity? Can it be a member of international organizations? Can its representatives enter into agreements with other entities? This is the concept used most frequently in international legal scholarship, but it has been employed by scholars and practitioners of international relations more generally.

The classic model of international law is a replication of the liberal theory of the state. The state is treated at the international level as analogous to the individual at the national level. Sovereignty, independence, and consent are comparable with the position that the individual has in the liberal theory of the state.[24] States are equal in the same way that individuals are equal. The concept of the equality of states was introduced into international law by Vattel in *Le droit de gens*, first published 1758. Vattel reasoned from the logic of the state of nature. If men were equal in the state of nature, then states were also free and equal and living in a state of nature. For Vattel a small republic was no less a sovereign state than was a powerful kingdom.[25]

The basic rule for international legal sovereignty is that recognition is extended to entities, states, with territory and formal juridical autonomy. This has been the common, although as we shall see, not exclusive, practice. There have also been additional criteria applied to the recognition of specific governments rather than states: the Communist government in China, for instance, as opposed to the state of China. These additional

---

[23] Keohane 1984, 1995.
[24] Weiler 1991, 2479–80.
[25] Brierly 1963, 37–40.

rules, which have varied over time, have included the ability to defend and protect a defined territory, the existence of an established government, and the presence of a population.[26]

The supplementary rules for recognizing specific governments, as opposed to states, have never been consistently applied. The decision to recognize or withhold recognition can be a political act that can support or weaken a target government. Weaker states have sometimes argued that the recognition of governments should be automatic, but stronger states, who might choose to use recognition as a political instrument, have rejected this principle. States have recognized other governments even when they did not have effective control over their claimed territory, such as the German and Italian recognition of the Franco regime in 1936, and the American recognition of the Lon Nol government in Cambodia in 1970. States have continued to recognize governments that have lost power, including Mexican recognition of the Spanish republican regime until 1977, and recognition of the Chinese Nationalist regime by all of the major Western powers until the 1970s. States have refused to recognize new governments even when they have established effective control, such as the British refusal in the nineteenth century to recognize the newly independent Latin American states until a decade after they had established effective control, the Russian refusal to recognize the July monarchy in France until 1832, and the U.S. refusal to recognize the Soviet regime until 1934. The frequency and effectiveness of the use of recognition or nonrecognition as a political instrument have depended both upon the distribution of power (conflicting policies by major powers reduce the impact of recognition policies) and the degree of ideological conflict.[27]

More interesting from the perspective of this study is not the fact that specific governments have been denied or given recognition, but rather that even entities, as opposed to specific governments, that do not conform with the basic norm of appropriateness associated with international legal sovereignty have been recognized. Entities that lack either formal juridical autonomy or territory have also been recognized. India was a member of the League of Nations and a signatory of the Versailles settlements even though it was a colony of Britain. The British Dominions were signatories at Versailles and members of the league even though their juridical independence from Britain was unclear. India and the Philippines were founding members of the United Nations even though they did not become formally independent until 1946 and 1947 respectively. The Palestinian Liberation Organization (PLO) was given observer status in the

[26] Fowler and Bunck 1995, chapt. 2; Thomson 1995, 228; Oppenheim 1992, 186–90; Crawford 1996, 500.

[27] M. Peterson 1982, 328–36; Peterson 1997, 32, 90–91, 187; Strang 1996, 24.

United Nations in 1974 and this status was changed to that of a mission in 1988 coincident with the declaration of Palestinian independence even though the PLO did not have any independent control over territory. Byelorussia and the Ukraine were members of the United Nations even though they were part of the Soviet Union.[28] Andorra became a member of the United Nations in 1993 even though France and Spain have control over its security affairs and retain the right to appoint two of the four members of its Constitutional Tribunal.[29] Hong Kong, a British colony and then part of China, became a founding member of the World Trade Organization even though China was not. The Order of Malta is recognized as a sovereign person by more than sixty states even though it lost control of Malta in 1798 and holds no territory other than some buildings in Rome.[30]

The uncertainty surrounding the recognition of specific governments, and even the violations of the principle that recognition should be limited to territorial entities that are juridically independent, have not reduced the attractiveness of international legal sovereignty for rulers or created an environment in which basic institutional arrangements have been challenged.

Almost all rulers have sought international legal sovereignty, the recognition of other states, because it provides them with both material and normative resources. Sovereignty can be conceived of as "a ticket of general admission to the international arena."[31] All recognized states have juridical equality. International law is based on the consent of states. Recognized states can enter into treaties with each other, and these treaties will generally be operative even if the government changes. Dependent or subordinate territories do not generally have the right to conclude international agreements (although, as with everything else in the international system, there are exceptions), giving the central or recognized authority a monopoly over formal arrangements with other states.[32]

Even though the differences in treatment can be blurred, it is better to be recognized than not. Nonrecognition is not a bar to the conduct of commercial and even diplomatic discourse, but it can introduce an element of uncertainty into the calculations of actors. Ex ante they may not be able to predict how particular governments or national court systems will respond to an unrecognized government.[33] Multinational firms might be more reluctant to invest.

---

[28] Oppenheim 1992, 145–46.

[29] Constitution of Andorra 1993, Article 66.

[30] Bradford 1972, 63–67, 117–23, 220, 226.

[31] Fowler and Bunck 1995, 12.

[32] Oppenheim 1992, 158, 245, 339–40; Thomson 1995, 219.

[33] For a discussion of the relationship between the Sovereign Immunities Act in the United States and recognition, see Movsesian 1996.

By facilitating accords, international legal sovereignty offers the possibility for rulers to secure external resources that can enhance their ability to stay in power and to promote the security, economic, and ideational interests of their constituents. The rulers of internationally recognized states can sit at the table. Entering into certain kinds of contracts, such as alliances, can enhance security by reducing uncertainty about the commitment of other actors.[34] Membership in international financial institutions opens the possibility, although not the assurance, of securing foreign capital. Even if rulers have entered into accords that have far-reaching effects on their domestic autonomy, such as the European Union, they have nothing to lose by retaining their international legal sovereignty, including their formal right to withdraw from any international agreements.

Recognition also provides a state, and by implication its rulers, with a more secure status in the courts of other states. The act of state doctrine holds, in the words of one U.S. Supreme Court decision, that "Every sovereign State is bound to respect the independence of every other sovereign State, and the courts of one country will not sit in judgment on the acts of the government of another done within its own territory."[35] In British and American courts recognition is consequential because the sovereign or public acts of a recognized state, as opposed to its private or commercial acts, cannot be challenged, and the property of a recognized state is immune from seizure. Traditionally only the citizens of recognized states have been able to appear as parties to litigation in the United States. If a government or state is not recognized either de jure or de facto, then American and British courts need not consider its legislation valid— for instance, in deciding whether a piece of property has been legally transferred.[36]

Recognition also provides immunity for diplomatic representatives from both civil and criminal actions. Representatives are not subject to any form of arrest or detention, although the host country can refuse to receive, or can expel, specific individuals. Diplomatic premises can not be entered by representatives of the host country. Diplomatic bags can not be opened.[37]

The attractiveness of international legal sovereignty can also be understood from a more sociological or cognitive perspective. Recognition as a state is a widely, almost universally understood construct in the contemporary world. A ruler attempting to strengthen his own position by creating

---

[34] Fowler and Bunck 1995, 142.
[35] The case is *Underhill vs. Hernandez*, quoted in Oppenheim 1992, 365–67.
[36] Brierly 1963, 149–50.
[37] Oppenheim 1992, 1072–97.

or reinforcing a particular national identity is more likely to be successful if his state or his government enjoys international recognition. Recognition gives the ruler the opportunity to play on the international stage; even if it is only a bit part, parading at the United Nations or shaking hands with the president of the United States or the chancellor of Germany, can enhance the standing of a ruler among his or her own followers. In an uncertain domestic political situation (a situation in which domestic sovereignty is problematic), international recognition can reinforce the position of rulers by signaling to constituents that a ruler may have access to international resources, including alliances and sovereign lending. Hence, international legal sovereignty can promote the interests of rulers by making it easier for them to generate domestic political support not just because they are in a better position to promote the interests of their constituents but also because recognition is a signal about the viability of a political regime and its leaders.

Like other institutional arrangements in the international environment, however, international recognition is not a constitutive act in the sense that the absence of recognition precludes the kinds of activities that recognition itself facilitates. Governments have maintained administrative contacts and signed agreements with governments they have not recognized; they have exchanged trade missions, registered trademarks, accepted consular missions, and concluded arrangements for the exchange of prisoners of war. Representatives of one state have had contacts with representatives of other states that they have not recognized; for instance, the United States sent a personal representative to the Holy See when the Vatican was not recognized by the United States; U.S. and mainland Chinese officials met in Geneva in 1954; the Vietnam peace negotiations in Paris from 1970 to 1973 took place when the United States did not recognize the North Vietnamese government; President Nixon went on an official visit to China in 1971 when the two countries did not recognize each other. National court systems have increasingly been given discretion by their own governments to decide whether the actions of nonrecognized governments will be given special legal standing. The U.S. Protection of Diplomats Act of 1971 provides for the protection of diplomats even if their governments have not been recognized by the United States. When the United States recognized the People's Republic of China as the legitimate government of China in 1979 and withdrew recognition from the Republic of China (ROC), it established a special status for Taiwan. The Taiwan Relations Act stipulated that the legal standing of the ROC in American courts would not be affected, that Taiwan would continue to be a member of international financial institutions, and that the American Institute in

Taiwan, a nongovernmental agency, would be created, in effect, to conduct the functions of an embassy.[38]

As the following chapters demonstrate, whatever international recognition has meant, it has not led rulers to eschew efforts to alter the domestic authority structures, policies, or even personnel of other states, or to enter into contractual relationships that compromise the autonomy of their own state. International legal sovereignty does not mean Westphalian sovereignty. Moreover, it does not guarantee that legitimate domestic authorities will be able to monitor and regulate developments within the territory of their state or flows across their borders; that is, it does not guarantee either domestic sovereignty or interdependence sovereignty.[39]

Indeed, international legal sovereignty is the necessary condition for rulers to compromise voluntarily aspects of their Westphalian sovereignty. Nowhere is this more apparent than in the European Union. In an interview shortly before the opening of the April 1996 European Union conference on governance in Turin, Jacques Chirac, the president of France, stated that "In order for Europe to be widened it must in the first instance be deepened, but the sovereignty of each state must be respected."[40] Chirac was arguing that the member states of the European Union must retain their international legal sovereignty, even while they were entering into agreements that compromised their Westphalian, interdependence, and domestic sovereignty since the European Union can regulate transborder movements; the European Court exercises transnational authority; and some European Union decisions can be taken by a majority vote of the member states.

Finally, it should be obvious that international legal sovereignty does not guarantee the territorial integrity of any state or even the existence of

[38] Oppenheim 1992, 158–73; M. Peterson 1997, 107–8, 140, 148–52, 197; United States, Taiwan Relations Act.

[39] With American troops about to leave Italy in the summer of 1947 following the ratification of the Italian Peace Treaty, George Marshall, the American secretary of state, indicated to the U.S. embassy in Rome that it must be stressed to General Lee (commander of allied forces) that "Govt Allied mil in Italy must respect scrupulously restoration Ital sovereignty upon coming into force treaty" (United States, FRUS, [1947, vol. 3], 1972, 931). This message was sent at time when the United States was intervening in Italian domestic politics by supporting the Christian Democrats, trying to restructure the Socialist Party, and attempting to weaken the position of the Communist Party in Italy. Marshall wanted to recognize Italy's international legal sovereignty, but he was completely unconcerned with Italy's Westphalian sovereignty, with the exclusion of American influence from Italy's domestic authority formations. See J. Miller 1986, 243–63.

[40] *Frankfurter Allgemeine Zeitung*, March 26, 1996, 1, translated by the author. The original quotation reads: "Um sich erweitern zu können, muss sich Europa zunächst vertiefen, wobei es die Souveränität seiner Staaten respektieren muss."

a state. Recognized states have been dismembered and even absorbed. The conquest of any particular state extinguishes the sovereignty of that state (domestic, Westphalian, interdependence, and usually international legal), but conquest is not a challenge to Westphalian and international legal sovereignty as institutional forms. It reconfigures borders but does not create new principles and norms.

Westphalian Sovereignty

Finally, sovereignty has been understood as the Westphalian model, an institutional arrangement for organizing political life that is based on two principles: territoriality and the exclusion of external actors from domestic authority structures. Rulers may be constrained, sometimes severely, by the external environment, but they are still free to choose the institutions and policies they regard as optimal. Westphalian sovereignty is violated when external actors influence or determine domestic authority structures.

Domestic authority structures can be infiltrated through both coercive and voluntary actions, through intervention and invitation. Foreign actors, usually the rulers of other states, can use their material capabilities to dictate or coerce changes in the authority structures of a target; they can violate the rule of nonintervention in the internal affairs of other states. Rulers may also themselves establish supranational or extranational authority structures that constrain their own domestic autonomy; they can extend invitations, sometimes inadvertent, that result in compromises of their own Westphalian sovereignty. While coercion, intervention, is inconsistent with international legal as well as Westphalian sovereignty, voluntary actions by rulers, invitations, do not violate international legal sovereignty although they do transgress Westphalian sovereignty.

The norm of nonintervention in internal affairs had virtually nothing to do with the Peace of Westphalia, which was signed in 1648. It was not clearly articulated until the end of the eighteenth century. Nevertheless, the common terminology is used here because the Westphalian model has so much entered into common usage, even if it is historically inaccurate.

The fundamental norm of Westphalian sovereignty is that states exist in specific territories, within which domestic political authorities are the sole arbiters of legitimate behavior. While autonomy can be compromised as a result of both intervention and invitation, the former has gotten much more attention. For many observers, the rule of nonintervention—which is always violated through coercion or imposition, as opposed to voluntary invitation—is the key element of sovereign statehood. Robert Jackson writes that: "The *grundnorm* of such a political arrangement (sovereign statehood) is the basic prohibition against foreign intervention which simultaneously imposes a duty of forbearance and confers a right of independence on all statesmen. Since states are profoundly unequal in power the rule is obviously far more constraining for powerful states and far more liberating for weak states."[41]

The principle of nonintervention was first explicitly articulated by Wolff and Vattel during the last half of the eighteenth century. Wolff wrote in the 1760s that "To interfere in the government of another, in whatever way indeed that may be done is opposed to the natural liberty of nations, by virtue of which one is altogether independent of the will of other nations in its action."[42] Vattel argued that no state had the right to intervene in the internal affairs of other states. He applied this argument to non-European as well as European states, claiming that "The Spaniards violated all rules when they set themselves up as judges of the Inca Athualpa. If that prince had violated the law of nations with respect to them, they would have had a right to punish him. But they accused him of having put some of his subjects to death, of having had several wives, &c—things, for which he was not at all accountable to them; and, to fill up the measure of their extravagant injustice, they condemned him by the laws of Spain."[43]

Weaker states have always been the strongest supporters of the rule of nonintervention. During the nineteenth century the Latin American states endorsed this rule at international meetings in 1826 and 1848. In 1868 the Argentine jurist Carlos Calvo published a treatise in which he condemned intervention by foreign powers to enforce contractual obligations of private parties. The foreign minister of Argentina, Luis Drago, argued in a note to the American government in 1902 that intervention to enforce the collection of public debts was illegitimate. The Calvo and Drago doctrines became recognized claims in international law. At the sixth International Conference of American States held in Havana in 1928, the Commission of Jurists recommended adoption of the principle that "No state has a right to interfere in the internal affairs of another." This proposal, however, was rejected, in large part because of the opposition of the United States. The United States had engaged in several interventions in Central America and the Caribbean. The American secretary of state, Charles Evans Hughes, argued that the United States had a right to intervene to protect the lives of its nationals should order break down in another country. At the seventh International Conference of American States held in 1933, the United States finally accepted the principle of nonintervention. The wording that "no state has the right to intervene in the internal or external affairs of another" was included in the Convention on

[41] Jackson 1990, 6.
[42] Quoted in A. Thomas and Thomas 1956, 5.
[43] Vattel 1852, 155.

Rights and Duties of States and accepted by the United States.[44] The Charter of the Organization of American States (OAS) stipulates that "No State or group of States has the right to intervene, directly or indirectly, for any reason whatever, in the internal or external affairs of any other State. The foregoing principle prohibits not only armed force but also any other form of interference or attempted threat against the personality of the State or against its political, economic, and cultural elements."[45] In the latter part of the twentieth century nonintervention has been routinely endorsed in major international agreements such as the United Nations Charter and the 1975 Helsinki agreement, albeit often along with other principles such as human rights that are in tension with nonintervention.

While Westphalian sovereignty can be compromised through invitation as well as intervention, invitation has received less notice in the literature because observers have confounded international legal and Westphalian sovereignty. Intervention violates both. Invitation violates only Westphalian sovereignty. Invitation occurs when a ruler voluntarily compromises the domestic autonomy of his or her own polity. Free choices are never inconsistent with international legal sovereignty.[46]

Invitations can, however, infringe domestic autonomy. Rulers may issue invitations for a variety of reasons, including tying the hands of their successors, securing external financial resources, and strengthening domestic support for values that they, themselves, embrace. Invitations may sometimes be inadvertent; rulers might not realize that entering into an agreement may alter their own domestic institutional arrangements. Regardless of the motivation or the perspicacity of rulers, invitations violate Westphalian sovereignty by subjecting internal authority structures to external constraints. The rulings of the European Court of Justice, for instance, have legitimacy in the judicial systems of the member states of the European Union. IMF conditionality agreements, which may include stipulations requiring changes in domestic structures, carry weight not only because they are attached to the provision of funding but also because the IMF has legitimacy for some actors in borrowing countries derived from its claims to technical expertise. Human rights conventions can provide focal points that alter conceptions of legitimacy among groups in civil society and precipitate possibly unanticipated changes in the institutional arrangements of signatory states.

Violations of Westphalian sovereignty can arise in a sovereign state system because the absence of a formal hierarchical system of authority, the

---

[44] A. Thomas and Thomas 1956, 56–62.

[45] Quoted in Damrosch 1993.

[46] Oppenheim (1992, 431), for instance, writes that intervention only occurs when one state engages in forcible or dictatorial measures related to matters over which another state

defining characteristic of any international system, does not mean that the authority structures in any given political entity will be free of external influence. Wendt and Friedheim have defined informal empires as "transnational structures of de facto political authority in which members are juridically sovereign states."[47] Formal constitutional independence does not guarantee de facto autonomy. A recognized international legal sovereign will not necessarily be a Westphalian sovereign.

In recent years a number of analysts have used the Westphalian model as a bench mark to assert that the character of the international system is changing in some fundamental ways. Writing of the pre-1950s world, James Rosenau contends that "In that system, legitimate authority was concentrated in the policy-making institutions of states, which interacted with each other on the basis of equality and accepted principles of diplomacy and international law. Their embassies remained inviolable and so did their domestic affairs. Intrusion into such matters were met with protests of violated sovereignty and, not infrequently, with preparations for war. For all practical purposes, the line between domestic and foreign affairs was preserved and clearly understood by all. The norms of the Western state system lodged control over external ties in the state and these were rarely defied and even more rarely revised." Philip Windsor states that "It is fashionable, at present, to suggest that the old Westphalian system of a world of non-interventionist states is on the decline, and that the dangers of growing intervention by different powers in the affairs of other states have been on the increase. The Westphalian system represented some remarkable achievements: the absolute sovereignty of a state rested on a dual basis whereby internal authority was matched by freedom from external interference; and in this way the principle of *cuius regio, eius religio*, codified in the Religious Peace of Augsburg, laid the foundation of the modern states system."[48]

The way in which some analysts have understood sovereignty in terms of the Westphalian model is brought out clearly by authors who have studied minority or human rights, because claims about such rights are seen as a contradiction of sovereignty. In one of the most important studies of minority rights in the interwar period C. A. Macartney writes, "The doctrine of state sovereignty does not admit that the domestic policy of any state—the policy which it follows towards its own citizens—can be any concern of any other state." In a more recent study of human rights Forsythe suggests that "The most fundamental point about human rights law is that it

---

has the right to exercise sovereignty, such as "its political, economic, social and cultural systems, and its foreign policy."

[47] Wendt and Friedheim 1996, 245.

[48] Rosenau 1990, 109; Windsor 1984, 45.

establishes a set of rules for all states and all people. It thus seeks to increase world unity and to counteract national separateness (but not necessarily national distinctions). In this sense, the international law of human rights is revolutionary because it contradicts the notion of national sovereignty—that is, that a state can do as it pleases in its own jurisdiction." Writing in the 1990s about the status of minority groups Kay Hailbronner claims that "Modern public international law seems to have broken through the armour of sovereignty." Similarly Brian Hehir has asserted that "In the Westphalian order both state sovereignty and the rule of nonintervention are treated as absolute norms." He then goes on to suggest that this Westphalian system is under an unprecedented level of assault.[49]

Despite these claims about unparalleled change, the most important empirical conclusion of the present study is that the principles associated with both Westphalian and international legal sovereignty have always been violated. Neither Westphalian nor international legal sovereignty has ever been a stable equilibrium from which rulers had no incentives to deviate. Rather, Westphalian and international legal sovereignty are best understood as examples of organized hypocrisy. At times rulers adhere to conventional norms or rules because it provides them with resources and support (both material and ideational). At other times, rulers have violated the norms, and for the same reasons. If rulers want to stay in power and to promote the security, material, and ideational interests of their constituents, following the conventional practices of Westphalian and international legal sovereignty might or might not be an optimal policy. After the Second World War it was preferable for the rulers of western Europe to sign the European Human Rights Convention, which compromised their Westphalian sovereignty, than to insist that the domestic autonomy of their polities be unconstrained. In the late 1990s it was better for the rulers of China and other states to allow Hong Kong, which did not have juridical independence after its return to China, to enjoy international recognition; Hong Kong continued its participation or joined international organizations, including the World Trade Organization, whose members denied China itself the right to become a founding member.

In sum, analysts and practitioners have used the term sovereignty in four different and distinct ways. The absence or loss of one kind of sovereignty does not logically imply an erosion of others, even though they may be empirically associated with each other. A state can be recognized, but its authority structures can be de facto subject to external authority or control. It can lose control of transborder movements but still be autonomous.

---

[49] Macartney 1934, 296; Forsythe 1983, 4; Hailbronner 1992, 117; Hehir 1995, 6.

Rulers have almost universally desired international legal sovereignty,[50] but this has not meant that they have universally followed the rule of recognizing only juridically autonomous territorial entities. Rulers have recognized entities that lack formal juridical autonomy or even territory, and they have denied recognition to governments that have exercised effective control over the territory of a recognized state. Recognition can be a political act, one designed to support a specific government or legitimate the claims to territorial autonomy of particular rulers, and adherence to the basic principle of international legal sovereignty might, or might not, enhance these purposes.

The tensions between the conventional rule and actual practice have been more severe for Westphalian than international legal sovereignty. Rulers have sometimes invited external actors to compromise the autonomy of their own state. Westphalian sovereignty has also been violated through intervention; more powerful states have coerced their weaker counterparts into altering the domestic institutional arrangements of their polities. Following the rule of Westphalian sovereignty—preserving the de facto autonomy of a territorial political entity—might, or might not, further the interests of rulers.

The international system is complex. Information is imperfect. There are no universal structures that can authoritatively resolve conflicts. Principles and rules can be logically contradictory. Power asymmetries can be high. Widely recognized and endorsed principles will not always promote the interests of rulers. Logics of consequences can trump logics of appropriateness. Westphalian and international legal sovereignty, the major concerns of this study, are examples of organized hypocrisy. They are both defined by widely understood rules. Yet, these rules have been comprised, more frequently in the case of Westphalian than international legal sovereignty.

MODALITIES OF COMPROMISE

Deviations from institutional norms and rules, whether of international legal or Westphalian sovereignty (or any other institutional arrangement for that matter) can occur in four ways: conventions, contracts, coercion, and imposition. These four modalities are distinguished along two underlying dimensions. First, does the behavior or policy of one ruler depend

---

[50] There have been cases where rulers have sought to abandon international legal sovereignty. For instance, the leaders of Nicaragua and Guatemala asked to join the United States in the 1840s and the president of Belarus contemplated joining with the Soviet Union in 1990s.

on that of another: is it contingent? Second, is at least one of the parties better off and none worse off: is the transgression Pareto-improving?

Rulers can join international *conventions* in which they agree to abide by certain standards regardless of what others do. Rulers can enter into *contracts* in which they agree to specific policies in return for explicit benefits. Rulers can be subject to *coercion*, which leaves them worse off, although they do have some bargaining leverage. Finally, rulers or would-be rulers can suffer *imposition*, a situation that occurs when the target ruler cannot effectively resist.

The Westphalian model has been violated through all four of these modalities: rulers have issued invitations that compromise their autonomy by joining conventions or signing contracts, and they have intervened in the internal affairs of other states through coercion and imposition. Departures from international legal sovereignty, especially with regard to recognizing entities that lack juridical independence or autonomy, have occurred less frequently and have depended primarily on contracts, Pareto-improving mutual agreements.

The distinctions between conventions, contracts, coercion, and imposition are summarized in Figure 1.1. A convention makes rulers better off—otherwise they would not have accepted it—even if not all parties honor its terms. Contracts make at least one ruler better off and none worse off, but only if the participants honor their commitments. If one party reneges, so will the other. For rulers contemplating entering into conventions and contracts, the status quo remains available. Rulers are no worse off if they do not participate. Conventions and contracts are voluntary accords.

Coercion and imposition leave one of the parties worse off. In situations of coercion one ruler threatens to impose sanctions on another if the target ruler does not alter his or her policies. The target can reject these demands, in which case it suffers sanctions, or accept them. In either case the target is worse off. The status quo ante is no longer an option. The target can either suffer sanctions or make changes.

Imposition is the logical terminus of coercion. It involves a situation in which the target has no choice but to accept the demands of the initiator: your money or your life is not a question that encourages bargaining. The target is so weak that it cannot effectively resist. In the extreme the weaker ruler would either be removed from office or, in the case of rulers of would-be states, never be allowed to assume office in the first place.

With regard to concerns of this study, invitations, which compromise autonomy through conventions and contracts, violate Westphalian sovereignty but not international legal sovereignty; in fact, all contracts and conventions are facilitated by and are a confirmation of international legal sovereignty. What is critical for international legal sovereignty is that the

Pareto Improving

		Yes	No
Contingent	Yes	Contract	Coercion
	No	Convention	Imposition

Figure 1.1. Modalities of Compromise

ruler formally retains the right to terminate the contract and that the contract or convention is voluntary.

Coercion and imposition involving issues of autonomy are violations of both international legal sovereignty and Westphalian sovereignty. Both coercion and imposition leave one of the parties worse off. The weaker actor would not have accepted an outcome inferior to the status quo ante if it were not faced with the threat of sanctions, possibly including the use of force. In the most extreme case, the target could be eliminated. Coercion and imposition violate a basic norm of international legal sovereignty, which is that states have the right to act voluntarily. Rulers would never voluntarily accept an arrangement that leaves them worse off.

The modality through which norms might be violated depends on configurations of power and interest. Imposition can only occur when interests are different and power asymmetries high. The initiator must have overwhelming power, the ability to determine the life or death, figuratively and sometimes literally, of rulers in the target entity (state or would-be state). Often this power takes the form of military resources, but in some cases it has involved the initial recognition not just of a particular government but of the state itself. Already established and powerful states have engaged in imposition by conditioning recognition on the target's acceptance of conditions related to domestic political structures. Rejection would mean that the target never becomes an actor. The status quo is an option, but the status quo, an absence of international recognition, would leave the ruler without a state to rule.

Coercion also can take place if the preferences of rulers are different and if there are asymmetries of power. For coercion, however, the asymmetries are less than is the case for imposition. The initiator cannot annihilate the target. The target ruler is worse off if he or she resists and suffers the imposition of sanctions, but the ruler does not cease to exist. The target is faced not with the alternatives of capitulation or nonexistence but with a choice between suffering the costs of sanctions or the costs of acceding to the initiator's demands. In situations of coercion the status quo ante is no longer an option. Rulers in the target state cannot simply reject the demands of the initiator without suffering negative consequences.

For contracting to occur, there must be opportunities for cooperation; actors must have complementary interests, but power can also matter. All rulers are better off as a result of a contract, although some may be better off than others. Acceptance is always voluntary. The status quo ante remains an option; the ruler is no worse off if the contract is rejected. The terms of a specific contract may depend on the bargaining power of rulers, their ability to threaten credibly to stay with the status quo rather than conclude an agreement. In contracting, however, one ruler is never worse off.

Conventions only involve interests, usually ideational rather than material. Power is irrelevant. Rulers are not forced to join conventions; they can remain with the status quo and be no worse off. The behavior of one ruler, the extent to which he (or she) implements a convention, is not contingent on the behavior of others. Conventions are not likely to involve security or economic interests where contingent behavior matters because the utility of one ruler depends on other rulers honoring the terms of the agreement; if one actor reneges, so will others. Rulers may, however, find that their ideational interests can be furthered, regardless of whether other signatories to a convention honor their commitments. Conventions can only occur if rulers have complementary or identical interests.

Violations of Westphalian sovereignty have been almost routine in international politics even though observers have been blinded to their frequency by the assumption that the Westphalian model has been operative. Violations of international legal sovereignty have been less common. They have almost always been the result of voluntary decisions, contracting or conventions; rulers have mutually agreed to departures from the norm that international recognition should be accorded to juridically autonomous territorial entities.

Some of the empirical data of the following chapters, arrayed according to the modalities through which Westphalian sovereignty has been compromised, is summarized here. Selection bias is an issue, especially with regard to minority and human rights, issues that are thematically discussed in Chapters 3 and 4. Cases involving minority rights and human rights have been sampled on the dependent variable; situations where the Westphalian model has not been challenged have not been investigated. Nevertheless, the empirical evidence associated with the extent to which relations between rulers and ruled have been subject to external pressures or authority structures should not be dismissed as simply the result of scavenging for examples that support the argument presented here. First, almost all minority rights cases are associated with the major peace treaties of the last four centuries—Westphalia, Vienna, Berlin, Versailles—as well as other settlements linked to salient conflicts such as the Peace of Paris, which ended the Crimean War, and the Dayton accords, which brought some stability to Bosnia. These treaties are not the result of selection bias. This study could have been organized around an examination of the multiple norms that have been incorporated in major peace settlements. Second, most of the countries of eastern and central Europe have had autonomy with regard to their national legal order regarding minority rights or human rights for only a fraction of their existence as international legal sovereigns, namely the period from the Second World War until the end of the cold war, and during these years the Westphalian sovereignty of most of these countries was compromised in even more dramatic ways by Soviet intervention. Hence, perhaps half of the countries of Europe have never enjoyed Westphalian sovereignty for a single moment of their existence as international legal sovereigns. Third, although situations where states have been autonomous with regard to minority and human rights are not examined systematically, the data presented in this study suggest that more powerful states are unlikely to lose their Westphalian sovereignty unless they invite external authority through conventions or contractual arrangements. Only weaker states have been the targets of intervention through coercion or imposition.

Sovereign lending is an issue area where violations of the Westphalian model have been pervasive for weaker states. When rulers, or governments, or international financial institutions have extended loans to other rulers, they have often demanded direct authority and control over revenue-generating activities; they have not just set terms of repayment, but also stipulated changes in policies, personnel, or institutions. This is true for virtually all of the lending that has been conducted by international financial institutions since the 1950s and for much of the lending to weaker states in the nineteenth century. Chapter 5 presents a wide array, if not the full universe, of cases of sovereign lending. Sovereign lending has been associated with violations of Westphalian norms through imposition, coercion, and contracting.

Chapters 6 and 7 examine the extent to which constitutional structures in all of the states that were created in the nineteenth and twentieth centuries were subject to some external authority structure. There is no sampling on the dependent variable. Almost the entire universe of cases is explored. Could rulers or would-be rulers and their constituents choose the constitutional structure that they preferred or were basic organizational characteristics of their polities determined or influenced by external actors? In the nineteenth century the new states in the Balkans were subject to external coercion or imposition; their counterparts in Latin America were not. In the twentieth century violations of the Westphalian model took place primarily in Central America and the Caribbean and, perhaps ironically, in Europe itself, but were less extensive in the newly independent African and Asian states, because the major powers cared less.

Conventions

The conventions[51] examined in this book relate to Westphalian sovereignty. These conventions are voluntary agreements in which rulers make commitments to follow certain kinds of practices involving relations between rulers and ruled within their own borders; commitments that are not contingent on the extent to which other signatories honor the same accord. These agreements can expose domestic practices to external scrutiny. To one degree or another a convention can violate Westphalian principles by undermining the autonomy of the state; conventions invite, although do not inevitably result in, external actors having some influence on domestic authority structures. In the most compelling example of a convention that violates Westphalian sovereignty, the European Human Rights regime, individuals within signatory states can bring cases against their own government in the European Court of Human Rights and the decisions of the court are binding on national judiciaries. In the weakest cases, signing a convention might have no effect on the de facto autonomy of a signatory state whose rulers might simply ignore its provisions.

All of the empirical instances of conventions discussed in this study deal with either the rights of minorities or other specially designated groups such as guest workers, or with human rights, which apply to all individuals. It is conceivable that conventions could occur in other issue areas such as security or economic exchange, but not likely. In matters of material well-being and defense, agreements will almost certainly be contingent; the behavior of one ruler will depend upon that of others.

Conventions are primarily a development of the twentieth century. The only example of a convention in the nineteenth century that I have discovered involves the rights of Polish nationals after the Napoleonic Wars. As part of the Vienna settlement, the rulers of the major powers committed themselves to preserving the national institutions of the Poles, even though Poland itself had been partitioned among Russia, Prussia, and Austria.

Many conventions have been signed in the twentieth century. In 1926 the League of Nations adopted a convention outlawing slavery. The International Labour Organization, which was created after the First World

---

[51] I am indebted to Jay Smith for suggesting this term.

War, endorsed a number of agreements regarding the treatment and conditions of workers, all of which were conventions. For instance, the fact that one state violated the terms of the 1930 Convention Regarding Forced and Compulsory Labor, which stipulated that forced labor was to be paid at prevailing wages and would never be used in mines, did not mean that others would do so as well.[52]

After the Second World War, the number of conventions increased dramatically. About fifty agreements involving relations between rulers and ruled have been ratified. Most have been adopted within the United Nations system, including broad statements of general principle such as the commitment to human rights in the Preamble to the Charter of the United Nations and the United Nations conventions dealing with political rights and with social and economic rights, as well as accords on more specific issues such as slavery, women, children, refugees, stateless persons, genocide, and torture. There have been a number of regional conventions as well, the most consequential of which have been adopted in the Western Hemisphere and Europe.

The enforcement and monitoring mechanisms for these conventions vary enormously. Some, such as the Universal Declaration of Human Rights, do not have the status of a formal treaty and are devoid of monitoring provisions. Others—for example, the conventions on slavery, the status of refugees, and political rights of women—provide that disputes can be referred to the International Court of Justice. No human rights cases have, however, been referred to the court. Others, such as the conventions on racial discrimination, apartheid, and the rights of the child, provide for the creation of committees that receive information and can, with the approval of the concerned states, investigate alleged violations.

The European Convention on Human Rights, which entered into force in 1953, and subsequent protocols have by far the most wide ranging enforcement provisions and most elaborated organizational structure. The European Commission on Human Rights can hear complaints from individuals, nongovernmental organizations (NGOs), and states; it receives about four thousand communications a year. The European Court of Human Rights can make decisions that are binding on national jurisdictions. The jurisdiction of the commission (composed of independent experts) and the court has been recognized by more than twenty signatories to the convention. Decisions of the commission and the court have led to legal changes in Belgium, Switzerland, Germany, and Sweden.[53]

None of these conventions violates international legal sovereignty. The extent to which they have violated Westphalian sovereignty depends on

---

[52] Convention on Forced and Compulsory Labor, reprinted in Brownlie 1992, 246–56.
[53] Donnelly 1992, 82–83; Forsythe 1989, 19.

whether they have any actual impact on the domestic authority structures of signatory states. General statements of principle like the Universal Declaration of Human Rights can only affect Westphalian sovereignty indirectly if they in some way mobilize domestic groups that then influence authority structures. Conventions with formal reporting requirements might, or might not, change state practice.

The question of whether human rights conventions alter policy can only be answered by examining behavior, not simply by looking at the terms of the agreement. Andrew Moravcsik has pointed out that the formal provisions of the Inter American human rights regime are as, or more, organizationally elaborated than the European regime, but have been less consequential because there has been less domestic political support.[54] At least until the 1990s, and the collapse of the Soviet bloc, the correlation between the behavior of governments with regard to human rights and the number of United Nations accords they had signed was weak (see Chapter 5).

There is no single explanation for why countries sign conventions. Rulers could sign because they expect that this would strengthen values and practices that they are committed to by tying the hands of their successors or making particular principles and norms more attractive to other rulers. In the case of the European regime, the rulers of western Europe, especially in those countries where democracy was fragile, wanted to reinforce democratic values. The existence of the regime made it more likely that citizens would have a clearer view of what constituted illegitimate state acts.[55]

Where enforcement and monitoring provisions have been weak, as has generally been the case for human rights regimes, rulers might sign because, even though they are indifferent or antipathetic to human rights within their own state, they might believe that signing would make their regime appear more palatable to external and internal actors. Stalin's willingness to sign on to some human rights conventions could be viewed as a cynical act designed to make the Soviet Union more attractive to Communist sympathizers in other countries. The Helsinki accords, which included human rights provisions, altered the behavior of groups in civil society in eastern Europe, much to the dismay and surprise of their Communist overlords, who had signed because they believed that the provisions of the accord dealing with borders and economic exchange would strengthen their position.[56]

---

[54] Moravcsik 1994, 54–55.

[55] Moravcsik 1998. For a discussion of the importance of such views about what constitutes a transgression of rights, see Weingast 1997.

[56] D. Thomas 1997.

Rulers might also sign a convention because it is part of the script of modernity; it is something that a modern state does. Some rulers might not have an autonomous conception of appropriate behavior. When cognitive models provide the motivation for signing a convention, participation might, or might not, actually have an impact on domestic authority structures. In many cases, talk and action have been completely decoupled.

Contracts

A contract is an agreement between two or more rulers, or a ruler and another international actor, such as an international financial institution, that is mutually acceptable, Pareto-improving, and contingent. Contracts are always consistent with international legal sovereignty. Indeed, the ability to enter into agreements is one of the advantages of international legal sovereignty.

Contracts might, or might not, be consistent with Westphalian sovereignty. A contract can violate the Westphalian model if it alters domestic conceptions of legitimate behavior, subjects domestic institutions and personnel to external influence, or creates transnational authority structures. Obviously, many contracts between states do not transgress the Westphalian model. A military alliance, for instance, might commit one state to come to the aid of another, a trade agreement to end export subsidies, a financial accord to specify capital requirements for banks, an environmental treaty to limit fishing in international waters. Such arrangements do not alter domestic authority structures.

Rulers must regard a contract as Pareto-improving; otherwise they would not enter into it, since the status quo remains available. In contrast with conventions, however, the behavior of actors is mutually contingent. In contractual arrangements affecting Westphalian sovereignty rulers would not compromise the autonomy or territorial authority of their state unless the behavior of others also changed. If one actor abrogates the contract, others would do so as well. For both contracts and conventions rulers compromise Westphalian sovereignty through invitation; they are not the targets of intervention but rather voluntarily choose to insinuate external factors into their domestic structures of authority.

For more than three hundred years there have been contracts, often major international treaties, that have compromised Westphalian principles. It should hardly be surprising that under some circumstances rulers would find that their prospects for retaining office, or promoting the material, security, and ideational interests of their constituents would be enhanced by entering into contractual arrangements that conceded domestic autonomy. The Peace of Westphalia contained extensive provisions for religious toleration between Catholics and Protestants in Germany. Germany had been devastated by the Thirty Years' War, whose intensity was exacerbated by religious conflict. While Ferdinand III, the Habsburg ruler and Holy Roman emperor, would have preferred to repress the Lutherans and Calvinists, he lacked the resources to do so and, instead, accepted institutional changes in the empire that specified a consociational decision-making structure for religious questions.[57] In the Peace of Utrecht of 1713, the rulers of Europe agreed that France and Spain would never be unified under a single king, a decision that reflected a desire to enhance security by maintaining a system that could sustain a balance of power. The Treaty of Utrecht of 1731, in which France ceded Arcadia and the Hudson Bay to Britain, provided for the protection of the rights of Catholics living in these areas, a constraint on British autonomy that was accepted as part of the more general settlement from which Britain benefited. The Peace of Vienna protected the rights of Catholics living in the Netherlands; clauses stipulating religious toleration were included in the basic law of the Netherlands and could not, according to the treaty, be unilaterally changed by the Dutch themselves, because the major powers wanted to limit the possibilities of religious strife in the Low Countries.

Sovereign lending to weaker states in the nineteenth century, as well as the twentieth, frequently was conducted through contracts that violated Westphalian principles. When Greece was recognized as an independent state in 1832, it accepted a sixty-thousand-franc loan, but the terms involved a commitment of specific revenues as well as the presence of foreign officials approved by the major powers of Europe. In 1881 the Ottoman Empire established the Council of the Public Debt controlled by foreign bondholders, which collected revenues and even engaged in development projects. By 1910 it had more employees than the Ministry of Finance. Again, the Ottoman rulers would have preferred to control their own finances, but it was better to have the foreign loan with the Debt Council than not to have the loan without it. In 1895 Serbia accepted a six-member Monopolies Commission, two of whose members were appointed by France and Germany, which controlled revenues from the tobacco, salt, and petroleum monopolies, revenue that went directly to foreign bondholders and not into the treasury of Serbia.

In the twentieth century sovereign lending routinely involved violations of Westphalian autonomy. International financial institutions, such as the World Bank and the International Monetary Fund, have institutionalized and routinized practices that are inconsistent with Westphalian autonomy. These institutions do not simply offer funds on the condition that they be repaid; they extend resources only if borrowers are willing to accept changes in their domestic policies and often institutional structures

---

[57] Lehmbruch 1997.

as well. The European Bank for Reconstruction and Development, created after the collapse of the Soviet bloc, explicitly requires that member states have democratic regimes. Conditionality attached to loans from international financial institutions was initially supported by the United States but resisted at Bretton Woods by the representatives of European and Latin American states, who correctly assumed that they would be the targets of policies that were heavily influenced by American decision makers. Ultimately, the Americans succeeded in having conditionality written into the Articles of Agreement of the fund because the United States was the only source of significant capital in the 1950s.

Minority and human rights have also been promoted through contracts that violate Westphalian autonomy. Extensive minority rights agreements were concluded with all of the new states that were created at the end of the First World War. Most were the result of intervention through coercion or imposition. The leaders of most of the newly created states felt that they had no alternative but to accept the demands of the major powers. They did not want to guarantee minority rights. In a few cases, however, notably Czechoslovakia, Hungary, and the Baltic states, rulers offered invitations, voluntarily accepted protection for minorities, as part of a more general settlement that included their recognition as international legal sovereigns. After the Second World War Austria and Italy concluded treaties, contracts, covering the rights of the German-speaking minority in the South Tyrol. Germany and Denmark have made joint declarations about the status of minority speakers in the border areas of the two states.

Contracts have also been concluded that affected basic constitutional structures, not just specific institutions or policies. American practices in Italy and Germany after the Second World War involved contracts with national leaders that were designed to promote democratic regimes, or at least to exclude or repress Communist influence; national leaders invited the influence of their American counterparts. In Italy, the Christian Democrats were happy to enter into these arrangements, which enhanced their own ability to stay in power. American rulers also assiduously cultivated non-Communist leaders in Germany. They supported the Christian Democrats and other non-Communist parties. Even in Germany, which was formally occupied until 1955, American rulers could not simply dictate outcomes. They had to contract with local leaders.

The European Union, which raises issues about the principles of both territoriality and autonomy, has been created through contracts entered into by the rulers of the European states. In the Treaty of Rome, the Single European Act, Maastricht, and other agreements, rulers have promoted their interests by establishing new policies and institutional arrangements, some of which transcend territorial boundaries and compromise their domestic autonomy.

The regime for the law of the seas was developed in the 1980s and 1990s through a series of tacit and explicit contracts—that is, coordinated national policies and international agreements. One element of this regime is the exclusive economic zone (EEZ), which generally extends from twelve to two-hundred nautical miles from the shore. Within the EEZ littoral states have authority over mineral and fishing resources, but they do not have control over shipping. The EEZ does not violate autonomy; there is no exercise of external authority, but it does violate territoriality by creating an area within which states have authority over some issues but not others.

Hence, rulers have frequently concluded contracts that violate the principle of autonomy, and in some cases territoriality as well. They are better off with these agreements than without them; otherwise they would have stayed with the status quo. Better to have financial resources at lower interest rates and conditionality than to pay much higher rates or have no access to international capital markets at all. Better to have the European Court and mutual recognition (both of which violate autonomy) than not. Better for the rulers of Czechoslovakia to have an international regime for minority protection in 1919 than to leave the large German minority in the Sudetenland without any international guarantees, although in 1938 this did Czechoslovakia no good. Better for Italian Christian Democrats to accept aid and guidance from the Americans than to confront Italy's large Communist Party without external support.

Coercion and Imposition

Coercion and imposition, both examples of intervention, exist along a continuum determined by the costs of refusal for the target state. With regard to Westphalian principles, coercion occurs when rulers in one state threaten to impose sanctions unless their counterparts in another compromise their domestic autonomy. The target can acquiesce or resist, but is always worse off than in the status quo ante. Imposition occurs when the rulers or would-be rulers of a target state have no choice; they are so weak that they must accept domestic structures, policies, or personnel preferred by more powerful actors, or else be eliminated, or, if they are weak polities that have not been recognized, remain in oblivion. The higher the cost of refusal for the target, the more a particular situation moves toward the pole of imposition. When applied against already established states, coercion and imposition are violations of the international legal, as well as the Westphalian, meaning of sovereignty. When applied against the would-be rulers of not yet created states, coercion and imposition are violations of the Westphalian model because the autonomy of any state that does emerge has been constrained by external actors, but not of international law concepts of sovereignty, which only apply once a state has secured international recognition.

Coercion and imposition, unlike conventions and contracts, must involve power asymmetry. Imposition entails forcing the target to do something that it would not otherwise do. There is no bargaining. Effective coercion can only occur if the initiator can make credible threats to impose sanctions, which requires that the initiator would be better off if the target resists and the sanctions are imposed, than if the initiator fails to act. The initiator has the ability, the power, to remove the status quo from the set of available options.

Coercion is not a common occurrence in the international system because the conditions under which it can occur are stringent. The initiator must be able to make a credible threat. Since there is usually a cost to applying sanctions, credibility is often problematic.

The clearest cases of coercion with respect to the Westphalian model have involved the use or threat of economic sanctions. In the twentieth century sanctions have been applied more than twenty times in attempts to improve human rights or alter the domestic regime of the target either by removing the ruler or changing institutional structures. Collective sanctions against South Africa with the aim of ending apartheid were authorized by the United Nations from 1962 until 1994. The United Kingdom enacted sanctions against Uganda from 1972 to 1979 to force out Idi Amin. The European Community used economic pressure against Turkey in 1981–82 to encourage the restoration of democracy. Between 1970 and 1990 the United States imposed sanctions against more than a dozen countries for human rights violations.[58] In all of these cases the target, even if it did not comply with the sanctions, was worse off than it had been because it could not both avoid sanctions and maintain its ex ante policies. Either it suffered sanctions, at least for some period of time, or it had to change its policies.

Imposition occurs when the target is so weak that it has no choice but to accept the demands of the more powerful. It has taken place more frequently than coercion. Force is the most obvious instrument of imposition. Imposition has been possible when there has been either a condominium among the major powers or the acceptance of spheres of influence. Great powers have been cautious about attempting to impose violations of the Westphalian model when such policies have been opposed by their major rivals, because mutual antagonism among the strong gives potential targets opportunities to maneuver.

Imposition has been employed in cases associated with minority rights, sovereign lending, and the basic constitutional structures of weaker states.

---

[58] Hufbauer et al. 1990.

In the nineteenth century the British not only signed agreements, contracts, with major European powers, to end the slave trade; they also used military force. In 1839 Britain unilaterally authorized its ships to board suspected slavers flying the Portuguese flag, arguing that Portugal had failed to honor its treaty commitments to end the slave trade. In 1850 British warships entered Brazilian ports and burned ships that were thought to be involved in slaving.

Imposition through military force has been used to secure repayment of sovereign debt. Gunboat diplomacy in the nineteenth century involved the use of naval power to seize control of customhouses so that tariffs (the most important source of revenue for most governments) could be used to repay foreign obligations. European powers forcibly seized the customs receipts of a number of Latin American countries, activities that prompted Latin American jurists such as Calvo and Drago to explicate doctrines upholding the norm of nonintervention. Following nationalist protests against increasing foreign financial control, the British army invaded Egypt in 1882, then formally a part of the Ottoman Empire, and established a protectorate that included control of Egypt's domestic finances. Partly in response to financial problems, U.S. leaders sent marines into the Dominican Republic in 1911, and in 1916 forced out the president, declared martial law, and appointed U.S. officials as ministers of war and the interior. Similar pressure was applied against Nicaragua at the same time, with American officials selecting the Nicaraguan president in 1916.

U.S. imposition in the Caribbean has not been limited to financial issues. American rulers made acceptance of the 1901 Platt amendment, which included provisions limiting Cuban debt, authorizing American intervention if Cuban independence was threatened, and establishing an American naval base at Guantanamo, a condition for the withdrawal of U.S. troops. American decision makers have sent troops into Haiti almost a dozen times, wrote the Haitian constitution in 1915, and appointed the president. In 1994 American military action restored a Haitian president who had been overthrown by the military. Panama became an independent state in 1903 with the support of American leaders who wanted to build a canal across the isthmus. In 1989 American troops invaded Panama, arrested its president, Manuel Noriega, and brought him back to Florida, where he was tried and convicted of criminal drug charges.

The smaller states of central and eastern Europe, like their Caribbean and Central American counterparts, have also frequently been subject to impositions that violate the Westphalian model. These states all emerged from the Habsburg and Ottoman empires. The initial existence of some of these states depended on recognition by the major powers. For rulers with limited material strength, international legal sovereignty, recognition, was valued because it could provide external resources and enhance internal legitimacy. Unlike Lenin and Mao, the would-be rulers of Serbia, Greece, and Montenegro could not secure effective territorial control and authority on their own. The major powers were not willing to recognize these states unless their would-be rulers accepted externally dictated conditions regarding domestic political structures, policies, or personnel. The alternative to acceptance was nonexistence.

When Greece was created in 1832 the form of government, a monarchy, the monarch (Otho, second son of the king of Bavaria), ministers, army officers, and financial policies were all dictated by the major European states whose military intervention gave Greece life in the first place. When Otho was overthrown in 1863, the major powers appointed his successor.

The Treaty of Berlin of 1878 recognized Serbia, Montenegro, and Romania as independent states, and Bulgaria as a tributary state of the Ottoman Empire, but only after the would-be rulers of these new states had been compelled to accept limitations on their authority regarding commercial arrangements and minorities. Moreover, the lower Danube, which flowed through Romania, was to be controlled by an independent European commission. The first Albanian constitution was drafted not by Albanians, but by representatives of the major European powers in 1914.

During the cold war the Soviet Union dictated the domestic institutional structure and the policies of its east European satellites. Poland, Hungary, Romania, Czechoslovakia, and Bulgaria were not Westphalian states. Their militaries could not operate independently. In some cases their internal security forces reported directly to Moscow.[59] Although their rulers did have some autonomy they could not stray too far from the Kremlin's preferences, and abandoning Communist regimes was out of the question until the late 1980s.

One of the more enduring examples of imposition under great-power condominium has involved efforts to secure minority rights in eastern and central Europe during the nineteenth and twentieth centuries. All of the states that emerged from the Ottoman and Habsburg empires were compelled to accept provisions for minority protection as a condition of international recognition. This was true for Greece in 1832, and for Serbia, Montenegro, Romania, and Bulgaria at Berlin in 1878. The would-be rulers of the target states did not want to grant minority rights, but they acquiesced to the demands of the rulers of the major European powers because international recognition with minority rights provisions, which might be evaded, was better than no recognition at all.

The would-be leaders of all of the states that were created after the First World War (or were successors to the defeated empires) had to accept extensive provisions for the protection of minorities. As in Greece in 1832,

---

[59] Rice 1984, chapt. 1.

these would-be rulers had limited bargaining leverage. Austria, Hungary, Bulgaria, and Turkey were defeated states, and minority protections were written into their peace treaties. Poland, Czechoslovakia, Yugoslavia, Romania, and Greece were new or enlarged states. They signed minority rights treaties with the Allied and Associated Powers. Albania, Lithuania, Latvia, Estonia, and Iraq made declarations as a result of pressure that was brought upon them when they applied to join the League of Nations. With only a few exceptions, notably Czechoslovakia, Hungary, and the Baltic states, the would-be rulers of these new states were not sympathetic to minority rights. They did not want their constitutional arrangements to be dictated by external powers.[60]

The United States and especially the major powers of western Europe attempted to secure minority rights in the states that emerged out of Yugoslavia after 1991. Recognition of Slovenia and Croatia by the European Community in December of 1991 was conditioned on protection for minorities, including a guaranteed number of seats in the Croatian Parliament. The 1995 Dayton accords provided for the establishment of a commission for minorities, a majority of whose members were foreign, as well as an ombudsman who was initially to be appointed by the major European states. These were highly coercive if not imposed arrangements that would have been rejected by the states that emerged from the former Yugoslavia had they not been subject to external pressure.

CONCLUSIONS

The term sovereignty has been used in four different ways: domestic sovereignty, interdependence sovereignty, international legal sovereignty, and Westphalian sovereignty. The latter two, and most particularly Westphalian sovereignty, are the subject of this study. Both international legal and Westphalian sovereignty are best conceptualized as examples of organized hypocrisy. Both have clear logics of appropriateness, but these logics are sometimes inconsistent with a logic of consequences. Given the absence of authoritative institutions and power asymmetries, rulers can follow a logic of consequences and reject a logic of appropriateness. Principles have been enduring but violated.

For Westphalian sovereignty the violations have taken place through conventions, contracting, coercion, and imposition. Conventions and contracting are voluntary; rulers have invited violations of the de facto autonomy of their own polities because it leaves them better off than in the status quo ante. Coercion leaves one of the parties worse off; the target must alter its domestic policies or institutions or accept the costs of sanc-

---

[60] Claude 1955, 16; D. Jones 1991, 45; Bartsch 1995, 81–85.

tions. Imposition occurs when the target is so weak that it has no choice but to comply either because the ruler or would-be ruler is faced with military force or because the failure to secure international legal sovereignty, recognition, would threaten the very existence of the state. Coercion and imposition are examples of violations of Westphalian sovereignty through intervention rather than invitation.

For international legal sovereignty violations have primarily been the result of contracting and conventions. Rulers have recognized entities that lacked formal juridical autonomy or, in the case of the Knights of Malta, even territory. Rulers have also refused to recognize governments that have demonstrated domestic sovereignty, and extended recognition to governments that have not exercised effective control over their own territory. These have often been unilateral actions that have not been contingent on the policies of other states.

The logic of appropriateness that is associated with the Westphalian norm of autonomy has mattered in the calculations of rulers, but so have alternatives such as human rights, minority rights, international stability, and fiscal responsibility. Rulers have different constituencies. They respond primarily to domestic supporters who hold different values in different states. The material interests of states often clash. Power is asymmetrical. There is no hierarchical authority. Logics of consequences have trumped Westphalian logics of appropriateness.

The basic rule of international legal sovereignty has been more robust and more widely adhered to. Once rulers have recognition, they hardly ever want to give it up. International legal sovereignty provides an array of benefits, including reducing the transaction costs of entering into agreements with other entities, facilitating participation in international organizations, extending diplomatic immunity, and establishing special legal protections. Because international legal sovereignty is a widely accepted and recognized script, it makes it easier to organize support from internal as well as external sources. Especially in polities with weak domestic sovereignty, international legal sovereignty, international recognition, can provide a signal to constituents that a regime and its rulers are more likely to survive and thereby make it more likely that these constituents would support the regime.

Nevertheless, international legal sovereignty like Westphalian sovereignty is not a Nash equilibrium, nor is it taken for granted. Rulers have had reasons to deviate from the rule and have invented other institutional forms when it has suited their purpose. The British Commonwealth, with its high commissioners rather than ambassadors, was an alternative to international legal sovereignty. Meetings of the major industrialized states include not only the representatives of international legal sovereigns—the presidents, premiers, and prime ministers of this and that country—but also the commissioner of the European Union. The consequences for Taiwan of losing its international legal sovereignty in the 1970s have been mitigated by the fact that some countries, notably the United States, have invented alternative arrangements that provide the functional equivalent of recognition.

Of all the social environments within which human beings operate, the international system is one of the most complex and weakly institutionalized. It lacks authoritative hierarchies. Rulers are likely to be more responsive to domestic material and ideational incentives than international ones. Norms are sometimes mutually inconsistent. Power is asymmetrical. No rule or set of rules can cover all circumstances. Logics of consequences can be compelling. Organized hypocrisy is the norm.

CHAPTER 2

Theories of Institutions and International Politics

THE MAJOR THEORIES of international politics—neorealism, neoliberalism, the English school, constructivism, world culture—are examples of more general perspectives on the nature of social life. One fundamental divide is between actor-oriented theories that take actors as the ontological givens and sociological (for lack of a better word) theories that take institutional structures as the ontological givens. These two approaches have different understandings about the nature of actors or agents and institutions. Indeed, such basic terms as actor and institution can only be comprehended from within a particular theoretical context. Webster's dictionary is not helpful.

For actor-oriented perspectives, the actors and their preferences are exogenous; actor-oriented theories do not attempt to explain them. Institutions are formal or informal structures of norms and rules that are created by actors to increase their utility by, for instance, providing additional information or enforcing contracts. The strategies of actors, their policy choices, but not their underlying desires, their preferences, can be affected by institutions. This does not mean that institutions always produce optimal outcomes. Suboptimality might result, for instance, from path-dependent processes, or limited information.

This study begins with an actor-oriented perspective. The actors, however, are not states, as is the case for neoliberalism and neorealism. Assuming states as the starting point is not useful because the aim of this project is to understand how certain attributes associated with statehood—international recognition and autonomy—have actually operated. Rather, this study takes rulers, political leaders who make policy decisions, as the ontological givens. I assume that rulers want to remain in office, whatever that office might be, and to promote the security, prosperity, and values of their supporters, whether they be a national electorate or the presidential guard.

Sociological theories begin with institutional structures. Institutions are formal and informal rules and norms that generate other more specific entities or agents. Professors could not exist without universities or generals without armies. Relations among individuals or groups are conditioned by, or a manifestation of, the institutional arrangements within which they are embedded. The interests and power of actors are defined by the roles they play in larger institutional structures: police can arrest, soldiers can kill, professors can grade, surgeons can cut, judges can sentence.

Neorealism and neoliberalism are actor-oriented theories. They begin with states understood as unified autonomous actors. The English school is a sociological theory. It begins with a set of institutional structures that define the roles that are played by states and, indeed, with the very fact that the actors in the international system are states and not empires, city-leagues, religious organizations, or tribes. Actor-oriented theories are engaged in analysis in the sense of specifying cause-and-effect relationships. Sociological theories are engaged in understanding in the sense of imputing underlying institutional structures, which cannot be directly observed, from manifest behavior and the justifications that are offered for it.

These major approaches to the study of international politics whether actor-oriented or sociological reflect more general discussions about the nature of institutions and agency that can be arrayed in a space defined by two dimensions: institutionalization and durability. Institutionalization, the extent to which actual behavior conforms with principles and norms, can be high or low. Durability, the extent to which principles and norms endure in the face of changing circumstances, can also be high or low. Institutions can be deeply embedded, enduring and highly consequential for action; they can be brittle stalks, consequential but brittle in the face of changing conditions; they can be inconsequential and short-lived in a world of anarchy, and they can be characterized by organized hypocrisy, durable but often transgressed. The best-known approaches to international relations—neorealism, neoliberalism, and the English school—fall in the three quadrants defined by anarchical, brittle stalks, and embedded understandings of institutions (Figure 2.1). Organized hypocrisy has been much less well explored. Rulers have endorsed the principles associated with both international legal and Westphalian sovereignty for more than two hundred years, but in an environment characterized by multiple norms, power asymmetries, competing domestic demands, and the absence of any hierarchical authority, adhering to these principles has never been taken for granted.

CONVENTIONAL WISDOMS: SOVEREIGNTY AND THEORIES OF INTERNATIONAL RELATIONS

Westphalian sovereignty has been a central concept for the most well developed contemporary theories of international relations with the exception of Marxism. For neorealism and neoliberal institutionalism, Westphalian sovereignty is an analytic assumption. For the English school, Westphalian sovereignty is an internalized norm that has guided, although not determined, the behavior of political leaders. Recent constructivist theories have, like this study, emphasized the extent to which norms associated with sovereignty have been problematic and subject to challenge. While the empirical conclusions of several constructivist analyses are entirely in conformity with the evidence presented here, these studies have placed more weight on discourse and the impact of ideas, and less on power and material interests as explanations for the contested character of Westphalian sovereignty.

Any theoretical perspective must make some assumptions about the nature of the world; that is, about the units that are the subject of study. Neorealism begins with the assumption that Westphalian sovereign states are the constitutive actors of the system.[1] Each state has the same basic purposes and functions. Each state is autonomous: it is free to choose the course of action that will best serve its own national interest subject only to constraints imposed by the external environment. States vary only according to their power capabilities. Outcomes are a function of interaction among states. Neorealism is an actor-oriented, functional, utilitarian theory in which the actors—in this case, rational, value-maximizing sovereign states—are taken as a given.[2]

Similarly, the Westphalian model is an analytic assumption for neoliberal institutionalism. The actors are Westphalian states, unified rational autonomous entities striving to maximize their utility in the face of constraints and opportunities that emanate from an anarchic although interdependent international environment. What distinguishes neoliberalism from realism is its different understanding of the characteristic problem for these Westphalian states: for neoliberal institutionalism the problem is the resolution of market failures; for realism it is security and distributional conflicts.[3]

The Westphalian model is also the critical element of international society or sociological perspectives including some international legal ap-

---

[1] Neo this and neo that is usually an indication that a theoretical perspective has not been clearly thought out; if it had been, the "neo" would not be necessary. I bow here, however, to conventional usage. Neorealism refers to a theoretical perspective in which states as autonomous unified actors are the ontological given. In contrast, traditional realism has been identified as a perspective in which levels of uncertainty are high and statesmen have more discretion. The ontological givens of traditional realism are, however, not clear. Are the actors states or are the actors the rulers of states? Traditional realist discussions such as those of Morgenthau and Kissinger emphasized distinctions between status quo and revisionist or revolutionary states, a distinction that Waltz aptly pointed out introduces variations in domestic political systems, not just the international distribution of power, as a causal factor. See Morgenthau 1948; Kissinger 1957; Waltz 1979.

[2] See Wendt 1987, 343, who offers a critical account of neorealism; Waltz 1979, chaps. 3–6, for the best-known, thorough, and elegant exposition of the theory.

[3] See Keohane 1984 for the seminal treatment of neoliberal institutionalism and Krasner 1991 for the distinction between market failure and distributional conflicts.

proaches, the English school, and some constructivist discussions. In contrast, however, with neorealism and neoliberalism, sovereignty is not an analytic assumption but is rather an empirical regularity that reflects intersubjectively shared understandings about territoriality, autonomy, and recognition. The ontological given for international society perspectives is the underlying institutional structure, a structure that is defined by a set of mutually shared norms and expectations. This structure cannot be directly observed. Rather, it is reflected in the behavior and explanations offered by individuals in their capacity as representatives of states.

Many students of international law have described the international system in terms of a set of shared values or rules that constrain the behavior of actors. For instance, according to Farer writing about the Yale school, the basis of "international order" is a set of consensus values. They hold international society together. Evidence for the existence of such base values is found in treaties, the decisions of international tribunals, resolutions of international organizations, the writings of authorities, and the statements and actions of national policy makers. There are four core values in the present international system:

1. The maintenance of minimum public order, meaning the avoidance of behavior that would risk general war.
2. Self-determination, although this term lacks any specific meaning beyond decolonization.
3. Minimum human rights, which consists of the notion that a state violates international norms if it denies an "identifiable group equal access to the political, economic, and social perquisites of that society."
4. Modernization, the assertion that living standards should be raised throughout the world.[4]

For students of international relations the English school is the best-known sociological perspective.[5] For the English school the defining characteristic of the present international system is that "the independent state has everywhere become the standard form of territorial political organization and all conflicting standards have been discredited and in most cases abandoned."[6] The individual participants in this drama—public officials, diplomats, statesmen, political leaders—have internalized the same basic rules of the game. Actions follow particular patterns not because they are dictated by some higher authority or coerced by the threat of force, or

---

[4] Farer 1968, 22.

[5] For a discussion of the differences between British and American approaches to international relations theory, see Buzan 1993.

[6] Jackson and James 1993, 4.

constrained by the power of other states, but because players in international society have a common world view.

For the English school, internal and external sovereignty (most closely associated with what is termed Westphalian sovereignty in this study) is the constitutive rule of international society. Internal sovereignty "means supremacy over all other authorities within that territory and population." States also assert external authority "by which is meant not supremacy but independence (what is termed in this study autonomy) of outside authorities." Sovereignty exists both at the normative and factual level. States assert sovereign rights and "they also actually exercise, in varying degrees, such supremacy and independence in practice. An independent political community which merely claims a right to sovereignty (or is judged by others to have such a right) but cannot assert this right in practice, is not a state properly so-called."[7]

The role of sovereign states permits some kinds of activities but not others. The rules of sovereignty give states full authority over activities within their own borders and prohibit intervention in the internal affairs of other states. Hedley Bull, the best-known exponent of the English school, writes: "From the perspective of any particular state what it chiefly hopes to gain from participation in the society of states is recognition of its independence of outside authority, and in particular of its supreme jurisdiction over its subjects and territory. The chief price it has to pay for this is recognition of like rights to independence and sovereignty on the part of other states." The existence of international society is reflected in diplomatic practices, the balance of power as a conscious policy not some automatic mechanical equilibrating mechanism, the rules of international law whose "binding force is an especially strong one" because they have the force of law not merely morality, and international institutions created to regulate interdependencies.[8]

For the English school an international society is the product of a shared civilization. For an international society to exist there must be "an international social consciousness, a world-wide community sentiment."[9] The contemporary sovereign state system is a product of beliefs that are rooted in Christian notions of natural law. These European concepts have spread, to one extent or another, to other areas of the world. Where there is no shared civilization, no shared sense of values, there is no international society, although there may be an international system, a situation in

---

[7] Bull 1977, 8–9; Bull and Watson 1984; Watson 1992. For other sociological analyses that emphasize the importance of the sovereign state, see Cerny 1990, 3; Tilly 1990b, 2–3.

[8] Bull 1977, 17, 104–6, 142–43. Also see Wight 1968, 96–97.

[9] Wight 1968, 96–97.

which there is interaction but no constraining norms. According to the English school, there were, for instance, no common rules affecting relations between Genghis Khan and those he conquered, between the Spanish and the Aztecs, or between the Christian and Moslem worlds. There have been other international societies aside from the sovereign state system including the classical Greek city-states, the Islamic world, the Chinese tributary state system, and the Indian international order. During the cold war the sense of shared culture among the great powers was less intense than it had been in the eighteenth and nineteenth centuries.[10]

The adherents of the English school have never claimed that behavior in the international system is solely determined by an internalized set of norms. Bull, Wight, and others recognized that norms are violated. Some aspects of the international system can be explained in purely Hobbesian terms, a war of all against all with no shared sense of community. Other aspects reflect the behavior of nonstate actors. Bull himself edited a volume on intervention, a practice that violates the constitutive principle of the sovereign state system. The great powers are often in position to do what they like. The disintegration or absence of an international society occurs not when there is simply a violation of the rules (there is always sin) but rather when there is an appeal to conflicting principles.[11]

What has come to be termed constructivism is another approach, which, like the Yale school of international law and the English school, argues that international relations can only be adequately understood from a perspective that emphasizes shared norms and values. The identities and associated roles of actors are generated and reproduced by mutual interaction, which involves not just behavior but also shared conceptions and intersubjective understandings. "Discourse—whether political or scientific—is actively involved in the construction of reality."[12] Brute physical factors, such as the distribution of power among states, only have significance in the context of given social structures.[13]

Aside from agreeing on the importance of intersubjectively shared norms, however, analysts associated with constructivism as a general research program have had deep epistemological and analytic disagreements. What might be termed conventional constructivists have accepted the possibility of objective social scientific investigations. Postmodernists, in contrast, have expressed skepticism about the possibility of any objective real-

[10] Bull 1977, 12–13, 16, 44, 115; Bull and Watson 1984.

[11] Bull 1984; Wight 1968, 101–2, 111, 117–20; Bull 1977, xi–xii, xiv, 7, 41–43, 67–68, 138.

[12] Bartelson 1995, 18–19.

[13] Wendt and Friedheim 1996, 242, 248–54; Wendt 1994; R. Hall 1997, 594; Strang 1996, 22. See Katzenstein 1996 and J. Ruggie 1998 for excellent expositions of the constructivist project.

ity. The observer is always insinuated in that which is being observed. Different analysts may have different truths.[14]

John Searle has pointed to the fundamental fallacy in the postmodern project. There can be a subjective ontology but an objective epistemology. Human institutions are the result of intersubjective shared understanding. They are not brute physical facts. If human beings disappeared, American currency would just be green pieces of paper, but because human beings agree that these pieces of paper represent value, they can be exchanged for goods. The fact that the objects of study, human institutions including sovereignty, exist only because individuals share the same intersubjective understanding of their status functions does not preclude an objective epistemology. Investigators can make objective judgments about the character of institutions.[15]

Most contructivists have rejected postmodernism. Conventional constructivists accept that propositions can be tested against evidence, including evidence based on claims about institutions that exist only because of the characteristics that humans attribute to them. The issue then is, What are the characteristics of these institutions? How should sovereignty be understood?

The analytic claims of constructivists have varied. Some have argued that sovereignty has a taken-for-granted quality. Alexander Murphy, for instance, writes that "The political geographic importance of the ideal was no less than to crowd out competing conceptions of how power might be organized to the point where the sovereign territorial ideal became the only imaginable spatial framework for political life."[16] Like the claims of this study, however, most recent work from a constructivist perspective has suggested that the attributes associated with sovereignty have been problematic and contested. Established agreements can change quickly. Sovereignty is constantly being constructed and deconstructed through interactions among agents and between agents and structures. Neither the state nor sovereignty can be taken as given. Rather the state as an agent and sovereignty as an institution or discourse are mutually constitutive and constantly being transformed and changed.[17]

Wendt and Friedheim have suggested that authority among states can be ordered in a variety of ways of which sovereign statehood with its claims of Westphalian autonomy is only one. Authority can be internationally shared as in the European Union. It can be formally hierarchical as in an

---

[14] Bartelson 1995 offers one example of a postmodern examination of sovereignty.

[15] Searle 1995.

[16] Murphy 1996, 91.

[17] Biersteker and Weber 1996, 3, 11; Weber and Biersteker 1996, 282; Onuf 1991, 431; Doty 1996, 121.

empire. It can be informally hierarchically ordered among formally independent states as in the case of what they term informal empires. There have been three informal empires in the postwar period, Wendt and Friedheim argue, those of the United States, the Soviet Union, and France. These have been based not simply on material capability but also on intersubjective structures of authority. To create an informal empire, a more powerful state must intervene in a weaker one to create a regime that is friendly to it. This may happen with, or without, the weaker state's consent. Informal empires are institutionalized by allowing the more powerful state to have some control over the domestic and foreign policies of the weaker state in exchange for the provision of security, and by securing the rule of actors in the subordinate state who would otherwise have to make concessions to domestic rivals or would not be able to rule at all. Informal empire creates identities that institutionalize this arrangement. Clients become dependent on and identify with their patrons. The shared beliefs involved in informal empire will typically be embodied in an ideology and given some formal organizational form such as the Warsaw Pact.[18]

Wendt and Friedheim's conception of informal empires captures exactly the descriptive claims of this study. Westphalian sovereignty has never been taken for granted. The exercise of informal authority has been pervasive in the international system. What distinguishes this study from those constructivist approaches that have emphasized the problematic nature of sovereignty is not the empirical description of reality but rather the weight that should be given to different explanatory factors. For all constructivist arguments, shared principles and norms are the critical determinants of actual outcomes. These norms, not directly observable, are the underlying structure that is manifest in actions and the reasons that are offered to justify them. Power is not ignored but is comprehended as being embedded in an underlying institutional structure. Differences in material capabilities are never the fundamental motivating factor although they may play a proximate or intermediate role. Wendt and Friedheim, for instance, note that an informal empire can only be established if there are power asymmetries so large that a stronger state can provide security for a weaker one.[19]

This study gives greater weight to the importance of power asymmetries. In the international environment rulers constantly scan for resources, material and ideological, that will enhance their ability to stay in power and promote the interests of their supports. Rulers are calculators, not agents manifesting some deeper international institutional structure, although they may be firmly embedded in well-established domestic ar-

---

[18] Wendt and Friedheim 1996, 247–52.
[19] Wendt and Friedheim 1996, 248–52; see also Reus-Smit 1997, 568.

rangements. International norms are often contradictory. The disparity in resources available to rulers in different states can be huge. Rulers may appeal to norms that do depend on intersubjective shared understandings, albeit understandings that can be manipulated, but they may also appeal to guns, and a bullet through the head has the same effect regardless of the cognitive perspective of the target. In the international environment, logics of consequences dominate logics of appropriateness. Norms, though not irrelevant, do not have the weight that constructivism has attributed to them.

The Westphalian model is an excellent starting point for analyzing (à la realism or neoliberal institutionalism) or understanding (à la international society perspectives) much of what goes on in the international environment. A great deal of activity is completely consistent with the Westphalian model, whether it is treated as an analytic assumption or behavioral regularity generated by intersubjective shared understanding. The claims of external actors are rebuffed. Authoritative decision makers declare war, form alliances, enter into trade agreements, and regulate migration. Within their own borders, rulers have autonomy.

As Chapters 4–8 show, however, there are many other situations in which the principle of territoriality or, more frequently, autonomy has been violated. A system based on the formal or constitutional autonomy of states (the exclusion of external authority) does not preclude the de facto influence of external entities. Rulers have voluntarily entered into agreements, have issued invitations, that have insinuated external authority structures within their own borders, and rulers in powerful states have intervened in the internal affairs of weaker ones. The right, or ability, of the state apparatus to exercise full authority within its own territorial borders has never been consistently established in practice and has been persistently challenged in theory.

The empirical inaccuracy of the Westphalian model is a particular problem for the English school and, more generally, for sociological arguments that conceptualize the international system as an international society with more or less taken-for-granted norms. These perspectives suggest that there are some aspects of international relations that are so deeply embedded in the world views of political leaders that they are not questioned. Bull and other members of the English school have recognized that norms may be overwhelmed or shunted aside by power, but this is only likely to happen if there is no shared civilization.

It is, however, difficult to find any practices in the international system that are consistent with the notion that there are some norms that are taken for granted, even those associated with international legal, as opposed to Westphalian sovereignty. Rules as apparently uncontested as the treatment of diplomats have been grossly violated. One striking aspect of the seizure of the American diplomats by Iran was the lack of international reaction. Iran did not become a pariah state. The United States broke diplomatic relations but other states did not. Iranian representatives were not excluded from international fora. What the Iranian case suggests is that rules, when they exist in the international system, are instrumental, not deeply embedded. It was in the interest of the new Iranian regime to seize the American diplomats. It served a domestic if not an international political purpose. It was not in the interest of the other states, which wanted to maintain communication, to isolate Iran.

The rules regarding the treatment of diplomats, which are associated with international legal sovereignty, are among the least contested exactly because they are instrumentally useful. More generally the defining rule of international legal sovereignty—recognize entities that have territory and constitutional autonomy or independence—has been generally but, again, not universally honored. The participation of members of the British Commonwealth in international organizations before 1940, the acceptance of the European Union as a sovereign entity, the membership of Byelorussia and the Ukraine in the United Nations, the recognition of the Knights of Malta, and the inclusion of Hong Kong as a member of the World Trade Organization are all violations of international legal sovereignty that were agreed to by rulers because it served their instrumental interests.

Violations of Westphalian as opposed to international legal sovereignty have been more pervasive even within areas such as western Europe that must be characterized as sharing the same civilization. Formal independence has not guaranteed the exclusion of external powers. Religious toleration, minority rights, human rights, fiscal responsibility, and international security are principles that have persistently been invoked to justify violations of defacto autonomy, either coercively or voluntarily. States have endorsed mutually contradictory norms, often in the same documents. The international environment has been characterized by competing and often logically contradictory norms, not some single coherent set of rules.

The inaccuracy of the Westphalian model is also problematic for neorealism and neoliberal institutionalism. For both of these approaches, self-help and autonomy, are analytic assumptions, not claims of empirical validity. Support for these theories comes from propositions derived from their assumptions that are consistent with evidence. It helps, however, if the assumptions themselves appear to be empirically valid—that is, if states really do seem to be motivated by the desire to protect their territorial and political integrity and to enhance their material well-being. If there are states in the international system whose actions are inconsistent with these assumptions, then it is difficult to see how neoliberal or neorealist approaches would be applicable.

Neorealism and neoliberalism offer compelling analyses of some issues, indeed, for many of the biggest and most important issues in international relations, such as major wars or the possibility of cooperation among the great powers; but they cannot offer much guidance in situations where their basic ontological assumption that states are autonomous actors is violated. If authoritative decisions within a state are constrained by external actors, then outcomes cannot be the result of autochthonously generated preferences whose realization is determined only by the external power and preferences of other states. For instance, during the cold war the foreign policy of Poland or Bulgaria could not be explained in conventional realist terms. These countries did not have the option of weighing the relative merits of "bandwagoning" versus balancing, not just because the Soviet Union was powerful but because their domestic political structures were thoroughly penetrated. Neorealism and neoliberalism have been wonderfully productive theories but they have blinded analysts to a large set of international interactions that have involved efforts by rulers to alter the domestic structures and policies of their own or other states.

For neorealism and neoliberalism, the Westphalian model presents a logical paradox, not just empirical anomalies. Two of the basic assumptions of neorealism—self-help and autonomy—are logically inconsistent.[20] Self-help follows from anarchy; there is no higher authority to judge or dictate policy. A state can consider any policy that is in its self-interest. Yet the assumption of autonomy implies that some policies will not be pursued: rulers will not engage in actions that would compromise the internal integrity of their own or other polities. If there is no way to preclude some policies, then compromising the internal autonomy of another state, or even one's own polity, is one option among others. A state might choose to promote its objectives by applying external pressure through military threats and economic embargoes, policies perfectly consistent with neorealism, or it might weaken its opponent through internal subversion or by altering the domestic institutional structures of the target state, policies that contradict a neorealist ontology. A state might defend the financial interests of its foreign investors by limiting capital flows, or it might directly appropriate taxes by assuming control of customhouses, making the debtor something less than a fully Westphalian sovereign.

If there is self-help, there will be some circumstances when political leaders will decide that constraining some aspect of the domestic policies or institutions of another state, or accepting such constraints on one's own state, is the best policy option. In these cases self-help undermines autonomy. A theory that asserts that actors, in this case states, can do everything they please subject only to the reactions of other autonomous

---

[20] Hoffmann 1984.

states, but at the same time cannot do some other things, is not logically coherent.

The Westphalian model, whether deployed as an analytic assumption by neorealism and neoliberal institutionalism or treated as an empirical regularity by international society perspectives, is problematic. Neorealism and neoliberalism elide over the logical contradiction between self-help and autonomy by focusing on issues such as great-power wars or economic bargaining among major powers, where autonomy is rarely an issue. International society perspectives are refuted by empirical evidence: the actions of political leaders are not consistent with the rules and principles of Westphalian and international legal sovereignty. In an environment in which there are many norms from which to choose, constructivism's emphasis on intersubjectively shared understandings provides only limited guidance.

Constructivism, neorealism, neoliberalism, the English school, are not, of course, the only theoretical approaches to understanding international politics. There are other perspectives that have not deployed the Westphalian model. Marxist theories of various kinds never assumed that states were unified autonomous actors. On the contrary, the starting point for Marxism, the ontological given, is the economic structure. The economic structure is defined by the pattern of ownership of the means of production and the extent to which individuals are free to sell their own labor. Capitalism is a system defined by private ownership of the means of production, and a free market for labor.

Dependency theory, which draws on Marxist analytic categories and reasoning, unambiguously rejects the Westphalian model. Indeed, the gravamen of the argument is that weak states in the periphery are penetrated by actors from the core, such as multinational corporations, military advisors, diplomatic agents, and covert operatives. Peripheral states are not autonomous unitary actors; they are fragmented entities, much of whose behavior is determined by external forces. The economic and political choices of peripheral countries are limited not just by the external environment but also by the fact that both public and private decision-making networks are penetrated or even directly controlled by core actors. For dependency theory, violations of the Westphalian model are no surprise, in fact, they are exactly what would be expected in a world capitalist system.[21]

Dependency theory has been empirically demolished by the huge variation in growth rates among African, Asian, and Latin American countries, all of which were, at some point, part of the periphery. The financial crisis of the late 1990s notwithstanding, the newly industrializing countries of East Asia have grown at historically unprecedented rates, while most Afri-

---

[21] Evans 1979; Wallerstein 1974; Cardoso and Faletto 1979.

can states have remained mired in poverty. National rather than international factors offer the most compelling explanation for these variations.

Another alternative to approaches for which Westphalian sovereignty is a central concept is the world culture perspective, which underscores the similarity of domestic organizations across states. In the contemporary international system there is an astonishing degree of correspondence among the domestic laws and formal institutions of states with radically different levels of socioeconomic development, religious commitments, geographic location, and cultural heritage. Large numbers of states arrange their school systems in the same way, conduct censuses, provide for social security, stipulate rights for women, and establish privileges for guest workers.[22]

These similarities cannot be explained by the domestic characteristics of countries, since these vary so dramatically. These organizational isomorphisms are, according to the world cultural perspective, a product of a global institutional structure within which individual states are embedded. States seek rules of appropriate behavior. They follow externally provided scripts that are based on a globally accepted culture of modernity, progress, and rationality. Domestic structures are not a reflection of autochthonously generated purposes or reasoning, but exhibit an effort to be institutionally isomorphic with legitimated global values.[23]

The world culture perspective, however, suggests a degree of uniformity that is belied by the empirical evidence presented in this study. The extent to which external actors have compromised the Westphalian model has varied across states and has been determined primarily by power and interest. The most powerful states in the international system, the United States being the most notable example, have responded primarily to internally generated interests and norms. The United States has been a Westphalian state from its inception. Smaller weaker states have been much more subject to external pressures.

In sum, neither neorealism, neoliberalism, nor the English school provides an adequate understanding of the many developments in the international system that are inconsistent with the Westphalian model. Belying neorealist and neoliberal assumptions, many states have not been autonomous unified actors. Empirically, the frequency with which the domestic autonomy of states has been violated suggests that the shared norms and internalized constraints stipulated by the English school do not exist at

---

[22] Strang and Chang 1993; Finnemore 1996b; Soysal 1994; Meyer et al. 1997.

[23] Finnemore 1991; Finnemore 1996a, chap. 1; Finnemore 1996b; Meyer, Boli, and Thomas 1987, 13; Meyer, et al., 1997; Meyer and Rowan 1991, 45–46; Jepperson and Meyer 1991, 206. See Scott 1995 for a discussion of the distinction between sociological theories that emphasize normative socialization and those, like Meyer's, that conceptualize action and rhetoric in terms of cognitive scripts.

least with regard to the Westphalian model. Even the rules associated with international legal sovereignty are not taken for granted. Some constructivist analyses have emphasized the contested nature of international norms but, in contrast with this study, they have sought to explain variation in terms of intersubjectively shared ideas rather than the calculations of rulers who are free to choose among material and ideological resources.

Other theories, notably Marxism, dependency theory, and the world systems perspective do not use the Westphalian model as either an assumption or an empirical reality. They too, however, fail to provide an adequate understanding of the empirical issues investigated in this study. Many of the reasons for violating the domestic autonomy of weaker states, especially those associated with human and minority rights, cannot be explained from a Marxist perspective. Analysts working from a world culture perspective have demonstrated uniformity in the formal organizational arrangements of many states, but this theory cannot explain variations in the extent to which states with different amounts of power have been differentially affected by prevailing scripts.

INSTITUTIONS AND INSTITUTIONAL THEORY

Studies of international politics have not developed in isolation from more general investigations of the nature of social life. In recent years institutions have become a particular focus of attention. Institutions can be categorized along two dimensions: *institutionalization*—the extent to which behavior conforms with institutional structures, that is with some set of principles, norms, and rules (institutions can be formal or informal, explicitly articulated or embedded in culture).[24]—and *persistence or durability*—the extent to which a particular set of principles, norms, and rules persists over time in the face of changing conditions.

The greater the conformity between behavior and institutional rules, the higher the level of institutionalization. The most highly institutionalized patterns are those that are taken for granted. Institutional structures and associated patterns of behavior are taken for granted if actors either cannot conceive of alternatives or, if they can, regard the existing constraints as absolute and fixed in nature. Taken-for-granted institutions are often dignified by tradition or become identified with common sense.[25] The most weakly institutionalized environments are those in which institutional structures exist but have only the most limited impact on the actual pattern of behavior. Lip service might be given to particular norms

---

[24] See North 1990, 53, for a discussion of formal and informal institutions.
[25] Jepperson 1991, 147; Swidler 1986, 278–80.

and rules, but nothing more. An environment devoid of institutional structures would be akin to a state of nature in which behavior is driven only by short-term calculations of interest and action is constrained only by the power of others.

If institutionalization is one measure of the importance of institutions, then durability is a second. An institution, a set of principles, rules, and norms, is durable if it persists over time or across issue areas despite changing external circumstances. One way to show that institutions, as opposed to simply the power and interests of actors, matter is to demonstrate that they endure even though the interests and capabilities of specific actors differ.[26]

Rules or norms can, however, endure but have only a limited impact on actual behavior. Actors can say one thing and do another. They may pick and choose among different, and mutually incompatible, norms. They may adopt institutional arrangements that are inappropriate for their own material circumstances. Their identity, and the identity that they present to others, may be influenced by abiding principles and norms, but their actual behavior may be driven by a logic of consequences that is detached from principle.

The efficacy of institutional arguments rests on their ability to demonstrate either institutionalization (the congruence of institutions and behavior) or durability (the persistence of institutions in the face of changing circumstances), or both. If there is neither institutionalization nor durability, then institutional arguments cannot illuminate social phenomena. There is no point in going beyond the interests and power of actors. In contrast, institutions could be consequential either because they have a strong impact on behavior during a particular period and then disappear, or because, even if their impact is weak or uneven, they are enduring. All of the major theories about institutions can be arrayed in a space defined by the dimensions of institutionalization and durability (Figure 2.1).

Toward the southwest corner of Figure 2.1 institutions are of limited relevance; they are neither resilient nor consequential. In a situation of pure anarchy, institutions do not exist at all. In the southeast corner institutions are brittle stalks. Rules constrain behavior but they can change rapidly if the interests or power of actors changes; institutions have conse-

---

[26] Some of the most powerful arguments about the nature of specific polities are exactly designed to show that similar problems are handled in very different ways because basic institutional arrangements—norms, rules, and decision-making procedures—vary from one polity to another. See, for instance, Katzenstein and Okawara 1993 and Katzenstein 1993 on Japanese and German approaches to terrorism, M. Ruggie 1984 on the treatment of working women in Britain as opposed to Sweden, Soysal 1994 on the treatment of guest workers in different European countries, and Hartz 1955 on the influence of Lockeian liberal norms on the United States.

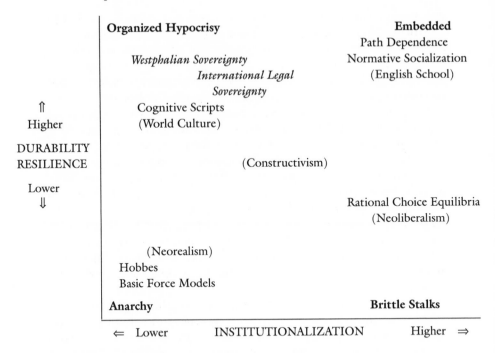

Durability Resilience: Persistence of norms in the face of changing conditions.

Institutionalization: Conformity between norms and behavior.

Italicized entries: Major concerns of this study.

Bracketed Entries: Theories of international relations.

Other Entries: General theories.

Figure 2.1. How and Why Institutions Matter

quences but are not durable or resilient. In the northeast corner institutions are embedded; they are both consequential and resilient, enduring even if the power and preferences of actors change. In the northwest corner institutions are characterized by organized hypocrisy; they are long-lasting but their impact on behavior is weak or uneven; the rules are followed in some circumstances but not others.

Under conditions of pure anarchy only the power and interests of actors matter. Hobbes's state of nature is one example. Every man must fend for himself. There are no constraints except the power of other individuals. Life is nasty, brutish, and short.

In the study of international relations, neorealism is a theory for which institutions may have some limited consequence, but they cannot be durable. The exemplary problems in international politics involve either zero-sum or distributional conflict. States struggle along the Pareto frontier; what makes one better off will make others worse off, regardless of whether they are interested in relative or absolute gains.[27] Institutions, conceived of as a set of rules and norms often embodied in formal organizations, reflect the policies of powerful states. They are to one extent or another the result of coercion. Institutions can reduce transaction costs by, for instance, providing salient solutions or signaling preferences. Alliances might make the intentions of actors clearer; a trade agreement could clarify the desires of the strong, making it easier for the weak to avoid inadvertent transgressions and reducing enforcement costs. But, if the interests or the power of states changes, then the rules will change as well. Weaker states will always be looking for opportunities to escape from the constraints that have been pressed upon them by the powerful. Outcomes, including institutions, are a product of the power and interests of actors.

There are several theories, primarily derived from rational choice actor-oriented analyses that explain why institutions could be consequential and also, to one extent or another, durable, why they could be expected to operate within the space defined by the right-hand side of Figure 2.

For rational choice institutionalism, principles, rules and norms are equilibrium outcomes, the result of self-interested voluntary choices. They alter strategies but not preferences. Solutions to simple coordination problems, like driving on the right- or left-hand side of the road, are the most obvious examples of stable equilibria. It does not really matter, at least at the outset, which side of the road is chosen but it is definitely advantageous for all drivers to choose one side or the other. Likewise battle-of-the-sexes payoff matrices, in which both players prefer doing something together rather than apart but their first best choices are different, going to the opera versus the ballet, for instance, are also situations in which there is no incentive to defect once a decision has been made.

When actors confront more complicated situations, institutions can establish stable equilibria in several ways. They can have a channeling effect by, for instance, creating monopoly proposers and veto groups, and making some kinds of comparisons infeasible.[28] Constitutions or pacts, can create self-enforcing focal points that enhance the prospects for stable democracy by coordinating group responses to potential abuses of power by rulers.[29] Once an institution is in place, regardless of how it got there in the first place, it can generate shared expectations that become a force for stability. Positions are formulated with the expectation that existing

[27] Krasner 1991; see also Grieco 1988, 1990 for a discussion of relative gains.
[28] Shepsle 1986, 64.
[29] Weingast 1997.

practices will continue.[30] Violations of institutional arrangements elicit more severe reprisals than disagreements about specific policies because institutional arrangements cover a range of policy options stretching across issue areas and time. An actor committed to institutional transformation must believe that new rules and norms would be beneficial not only for the particular policy choice at stake but for all other policy choices that might arise, a claim that other actors might find problematic.[31]

For rational choice approaches, institutions will always be consequential, located on the right-hand side of Figure 2.1, otherwise actors would not have accepted them in the first place. The durability of institutions varies depending upon the costs of transition. If these costs are negligible, then institutions would be brittle stalks, the southeast corner of Figure 2.1; they would affect actor behavior but they would not last if circumstances changed. In contrast, if the development of new institutions involves start-up costs such as transitional disequilibria, negotiations, organizational design, and personnel training, then institutions could be more durable.[32] If the start-up costs are high enough, then old institutions would be maintained, even if circumstances change. Rational choice approaches, however, do not view institutions as embedded, unchanging, and consequential. Such an outcome would be problematic for an approach that sees rules and norms as a result of choices made by always calculating actors.

The best-known international relations theory drawing on rational choice approaches is neoliberal institutionalism. As in neorealism states are assumed to be rational, unitary, autonomous actors.[33] For neoliberalism, however, the exemplary problems in international politics involve market failures, not relative gains or distributional conflicts along the Pareto frontier. Actors, pursuing their individual self-interest will not necessarily secure Pareto-optimal outcomes. The hidden hand of Adam Smith can fail as a result of collective goods problems, externalities, prisoners' dilemma payoff matrices, information imperfections and asymmetries, or commitment problems. Institutions are voluntary contractual arrangements that are created by actors to resolve market failures by providing information, establishing salient solutions, defining cheating, reducing transaction costs, increasing iterations, and offering opportunities for issue linkage. For neoliberal institutionalism cleverness, institutional design, not state power is the most important explanatory variable.[34]

---

[30] Moe 1987, 255–56.

[31] Shepsle 1986, 70–74.

[32] Aoki forthcoming, chap. 9.

[33] Keohane 1984.

[34] O. Williamson 1975; Axelrod 1984; Stein 1990; Snidal 1991, Martin 1992; Martin 1995; Fearon 1995; Kreps 1990; North and Weingast 1989; Schultz 1996.

As Figure 2.1 suggests, institutionalization will be high for neoliberal theory. Institutions establish Nash equilibria. Actors adhere to the rules because they would be worse off if they defect. Institutions may also be resilient but not embedded because there are transition costs involved in finding new equilibrium outcomes.[35]

There are both economic and sociological approaches that explain how institutions can become embedded, why they would occupy the northeast corner of Figure 2.1. Path dependence is an actor-oriented theory that explains how suboptimal institutions might persist as a result of random initial choices coupled with lock in effects. Normative socialization begins with an institutional structure into which individual agents are socialized, a process that defines both their interests and their capabilities.

Path-dependent arguments begin with actors whose preferences are exogenously given. Once an institutional choice is made, often for haphazard reasons, it can be locked in. More attractive arrangements are never considered. Equilibrium outcomes can be suboptimal.

Lock-in can occur for a number of different reasons. Increasing returns to scale is the most obvious. If a particular form of production—for instance, manufacturing computer chips—is characterized by increasing returns to scale, then the initial manufacturing process will be locked in even though there might have been some alternative that would have been more efficient in the long run. There will be no incentive to change to the new technique because it would have higher per unit costs in the short run even though it might have lower costs in the long run. The system is locked in by initial choices.[36]

Path dependency may also result from network externalities. The more people that choose a particular institutional structure, such as a given telephone system, the more useful that structure becomes. A phone system with 100 users is a lot less attractive than one with 100,000 even if the transmission quality of the former is better. Over time the changeover gap, the amount that would have to be spent to make some alternative routine equally attractive, increases.

Decisions may also be locked in by agglomeration externalities in particular geographic areas. Once a particular industry is established, ancillary services—legal, financial, technical, educational—move to the same location. Relocation becomes costly because the existing network of services and information exchange cannot be reproduced. Once Silicon Valley is established, it is not easily dislodged.[37]

---

[35] The extent to which new institutions involve fixed costs is, of course, an empirical question. The proliferation of new international organizations suggests that the costs might not be all that high.

[36] Arthur 1985, 5.

[37] Arthur 1984, 10; 1986, 2.

Choices about certain kinds of software can lock the user into complementary kinds of hardware. Perhaps the best-known example of path dependence is the QWERTY typewriter keyboard. The conventional account suggests that the standard configuration of keys was chosen not because it was the most efficient arrangement, but because the individual who invented touch typing happened to have a Remington typewriter that used a QWERTY keyboard, one of several keyboards available at the time. This account has, however, been challenged with regard to both its historical accuracy and technical claims.[38] Another example of hardware-software compatibility is the triumph of VHS technology for video-tapes over Sony's Beta not because it was technologically superior but because the owners of VHS encouraged the production of tapes while SONY maintained proprietary control. For consumers, having more tapes with a weaker technology was more attractive than having fewer tapes with a better technology.[39] Similar accounts have been offered for the success of IBM and DOS, which encouraged the development of programs, over Apple, which tried to maintain control of the software that would operate on its machines.[40]

Unlike conventional neoclassical economics with its decreasing marginal returns to scale, a path-dependent world is not necessarily efficient. Actors do not always select optimal institutional arrangements. Utility is not always maximized. Processes are nonergodic; rather than returning to some equilibrium path, they shoot off to an extreme once some initial boundary conditions are breached. Nor are they predictable because small random initial choices can have irreversible long-term consequences. Beginning with rational utility maximizing actors, path dependence suggests why institutions might be embedded, long-lasting, and consequential, yet suboptimal.[41]

Some sociological perspective can also explain why institutional arrangements might be embedded. Sociological approaches take principles, norms, and rules as the starting point. Institutions generate agents, endow them with certain kinds of power, and determine their underlying interests, their preferences, not just their strategies. In the words of John Meyer and his colleagues: "Institutionalized rules define the meaning and identity of the individuals and the patterns of appropriate economic, political, and cultural activity engaged in by those individuals. They similarly constitute the purposes and legitimacy of organizations, professions, inter-

---

[38] For the conventional account, see David 1985; for the challenge, see Liebowitz and Margolis 1990, 1995.

[39] Katz and Shapiro 1994, 94–95.

[40] Arthur 1987, 2; North 1990, 95; Powell 1991, 190; Nelson and Winter 1982, 19.

[41] Arthur 1984.

est groups, and states, while delineating lines of activity appropriate to these entities."[42]

The task of the analyst is to reveal the character of the underlying institutional structures by observing behavior and the meaning attached to it. The beliefs and actions of individuals are an indicator of institutional structures, not an explanation for them. Friedrich Kratochwil distinguishes between the world of observable facts, the world of intentions, and the world of institutions. In the world of institutions, constitutive rules, intersubjectively shared cognitive constructs, are critical. It is impossible to understand activity in an institutionalized world without comprehending these constitutive rules and the larger game that they define. For instance, observing that twenty-two men are knocking each other down will not provide an understanding of what is happening in an American football game.[43] For actor-oriented arguments the actors create the institutions; for sociological arguments institutions generate agents.

For classical sociological analyses that focus on normative socialization, institutions are enduring and consequential; they are understood to be in the neighborhood of the upper right-hand corner of Figure 2.1. Such approaches dominated sociological claims from Durkheim through Parsons. Behavior was seen as embedded in normative structures that included both values (desired objectives) and norms (the way these objectives were to be pursued). Individuals were socialized into roles that were empowering, not just constraining—allowing a doctor, for instance, to engage in intimate acts associated with a physical examination that would otherwise be forbidden. The central question for an individual is not whether a rule is instrumentally useful but rather what is the right normative principle in a given situation. Certain kinds of actions are obligatory. Legitimacy derives from conformity with moral precepts. Conformity arises out of sense of a obligation to adhere to the norms of the community. Individuals internalize conceptions of self-interest that are generated by institutional structures. Institutional arrangements will persist if their norms are successfully inculcated.[44]

More recently, sociological approaches have given greater emphasis to cognitive scripts than to socialization into normative values. Scripts are classificatory schemes—cognitive models that filter perceptions and suggest appropriate behavior. Scripts might or might not be followed; they can be deeply constraining or invitations to hypocrisy.

---

[42] Meyer et al. 1987, 12.

[43] Kratochwil 1989, chap. 2. Some authors have understood constitutive rules as simply facilitating some kinds of activities and making others more difficult. Others have, however, a more restrictive concept in which constitutive rules make some kinds of activities possible and preclude others. Contrast Searle 1995, 43–51, with Dessler 1989, 453–56.

[44] Scott 1995, 12–13, 17–23, 38–40.

Institutions provide scripts, some of which may be taken for granted. The existence and characteristics of actors are "socially constructed and highly problematic," and actions are understood as "the enactment of broad institutional scripts rather than a matter of internally generated and autonomous choice, motivation, and purpose."[45] Compliance may not be perfect because individuals may adopt scripts that are inappropriate for their own circumstances, even if they cannot explicitly formulate alternatives.

Identities rather than norms influence actions. They simplify the way in which one actor recognizes another, for instance, distinguishing a postman from a police officer, or an international legal sovereign from a nongovernmental organization. Identities are associated with prepackaged contracts that indicate how different agents should behave in different circumstances, for instance, providing immunity to diplomatic representatives of recognized states. Once institutionalized, cognitive beliefs become social facts, they anchor reality for individuals and become part of the objective social environment.[46]

Scripts are most frequently transmitted not through socialization into the norms of the institutions but by mimetic imitation. Individuals, or groups of individuals, are often unsure of what they should do. They scan the environment for appropriate models. In some cases instructors are available, such as international or nongovernmental organizations.

Analyses based on scripts suggest that actors are driven by a logic of appropriateness rather than a logic of consequences. They are not trying to maximize some objective utility function. Rather, they try to match their actions to appropriate rules. The same organizational forms are repeated in many different settings because individuals or groups are taught preexisting scripts. Given who I am—for instance, the ruler of an international legal sovereignty—how should I behave under these particular circumstances; what rule applies? In contrast, the actor-based theories on which most economists and political scientists rely, including realism and neoliberal institutionalism, are driven by a logic of consequences: institutions reflect the choices of actors attempting to maximize their utility.[47]

Approaches based on cognitive scripts offer insights into why principles and norms could be durable but not highly institutionalized, why institutions might be located in the northwest quadrant of Figure 2.1. From a cognitive perspective, decoupling, in which behavior is inconsistent with a particular script, or set of rules and norms can arise for several reasons.

[45] Meyer et. al 1987, 13.

[46] Scott 1995, 40–45; March 1994, 64–65.

[47] DiMaggio and Powell 1991, 10, 13–15, 29; Meyer and Rowan 1991; 41, 43–46; Douglas 1986, chaps. 5–6; Scott 1995, 30; March 1994, 57–59.

First, it may not be clear which of several possible scripts is most appropriate in a given context. Should the use of organs for transplants, for example, be subject to the logic of the market, or the logic of religion, or some other institutional script? Should the norm of nonintervention be invoked even if a ruler is torturing prisoners, or is autonomy trumped by universally endorsed standards of conduct?

Second, through mimetic imitation actors may adopt scripts that are inappropriate for their own circumstances. A world culture perspective suggests, for instance, that newly independent Third World states adopt scripts that have been developed in the more highly industrialized areas, although they do not have the resources to implement them. Third World states may legally guarantee universal primary education but then lack the money to build schools or hire teachers. They may legislate provisions for social security but not have the revenues to make payments. They may create national science organizations to promote research but not have scientists who could be supported. The identities of agents and the circumstances in which they operate are incongruent; talk and action are decoupled.[48]

Nils Brunsson has suggested that the decoupling between scripts and behavior may be a common state of affairs because to secure resources from the external environment organizations, any organization must honor externally legitimated norms and at the same time efficiently provide technical and material resources to its constituents. The requirements of efficiency may, however, be inconsistent with the norms emanating from the institutional environment. Ideally agents would prefer to decouple logics of appropriateness from logics of consequences in ways that avoid painful contradictions, but this might not be possible. Talk and action may go in different directions. An organization might adopt a new organizational chart in response to changing norms, but actual coordination within the organization would be accomplished through informal means. Legitimated scripts could prompt the collection of information that is never used, or the adoption of budgets that are ignored. Behavior is detached from rituals that are used for external display. Actions and norms are decoupled.[49]

Hypocrisy is an inherent problem for political organizations. Such organizations win support not by being consistent but by satisfying the demands of different interests. Talk, decisions, and products may be addressed to different constituencies. Political organizations win legitimacy and support through a logic of justification as well as through the provision of resources. A ruler might pay off his clients through import licenses

---

[48] Meyer et al. 1997.
[49] Brunsson 1989, 7, 168; March 1994, 197–98.

and at the same time claim to a wider group of voters that he was protecting his country from the depredations of global capitalism. IMF officials might impose conditions on loans that are consistent with the principles of neoclassical economics, while at the same time realizing that these conditions could not be honored because of the political pressures facing the ruling elite in the borrowing state. Legitimated policies might be important even if they do not alter outcomes, because good intentions can matter even if they have no result, or even an antithetical result.[50] How else could one possibly explain U.S. drug policy, which has been an abysmal failure but which responds to the fact that the public endorsement of drug legalization would not be a winning strategy for any major party presidential candidate?

Brunsson and other organizational theorists, who suggest that hypocrisy might be a normal state of affairs, have focused their attention on domestic political settings.[51] The logic of these analyses suggests that organized hypocrisy will be even more prevalent in the international environment. There are more constituencies to manage, because domestic actors are joined by international ones. Norms of appropriateness emanating from the international environment could be inconsistent with those originating from domestic sources. The authoritative decision-making role often assumed by courts in a domestic setting, which can sometimes resolve conflicts between conflicting rules, does not exist in the international environment.

Hence, some arguments that focus on the importance of cognitive scripts suggest why institutions might be enduring but, at the same time, not always consequential. Organized hypocrisy, the upper left-hand quadrant of Figure 2.1, occurs when the logic of appropriateness and the logic of consequences are in conflict. To secure resources from the environment, rulers must honor, perhaps only in talk, certain norms but at the same time act in ways that violate these norms, if they hope to retain power and satisfy their constituents.

With the exception of the northwest quadrant, the space defined in Figure 2.1 has been well explored. Situations characterized by an absence of institutions, by institutions that are consequential although not durable, and by institutions that are consequential and durable, even embedded, have been extensively investigated by social scientists. *Organized hypocrisy* in which institutional norms are enduring but frequently ignored has received less attention. As I hope to show in this study, however, organized hypocrisy characterizes many aspects of the international system, especially those associated with Westphalian and international legal sover-

[50] Brunsson 1989, 20–31, 195.
[51] See, for instance, Swidler 1986; Douglas 1986, chaps. 5–6; March 1994.

eignty. Rules, notably the norm of nonintervention, which is one defining characteristic of Westphalian sovereignty, have been widely recognized for more than two centuries but, at the same time, often violated. The tension between the logic of appropriateness associated with international legal sovereignty, recognize juridically independent territorial entities, and logics of consequences has been less severe than for Westphalian sovereignty. But even for international legal sovereignty, rulers have sometimes found that their interests are better served by recognizing entities that lacked juridical independence or even territory.

In sum, different theoretical perspectives have different views about the nature and impact of institutions. These perspectives can be arrayed in a space defined by durability or resilience along one dimension and the level of institutionalization, or the consequences of the rules for actual behavior, along the other. The major approaches to international politics have either implicitly or explicitly drawn on these theoretical frameworks. Neorealism locates international activity in the lower-left quadrant. International institutions, which are created by powerful states, could impact on behavior in modest ways by reducing uncertainty and transaction costs, but would never last beyond the preferences and power of the states that had created them in the first place. For neoliberal institutionalism market failures can be resolved by creating institutions that are consequential and may be durable, especially if start-up costs are high. The English school is an example of a sociological perspective based on normative socialization; statesmen from the same civilization will act according to some common set of norms. John Meyer, a sociologist, and his colleagues have developed a world culture perspective that is based on theories about cognitive scripts; norms of modernity generated in the West are accepted by, but decoupled from, action in Third World states whose material resources are severely constrained. Constructivist theories, whose common link is shared normative belief systems, can be arrayed across the upper half of Figure 2.1 with some arguing for the durability and consequences of norms[52] and others for a more fluid situation in which structures and agents are constantly reconstituted through mutual interaction.

INSTITUTIONAL THEORIES AND WESTPHALIAN AND
INTERNATIONAL LEGAL SOVEREIGNTY

One basic contention of this study is that none of the best-known approaches to institutions, which are all located in the anarchy, brittle stalks, or embedded quadrants of Figure 2.1, provides an adequate understanding of Westphalian or international legal sovereignty, both of which are

---

[52] See for instance J. Ruggie 1993.

better understood as examples of organized hypocrisy. Their rules are widely understood and enduring, but also violated, more frequently in the case of Westphalian than international legal sovereignty.

Westphalian Sovereignty and Institutional Theory

The Westphalian model has never become highly institutionalized even though it has been long-lasting because none of the mechanisms for embedding that have been suggested by either sociological or actor-oriented theories is applicable. The Westphalian model is not an equilibrium outcome. Rulers have often decided that they are more likely to retain power and promote the interests of their constituents if they invite compromises of the autonomy of their own polity, or intervene in the internal affairs of another.

The Westphalian model is also not characterized by path dependence: random choice followed by lock-in. The evolution of states as a dominant institutional form (including Westphalian sovereignty for the most powerful states) was not a random event but reflected functional advantages enjoyed by states over other structures such as feudalism, the Catholic Church, or city-states.[53] Once created, however, there were no lock-in mechanisms for Westphalian sovereignty, such as economies of scale, agglomeration externalities, network externalities, or hardware-software complementarities. Diplomacy, contracting, coercion, and war are not like making computer chips—it does not get cheaper the more you fight and talk.

Demonstrating that sociological arguments, especially normative socialization, are also not appropriate for understanding the Westphalian model must rely on empirical evidence. Chapters 3–7 present many instances in which the Westphalian model has been violated. Relations between rulers and ruled associated with minority and human rights, and international lending to weaker states, have frequently violated the principle of autonomy. In the nineteenth century the constitutional structure of the new states created in the Balkans was strongly influenced by the major powers, although those in Latin America were not, and in the twentieth century constitutional structures in Central America and the Caribbean and in Europe after the Second World War were often the result of coercion or imposition by either the United States or the Soviet Union. These violations have not been surreptitious, but have been justified, consciously justified, by alternative principles like minority rights and international stability. Every major peace treaty from Westphalia to Helsinki has included provisions that contradict the Westphalian model: religious toleration in

---

[53] Tilly 1990a; Spruyt 1994.

Westphalia, succession rights in Utrecht, minority rights and issues of legitimate order in Vienna, minority rights in the 1878 Treaty of Berlin, minority rights in Versailles, and human rights in Helsinki. If rulers are socialized into normative structures at all (and they may not be), these are most likely to be associated with domestic environments whose principles may, or may not, be consistent with those prevailing in the international system. The Westphalian model has never been taken for granted.

The Westphalian model is also, however, not a brittle stalk. It has been durable in the sense that it has affected the talk and conception of rulers since at least the end of the eighteenth century, despite substantial changes in the international environment including the disappearance of major empires (the Austro-Hungarian, German, Spanish, British, French, Portuguese, Soviet, and Ottoman), the rise of new powers (the United States, Japan, China, and the Soviet Union), the end of colonialism, the industrial revolution, the information revolution, and the spread of democracy. A system of political order that was first conceptualized in Europe is understood and invoked in all parts of the world. At the same time, however, behavior has often been inconsistent with Westphalian principles. Talk and action have been at odds.

The Westphalian model is an example of organized hypocrisy. It is a well-understood cognitive script, one that is sometimes honored and sometimes not. Rulers in more powerful states have justified violations of Westphalian principles by invoking alternative norms such as the illegitimacy of revolutionary regimes (the Holy Alliance), the provision of national security (the Platt amendment imposed on Cuba by the United States), problems of drug running (the 1989 U.S. invasion of Panama), or the protection of the Soviet commonwealth (the Brezhnev doctrine). Logics of consequences can be compelling. The justifications that rulers have offered are usually addressed in the first instance to their domestic constituents, and the principles embraced by these constituents have varied from one country to another. Rulers want to rule and to do that they can rhetorically invoke Westphalian principles even when they are at the same time endorsing contradictory norms or making instrumental decisions that undermine the autonomy of their own or other polities.

International Legal Sovereignty and Institutional Theory

International legal sovereignty is an institutional form that has been both consequential and resilient but not universally honored. The basic norm of international legal sovereignty is that recognition is extended to territorial entities that are formally independent (although as the violations of Westphalian sovereignty indicate, formal independence does not necessarily mean de facto autonomy). Rulers have almost always wanted recognition.

Recognition facilitates international agreements, provides diplomatic immunity, establishes a privileged status in the courts of other states, and may enhance domestic political support. Recognizing only juridically independent territories is not, however, a Nash equilibrium. Rulers have deviated from the norm by recognizing entities that lacked either formal independence or territory. These deviations have coexisted with rather than undermined the basic norm of international legal sovereignty.

International legal sovereignty is not embedded. As an institutional form, it has not been taken for granted. Rulers have recognized entities that were not formally independent and even in a few cases lacked territory. The United States accepted Byelorussian and Ukrainian membership in the United Nations to facilitate relations with the Soviet Union after the Second World War. The rulers of China did not block Hong Kong's membership in the World Trade Organization, and other international organizations, because for Chinese rulers it was better for Hong Kong to be in the WTO than out, and for the statesmen of other countries it was better to accept Hong Kong as a sovereign person than to deny recognition. Governments in exile have been recognized even though the territory of the state has been controlled by another regime.

Moreover, although recognition conveys benefits and imposes few, if any, costs, the absence of recognition does not condemn a political entity to death or oblivion. International legal sovereignty is not a constitutive rule that precludes alternative arrangements that can provide functional equivalents, for instance, to diplomatic immunity. The Soviet Union and the People's Republic of China did not wither and die when they were not recognized. The Taiwan Relations Act gave Taiwan a special status in U.S. law, more or less like that of an international legal sovereign, after recognition was withdrawn. Nonrecognition has not precluded state-to-state negotiations, or even official visits.

There have even been a few instances when rulers have explored the possibility of giving up international legal sovereignty. In 1849 the leaders of Nicaragua, Honduras, and Guatemala, fearing invasion by Mexico, indirectly suggested that their countries become part of the United States, but their demarche was rejected. In 1899 Mubarek, the ruler of Kuwait, agreed that his country would become a British protectorate because this placed him in a stronger position with regard to his internal opponents. In the 1990s, Alexander Lukashenka, the president of Belarus, toyed with the idea of becoming part of Russia because he thought it might promote his own political career on a larger stage.[54]

Like Westphalian sovereignty, international legal sovereignty is an example of organized hypocrisy, albeit one where the level of hypocrisy has

---

[54] LaFeber 1983, 25; Tetreault 1991; Blacker and Rice 1998.

been less pronounced. Most of the time recognition has been limited to juridically independent territorial entities. But on some occasions rulers, motivated by a logic of consequences, have pursued other strategies. These alternative policies have usually been less contentious than some violations of Westphalian sovereignty because they have been the result of voluntary consent rather than imposition or coercion. It was instrumentally useful for American leaders to accept Soviet demands for United Nations membership for Byelorussia and the Ukraine, and for the member states of the Council of Europe to accept Andorra even though it lacked juridical independence. In contrast, the seizure of American diplomats by the Islamic government of Iran in 1979 was highly visible and contentious but justified by arguing that the Americans were, in fact, spies and not diplomats.

CONCLUSIONS

There is a rich body of literature on institutions from both actor-oriented and sociological perspectives from which the major theoretical approaches to international politics—neoliberalism, neorealism, and the English school and other constructivist arguments—draw, either explicitly or implicitly. The simplest analyses, basic force models, see institutions as a product of the power and interests of actors. The strong may force their institutional choices on the weak. This is how institutions are understood by neorealism. In a realist world, institutions may be of limited consequence but they will not be durable.

Neoliberal analyses accord institutions a much more important role. Interests, not power, are what count. Institutions are designed to solve market failure problems. By providing information, monitoring, establishing salient solutions, encouraging iterations, and facilitating issue linkage, institutions can help states to reach the Pareto frontier. Neoliberal analysis suggests that institutions will fall along the right-hand side of Figure 2.1. They will be consequential—otherwise states would not have agreed to them in the first place—but their durability depends upon the start-up costs of alternatives. They will not, however, be embedded in the sense that alternatives that would make sense given a logic of consequences would be precluded.

Arguments about embeddedness in the international relations literature invoke approaches based on normative socialization. The English school and some other constructivist analyses understand institutions as generating agents that reinforce or enact, as a result of normative socialization into a common civilization, a particular set of principles, norms, and rules.

None of the best-developed approaches to international relations adequately conceptualize how international legal sovereignty and Westphalian sovereignty have actually functioned. Both are examples of organized hypocrisy. Their defining rules have endured and been widely recognized and endorsed but, at the same time, sometimes compromised—in the case of Westphalian sovereignty, frequently compromised.

Institutions have become a talisman for political scientists and economists as well as sociologists. Moving beyond purely actor-based analyses has shed new insights on many problems. The impact of institutions in the international system should, however, be approached with caution. The mechanisms that reinforce institutions, especially those that explain why particular institutional forms might become embedded, are much less salient in the international system than in stable domestic polities. In an environment characterized by multiple norms, power asymmetries, and the absence of authoritative structures that could resolve conflict, rulers can select among strategies that deploy normative as well as material resources in different and sometimes original ways. In the international system, no institutional arrangement, including international legal and Westphalian sovereignty, can be taken for granted. A logic of consequences can always prevail over a logic of appropriateness.

CHAPTER 3

Rulers and Ruled: Minority Rights

ACCORDING TO the Westphalian model relations between rulers and ruled ought not to be subject to any external actors. Rulers and their subjects or citizens can structure their own relationships independent of outside forces. They may enshrine individual human rights in their constitutional practices or ignore them; they may recognize that ethnic or religious minorities have specific rights or deny that such groups exist; they may provide symmetrical treatment regardless of gender or treat men and women differently; they may designate or reject indigenous peoples as a distinct category; they may legitimate slavery or prohibit it.

Empirically the Westphalian model has not provided an accurate description of the relationship between rulers and ruled that has existed in many states. By entering into contracts and conventions, rulers have extended invitations that engage external authority structures with their own polities. Through coercion and imposition, rulers in more powerful states have intervened in the internal affairs of their weaker counterparts.

This chapter examines one particular but pervasive issue where the Westphalian model provides limited understanding of actual practice, minority rights. Minority rights involve specific commitments by rulers or governments about the treatment of minority groups or specific individuals as a result of their membership in such groups. Minority groups have been defined in many different ways, although religion and ethnicity have been the most prominent; what they all have in common is some sense that the identity of the individual is associated with membership in a group and is distinct from the group identity embraced by other individuals within a given polity.

Internationally legitimated minority rights have most frequently been imposed or coerced, the exceptions being contractual arrangements for religious toleration in Europe beginning in the seventeenth century and a small number of cases involving ethnic groups in the twentieth century. Rulers in more powerful states have intervened to coerce or impose legal protections for minorities in weaker polities. Challenges to autonomy have always been grounded and justified by alternative principles. The Peace of Westphalia and a number of other sixteenth- and seventeenth-century treaties contained explicit provisions for religious toleration because the signatories wanted to contain the religious strife that threatened the stability of western Europe. Similar motivations informed the actions of the major European powers during the nineteenth century when they made the acceptance of religious toleration a condition of international recognition for all of the successor states of the Ottoman Empire. The provisions for the protection of minorities associated with the settlement of the First World War were, with a few exceptions, imposed on the states of central and eastern Europe, because the allied powers regarded such protections as essential for the establishment of stable democracies, which were in turn understood to be the underpinning for collective security and international peace. Likewise, protections for minorities were imposed on the successor states of Yugoslavia in the 1990s because the United States and the major powers of western Europe believed that this would promote stability in the Balkans and prevent the spread of ethnic violence to other countries in the Balkans and beyond.

In an environment that is as weakly institutionalized as the international system, there have always been a variety of often mutually inconsistent principles that have been used to legitimate policy. Even Vattel, the eighteenth-century jurist, who was one of the first to articulate fully the principle of nonintervention, also wrote that if the unjust rule of a sovereign led to internal revolt, external powers would have the right to intervene on the side of the just party when disorder reached the stage of civil war.[1] There has been no authority that could prevent rulers from offering invitations that legitimate external authorities in their own polity through conventions and contracts, or intervening through coercion and imposition with regard to the relationship between rulers and ruled in other polities. There has been no consensus on how the principles of autonomy and minority rights should be balanced against each other. Rulers in different states have had different conceptions about how minority rights should be defined, or whether they should exist at all, and how these rights should be weighed against the principle of autonomy.

The actual effect of external efforts to define relations between rulers and ruled in the area of minority rights has, however, been limited. Coercion and imposition have frequently failed: target rulers have accepted conditions regarding the treatment of minorities at moments when they have been most vulnerable, but then reneged when they became more powerful. The most commonly used method of coercion has been to condition recognition on the acceptance of specific stipulations about relations between rulers and ruled in the target state. Once, however, recognition is granted, it is not easily withdrawn; rulers in the target state can then rescind the promises they have made about the treatment of their own subjects. Intervention through coercion and imposition can work if

---

[1] Vatell 1852, book II, chap. IV, sec. 56.

the initiator can maintain pressure by, for instance, stationing military forces in the target state, or maintaining a credible threat to impose economic sanctions, but such sustained efforts have been unusual.

The few cases in which rulers have invited the influence of external authority through contracting have been more successful because such arrangements have involved commitments by one state to respect the rights of its minorities provided that the other party does the same. There is no problem of bridging time. If one state violates its guarantees, then the other will do the same and, because both parties know this, they are more likely to honor their contractual obligations.

The success of conventions, which have primarily been associated with human as opposed to minority rights, in influencing relations between rulers and ruled has depended primarily on the way in which such arrangements alter domestic attitudes.[2] Conventions have been most consequential when they have been reinforced by domestic actors whose position can, in turn, be strengthened by the convention. Rulers may make international commitments to treat individuals or groups in specific ways because these commitments conform with their own preferences and they anticipate that ratifying a convention will constrain their successors. A convention could legitimate at least verbal protests from other signatories, which could reinforce the position of domestic groups. A convention could provide for monitoring provisions that would make it more difficult for subsequent rulers to violate surreptitiously guarantees regarding the treatment of individuals or groups. It could, as in the case of the European human rights regime, establish judicial procedures that would give nonstate actors, including individuals, standing to bring complaints against their own government, again making it more difficult for future rulers to violate covertly the terms of a convention.

In sum, the Westphalian model notwithstanding, rulers have not always enjoyed autonomy over their relations with those they rule. Minority rights is one issue area where violations of the Westphalian model have been pervasive, including violations in the Peace of Westphalia itself. Other actors, especially rulers in the most powerful states, have intervened through coercion and imposition primarily because of their concerns that ruler-ruled interactions in weaker states could cause international instability. Rulers have also offered invitations to external authority structures by entering into contracts and conventions sometimes with the expectation of constraining the behavior of their successors. Many conventions, however, especially those with limited domestic support in signatory countries have had little impact on behavior.

[2] Moravcsik 1994.

Minority Rights

International attempts to influence the relationship between rulers and minority groups within their own country have been an enduring characteristic of international relations. For the European states, the first target of such efforts was the Ottoman Empire. European rulers made unilateral pledges to protect Christians as early as the thirteenth century. Numerous treaties were concluded between the Ottoman Empire and European states beginning in the sixteenth century. Every major peace treaty from Westphalia to Versailles contained some provisions for the protection of minorities, initially defined in terms of religious affiliation and later ethnic or linguistic identity. Most of these efforts involved intervention through coercion or imposition and most were unsuccessful because the more powerful states could not sustain their leverage over time; when pressure was relaxed, targets often abrogated their earlier commitments to minority rights. The major success story is the development of religious toleration in Europe. Religious toleration was a prominent feature of the Peace of Westphalia, a contractual agreement reluctantly accepted by rulers who, after the religious wars of the sixteenth and seventeenth centuries, recognized that they were more likely to keep their crowns, and their heads, if they acquiesced to religious differences rather than suppressing them.

The Ottoman Empire

After the Crusades the rulers of Christian Europe persistently asserted their right to protect Christians within the Ottoman Empire. These assertions continued after the Westphalian principle of nonintervention was widely recognized, and after the Ottoman Empire was explicitly accepted as a member of the community of states following the Crimean War. These pledges, which date back as far as the thirteenth century, were reaffirmed, for instance by Louis XIV in the seventeenth century. In 1535 Suleiman the Magnificent signed a treaty with Francis I of France, which provided that foreigners were to be judged by the laws of their home countries in consular courts, that foreigners were not subject to Ottoman taxation, and that customs duties on foreign goods would be limited. At the time these commitments were made, the Ottoman Empire was at the height of its power; the treaty was not an example of coercion. Treating foreigners differently was consistent with organization of political life within the Ottoman Empire, where the millet system gave religious communities considerable control over their own affairs.

As Ottoman power declined after the sixteenth century, the major European powers increasingly used coercion to secure rights for Christians.[3] In 1615 Austria and the Porte signed a treaty that guaranteed to Catholics the right to practice and build churches. In 1673 France secured concessions for the Jesuits and Capuchins. The Treaty of Karlowitz of 1699 gave the Polish ambassador the right to raise issues regarding the treatment of Catholics within the Ottoman Empire, and gave Austria the right to intervene on behalf of Catholics, a right that was renewed in 1718, 1739, and 1791. The Treaty of Kutchuk-Kainardju (1774) gave the Russian ambassador standing to represent all Christians. The European powers used these grants selectively when they served other political purposes. The pretense for intervention that these treaties gave the European powers increased instability in the empire.[4]

In dealing with the Ottoman Empire the rulers of the major European powers never accepted the principle of autonomy. Initially, when Europe was weak and the Ottoman Empire strong, they could do little more than offer often empty pledges to protect their coreligionists. Later, they signed treaties that validated Ottoman law. As the position of the Sultan weakened still further, they engaged in coercion, securing concessions that affirmed their right to protect Christians within the empire.

Religious Minorities in Europe

Every major peace treaty signed in Europe from Westphalia in 1648 (and even Augsburg in 1555) to Vienna contained provisions for the treatment of religious minorities. These arrangements were contracts, invitations, that provided for external scrutiny of domestic policies and practices. They violated the Westphalian principle of autonomy but they contributed to civic peace in Europe.

---

[3] Traditionally, Islamic polities divided the world into Dar-al-Islam, the House of Islam or the civilized world, and Dar al-Harb, the House of War inhabited by infidels. The first treaty in which the Ottoman Empire described a European power as a coequal was the Treaty of Sitvatorok (1606) between the Holy Roman Emperor and the sultan, which followed the Ottoman military defeat at the second siege of Vienna. In the Turkish text the emperor was given the same title that was used for the sultan. When Ottoman power had been at its height, a century before, there were no such treaties. The Ottomans had not regarded any Christian power as a juridical equal. See Lewis 1995, 120, 273. As the balance of power changed, Ottoman institutional arrangements changed as well; the logic of consequences dominated the logic or appropriateness. In 1987 a museum exhibition of rare prints and manuscripts dealing with Suleiman the Magnificent at the National Gallery in Washington, D.C., which was sponsored by the Turkish government, depicted the Ottoman Empire as another European power, a position that Suleiman himself would have found quixotic. See Rogers and Ward 1988.

[4] Macartney 1934, 161–63; Laponce 1960, 25; Blaisdell 1929, 24; Mansfield 1991, 80.

The development of religious toleration and later religious freedom was a triumph of European civilization that evolved out of both principled arguments about the illegitimacy of coerced beliefs and a recognition that religious strife could destroy political stability. Although the extent of repression varied, the persecution of religious minorities or heretics was characteristic of Christianity. After Constantine, the security and authority of the state in Europe were reinforced by Christianity. The Roman emperor Theodosius imposed the death penalty on a heretic in the fourth century. Saint Augustine endorsed persecution that was designed to open the minds of those who had embraced error, even though he rejected the death penalty. Catholic intolerance reached its peak at the end of the fifteenth century in Spain with the Inquisition. Although Luther started with a relatively accepting attitude once he began to build his own church, he became more prosecutorial. Calvin banished from Geneva those who did not subscribe to his doctrines. Luther and Calvin were interested in truth, not tolerance.[5]

The civil strife of the sixteenth and seventeenth centuries set Europe on the path to religious toleration. The Reformation ended any hope for unity in the Christian Church. By 1600 it was evident from experiences in France and the Netherlands that heretical beliefs could not be suppressed by the sword; the alternatives for rulers were political instability and even disintegration or some degree of toleration. The English Civil War destroyed the Stuart dynasty and even, for a time, monarchical rule. No conflict in Europe was more costly than the Thirty Years' War, which was exacerbated by religious conflict. Germany was devastated. The rural population might have declined by 40 percent, the urban by 33 percent.[6]

Practical experience was reinforced by a long-standing Christian view that true religious beliefs could not be coerced. Renaissance thinkers did not attack religious intolerance directly but they distinguished between the world of reason and the world of faith. In his *Utopia* written in 1516, Thomas More depicted a tolerant society, albeit one still grounded in religious belief. (More became much less tolerant of dissent after witnessing the initial consequences of the Reformation.) Before the outbreak of the religious wars in France, the first of which began in 1562, many educated Frenchmen had concluded that religious toleration was necessary not simply for political reasons (because the two sides balanced each other) but for moral ones as well. Support for toleration was also offered in France on practical political grounds. De l'Hopital, who was chancellor in the early 1560s, argued that while religious uniformity was preferable, efforts to repress Protestantism would tear the country apart. Bodin made similar

---

[5] Bainton 1951, 26, 38–53; Jordan 1932, 31.
[6] Beller 1970, 345–46, 357; Jordan 1932, 19–25, 38.

arguments in the *Six Books of the Commonwealth* published in 1576. Locke stated in his "Letter Concerning Toleration" published in 1689 that "neither Pagan nor Mahometan, nor Jew, ought to be excluded from the civil rights of the commonwealth because of his religion."[7]

Religious toleration was reflected in international agreements as well as changes in domestic policy. The Peace of Augsburg of 1555 endorsed the principle that the prince could set the religion of his territory (*cuius regio, eius religio*). *Cuius regio, eius religio* did not mean that rulers could do anything that they wanted regarding their subjects' religious practices. At a minimum dissenters were to be allowed to emigrate; they were not to be executed. There was a general view that, while the state could regulate public worship, it would not intervene in private practices. *Cuius regio, eius religio* was a break with the medieval world, which presumed a unified Christendom. This principle provided for equal international acceptance for Catholic, Lutheran, and later Calvinist rulers. Augsburg endorsed the view that one religion was necessary for the state but that it did not have to be the same religion for every state. Understood as the right of the ruler to set the religion of his territory, *cuius regio, eius religio* is entirely consistent with the Westphalian model; in fact Augsburg was more consistent with Westphalian principles than the Peace of Westphalia itself.

In a few specific areas, however, even the Peace of Augsburg violated state autonomy. In eight imperial cities of the Holy Roman Empire inhabited by both Protestants and Catholics, the emperor committed himself to accepting the existence of both faiths. In addition, the rulers of ecclesiastical states were prohibited from changing the religion of their domains, in effect contravening *cuius regio, eius religio*. The Habsburg ruler Ferdinand I also promised, in a secret agreement not formally part of the peace, that Lutheran nobles and townspeople living in ecclesiastical territories could continue to practice their faith.

Augsburg did not, however, provide for a satisfactory resolution of religious issues in the Holy Roman Empire. Populations were still intermingled. The position of ecclesiastical states, and Protestants within them, remained a bone of contention. Both Catholic and Protestant rulers violated the terms of the Augsburg settlement.[8]

While endorsing the principle of Augsburg, specific articles of the Peace of Westphalia (which consisted of two treaties: Osnabrück, between the empire and the Protestant states, and Münster, between the empire and the Catholic states) contravened the notion that the ruler could set the religion of his state. Territories were to retain the religious affiliation that

---

[7] Jordan 1932, 42; Skinner 1978, 244–54; Lewis 1992, 49.

[8] Scribner 1990, 195–97; Gagliardo 1991, 16–21; Jordan 1932, 36–37; Little 1993, 324–25.

they had on January 1, 1624, regardless of the desires of their ruler. Catholic orders were to stay Catholic; Lutheran orders were to stay Lutheran. Catholics who lived in Lutheran states or Lutherans who lived in Catholic states were to be given the right to practice their religions in the privacy of their homes and to educate their children at home or to send them to foreign schools. Subjects were not to be excluded from the "Community of Merchants, Artizans or Companies, nor depriv'd of Successions, Legacies, Hospitals, Lazar-Houses, or Alms-Houses, and other Privileges or Rights" because of their religion. They were not to be denied the right of burial nor were they to be charged an amount for burial different from that levied on those of the religion of the state. Dissenters (Catholic or Lutheran) who did not have any rights of religious practice in 1624 and who wanted to move or were ordered to move were to have the freedom to do so and were given five years to sell their goods.[9]

Cities with mixed Lutheran and Catholic populations (Augsburg, Dunckelspiel, Biberach, Ravensburg, Kauffbeur) were to have freedom of religious practices for Catholics and Lutherans. In the first four of these cities, offices were to be divided equally between Catholics and Lutherans. Members of the Silesian nobility who were Lutherans were granted by the emperor the right to build three churches and to continue to practice their religion provided that they "do not disturb the publick Peace and Tranquillity." Magistrates of either religion were admonished to forbid any person from criticizing or impugning the religious settlement contained in the agreement and in the earlier Treaty of Passau.[10]

The treaty provided that Catholics and Lutherans should be equally represented in the assemblies of the empire where religious issues were to be decided by consensus. Representatives to the imperial courts were to be divided by religion. If the judges of the two religions voted uniformly against each other in a case, the case could be appealed to the Diet. Rights given to Lutherans and Catholics were also extended to Calvinists.[11]

In the case of a situation in which the religion of the ruler of a particular territory changed from one Protestant sect to another (for instance, from Lutheran to Calvinist), the new ruler was to have the right of worship of his own religion, but he was prohibited from attempting to change the religion of his subjects or churches, hospitals, schools, and revenues. The new ruler was enjoined from giving "any trouble or molestation to the Religion of others directly or indirectly." The religious community was

---

[9] Treaty of Osnabrück 1648, 219–25, Article V.11–23; 229, Article V.28; and 229, Article V.28–30. Also see, Osiander 1994, 40.

[10] Treaty of Osnabrück 1648, 226, Article V.25; 217, Article V.7; 230–31, Article V.31; and 234, Article V.41.

[11] Treaty of Osnabrück 1648, 234, Article V.42; 238, Article V.45; and 239, Article VII.

given the right to name ministers, and the prince was to confirm them "without denial." Religious toleration was, however, limited to Lutherans, Calvinists, and Catholics.[12] The provisions of the peace applied only to the Holy Roman Empire. The king of France was obligated to the Catholic religion and to "abolish all Innovations crept in during the War" in those territories that were ceded to France by the treaty.[13] Austria, which was not part of the empire although ruled by the Habsburgs who were also the Holy Roman emperors, was also not included.

In sum, the Peace of Westphalia, often seen as the beginning or ratification of the modern state system, included extensive provisions for religious toleration that violated the principle of autonomy. The terms of the peace, which included stipulations regarding basic constitutional practices in the empire, were guaranteed by France and Sweden. The French argued that they were defending the traditional rights of the German princes against the emperor's efforts to establish absolute rule, and the king of Sweden, also a victor in the Thirty Years' War, became a member of the very medieval Diet of the Holy Roman Empire as the newly enfeoffed duke of Werden.[14] Ferdinand III, the Habsburg monarch and emperor, reluctantly pledged that religious issues would be decided by the principle of consensus within the empire but refused to accept toleration in other areas that he ruled. Westphalia was a contractual arrangement in which the emperor invited French and Swedish oversight of constitutional practices in the empire in exchange for an end to the Thirty Years' War.

After Westphalia, provisions for religious toleration were included in many international agreements. In the seventeenth and eighteenth centuries it was usual for a new sovereign taking over a territory to pledge to respect existing religious rights. The treaties of Oliva (1650), Nijmegen (1678), Breslau (1742), Dresden (1745), Hubertusburg (1763), and Warsaw (1772) all had provisions protecting the position of religious minorities. The Treaty of Utrecht of 1731, in which France ceded Hudson Bay and Acadia to Britain provided that the Roman Catholic subjects of these areas were entitled to practice their faith "insofar as the laws of England permit it." A similar provision was included in the Treaty of Paris of 1763 in which the king of Great Britain again agreed that his Catholic subjects in Canada would be entitled to the same rights as those in Britain.[15]

Over time the principle of toleration that was implied although not explicitly endorsed by the Peace of Westphalia did come to prevail in west-

[12] Treaty of Osnabrück 1648, 240, 241, Article VII.
[13] Treaty of Münster 1648, 32, Article LXXVII.
[14] Osiander 1994, 41, 65; Croxton 1998, 15–16.
[15] Laponce 1960, 23–24; Macartney 1934, 158–59. The quotation is from Laponce 1960, 24.

ern Europe. After 1648, there was a slow but general abatement of religious conflict. The treaties did work in the sense that the ecclesiastical boundaries set in 1648 remained more or less intact until as late as 1945. At first toleration was not regarded as either possible or desirable, but it was accepted in some specific areas as a matter of political necessity because efforts to repress one religious group or another would have precipitated unrest and even war.

In general, those states which (like France) could avert or reject the terms of Westphalia did so. While tolerating Protestants in such outlying areas as Silesia and Hungary, the Habsburgs kicked them out of Styria and Upper Austria—resettling them in Transylvania "for state economic reasons." The Habsburgs refused to abide by the provisions for the repatriation and restitution of Protestants and those prohibiting the expelling of unprotected dissidents after five years. Similarly, the powerful archbishop of Salzburg expelled Protestants in 1731. Such actions were typically followed by reprisals against Catholics in the Protestant northern states.[16]

Hence, one of the reasons for honoring international pledges of religious toleration was that in some cases violations by one ruler could lead to retaliation by others against religious minorities within their own territories. These early treaties, including the Peace of Westphalia itself, were contractual arrangements. The first best outcome for post-Reformation European rulers was the suppression of dissidents, a position embodied in the principle of *cuius regio, eius religio.* But mutual repression would lead to the worst possible outcome of political instability. The provisions of many seventeenth- and eighteenth-century treaties with respect to religious toleration provided a way out of this prisoners' dilemma, facilitating the development of religious toleration by providing an internationally legitimated focal point that clarified acceptable behavior. These arrangements were self-enforcing because it was evident that violations of religious toleration could lead to retaliation by other rulers, domestic unrest, and international conflict.

The Peace of Westphalia was a break point with the past but it is not the one understood by most students of international relations and international law. Westphalia did mark the transition from Christendom to reason of state and balance of power as the basic cognitive conceptualization informing the actual behavior of European rulers. But it accomplished this by violating the principle of autonomy. It was precisely the fact that rulers extended invitations, accepted internationally legitimated restraints on their own right to act as they pleased within their own territory, that made it possible to escape the state of nature resulting from sectarian warfare.

[16] Gagliardo 1991, 83–85, 178; Hughes 1992, 134–36; Holborn 1959, 370–71. The quotation is from Gagliardo 1991, 178.

Religious toleration continued to be a subject of concern even in the nineteenth century. The settlement of the Napoleonic Wars included provisions for the protection of religious minorities in parts of Belgium assigned to the Netherlands and in areas of Savoy ceded to Geneva. The agreement of July 21, 1814, with the Netherlands provided that Catholics in Belgium, which did not become independent until 1830, would have liberty of conscience, equal access to administrative positions, and representation in political bodies. These provisions were to be written into the Dutch constitution and could not be changed.

Article 3 of the protocol of May 29, 1815, ceded parts of Savoy, which had been ruled by the king of Sardinia, to Geneva. Savoy was Catholic; Geneva was Calvinist. The protocol stipulated that Catholics in the ceded territory would be able to continue their existing practices. In areas where the Catholic population exceeded the Protestant, the schoolmasters would always be Catholic, and no Protestant "temple"[17] would ever be established except in the town of Carrouge, where only one could be built. The mayor and vice-mayor would always be Catholic. If the Protestant population grew and exceeded the Catholic one, then there would be rotation in office and a Catholic school would always exist even if a Protestant one were built. The new government would continue to provide, at the existing level, support for the maintenance of the clergy and religion. In these areas Protestants could worship privately and could privately hire Protestant schoolmasters. Catholics were to have equal civil and political rights. Catholic children were to be admitted to public education institutions but religious instruction would be conducted separately. The king of Sardinia could bring complaints to the Diet of the Helvetic federation.[18]

The Vienna settlement also included for the first time explicit protection for an ethnic as opposed to a religious group. At Vienna, Castlereagh argued that the rights of the Poles ought to be guaranteed by the great powers within the three states that had participated in the partition of Poland (Prussia, Russia, and Austria). Efforts to make the Poles, he averred, "forget their existence and even language as a people has been sufficiently tried and failed."[19] Institutions had to reflect the desires of the population; otherwise, it would be impossible to maintain stability. The final act of the Congress of Vienna affirmed the rights of the Poles to preserve their nationality. Article 12 stated that there should be "institutions that assured to the Poles the preservation of their nationality."[20]

[17] Quoted in Laponce 1960, 26.
[18] Laponce 1960, 26–27, 39; Macartney 1934, 158–59.
[19] Quoted in Macartney 1934, 159–60.
[20] Quoted in Fouques-Duparc 1922, 122, translated by author.

These pledges had only a limited impact on actual policy. Austria strictly forbade any manifestations of political nationalism. Russia did establish distinct institutions for Poland, including a separate constitution and a parliament, after Vienna, but the 1830 revolt of Polish army cadets caused Nicholas I to end local autonomy. The French government protested. The British, however, anxious to avoid enmity with Russia, refused to take any significant action. The 1863 Warsaw Uprising precipitated more repression and more intense assimilative measures by Alexander II. Prussia engaged in Germanization campaigns after 1830 and 1848, and after 1867 excluded the Polish language altogether and expelled Russian Poles.[21]

In sum, in Europe religious toleration (and at Vienna even respect for an ethnic minority) was embodied in international agreements that prescribed national law and practices. These accords were usually contractual arrangements among the major powers concluded to end wars. These stipulations, including those found in the Peace of Westphalia, violated the Westphalian model. Rulers made international commitments about how they would treat the religious practices of some of their own subjects. In some cases foreign actors were recognized as having a legitimate right to monitor behavior and protest violations. In others, basic constitutional arrangements were specified in the agreement. These contracts were essentially invitations to compromise the autonomy of signatory states.

The development of religious toleration and later full religious freedom was an extraordinary accomplishment. It emerged out of a mutual recognition that religious disputes were so volatile that they could completely undermine political stability, a recognition driven home by bloody civil wars across western Europe in the sixteenth and seventeenth centuries, and reinforced by the principled argument that true religious belief could not be coerced but had to be voluntarily accepted.

The Balkans in the Nineteenth Century

At the conclusion of the Napoleonic Wars the Balkans were ruled by the Ottoman Empire. By the outbreak of the First World War all of the Balkans comprised states. Every one of the successor states to the Ottoman Empire—Greece, Romania, Serbia, Montenegro, Bulgaria, and Albania—as well as the Ottoman Empire itself, accepted constraints, often ineffectual, on how minorities would be treated. Initially these constraints were formulated in terms of religious affiliation, but later ethnic groups were included as well.

[21] Austria: Macartney 1934, 112. Russia: Fouques-Duparc 1922, 115, 122–26; Claude 1955, 7; Laponce 1960, 28–29; Pearson 1983, 72–74. Prussia: Pearson 1983, 128–29; Janowsky 1945, 25–27.

Unlike the evolution of religious toleration in western Europe, minority rights in the Balkans were the result of intervention through coercion or imposition rather than an invitation to external authority through contracting. Power asymmetries, at least at the point of independence, were high. The rulers or would be rulers of new states would have preferred complete autonomy with respect to the treatment of groups within their own borders. The rulers of the major powers, however, coerced or compelled them to make commitments regarding nondiscrimination. Leaders in Britain, France, Russia, and Austria-Hungary were motivated primarily by concerns about international stability; religious and ethnic strife could destabilize polities in the Balkans and draw other states into conflicts that they would have preferred to avoid. As World War I demonstrated these anxieties were all too prescient. There were other concerns as well, however, including the unwanted migration that could be generated by discriminatory policies.

These efforts to protect minorities were not successful. Monitoring was difficult. International recognition, an important source of leverage, lost its effectiveness once it was actually extended. After independence, the Balkan states secured more material resources. It became more difficult for the major powers to coerce by making credible threats or to compel by using force. Moreover, unlike religious toleration in western Europe, the protection of minorities did not enjoy support from groups within the Balkan polities.

Greece was the first state to become independent from the Ottoman Empire, a status that was secured only because of the intervention of Britain, France, and Russia. The Greek revolt began in 1821. By 1827 the Ottomans, with the help of a fleet provided by Mehmet Ali, the quasi-independent ruler of Egypt, were on the verge of suppressing the rebellion. A joint British, French, and Russian force then destroyed Mehmet Ali's fleet at the Battle of Navarino and the Ottoman army was then defeated.

Even before their military intervention, the major powers had discussed a number of institutional arrangements for Greece, including the creation of a tributary state within the Ottoman Empire. By 1830, however, they were committed to creating a formally independent state, but there was never any thought that this new Greek entity would be a Westphalian state. The British did not want any arrangement that would provide Russia with greater influence and naval access to the eastern Mediterranean. Russia did not have the military power to impose a settlement on its own. The Greek revolutionaries were themselves divided.[22]

[22] Schwartzberg 1988, 139, 301, 303; Temperley 1966, 406–8; Anderson 1966, 74–75; Dakin 1973, 289–90, 310–12; Jelavich and Jelavich 1977, 50–52.

The Greek polity was a creation of the major powers. Greek independence was recognized in 1832. Greece was established as a monarchy; most of the Greek revolutionaries would have preferred a republic. Otho, the underage second son of the king of Bavaria, was chosen as monarch because he did not have close ties with any of the major powers. Greece's use of its own revenues was constrained by the terms of a loan from the major powers. (These issues are discussed at greater length in Chapters 5 and 6.) Finally, the rulers of Great Britain, France, and Russia insisted that religious toleration be included in Greek law. The protocol, which they signed in 1830, stated that to preserve Greece from "the calamities which the rivalries of the religions therein professed might excite, agree that all the subjects of the new State, whatever their religion may be, shall be admissible to all public employments, functions and honours, and be treated on a footing of perfect equality, without regard to difference of creed, in their relations, religious, civil or political."[23]

Beginning with the accords following the Crimean War, the major powers also insisted on provisions for religious toleration in Wallachia and Moldavia, the two Ottoman provinces that were to become Romania. When Moldavia and Wallachia secured their independence in 1856 the Western powers sought to guarantee equal treatment for all, including Jews. The Treaty of Paris of 1858 implied that civil liberty and religious toleration should be granted to Jews, but the Romanian authorities ignored these vaguely worded provisions. The Romanian constitution of 1866 gave only Christians the right to apply for Romanian nationality. During the late 1860s leaders in both Britain and France protested against the treatment of Jews in Romania. In Britain Lord Stanley argued that the issue touched Christian as well as Jews, because, "if the suffering falls on the Jews, the shame falls on the Christians." Romania rejected foreign protestations, arguing that the principle of nonintervention ought to be upheld. The British claimed that the Treaty of Paris of 1858 gave the powers the right to enforce Article XLVI which provided for political and economic equality for Jews.[24]

In the Treaty of Paris of 1856, the European powers recognized Turkey as a completely sovereign state and eschewed interference in its internal affairs to protect the Christian minority, but only after the sultan, under pressure from the major powers, had issued the edict of Hatti-Humayoun, which made commitments both to administrative reform and to religious privileges for Christians. The charter for religious and administrative reform was included in Article IX of the Treaty of Paris of 1856.[25]

---

[23] Quoted in Macartney 1934, 164–65.
[24] Fouques-Duparc 1922, 98–106. The quotation is from p. 102, translated by author.
[25] Blaisdell 1929, 25.

The efforts of the major powers to establish religious toleration in the Balkans reached their apogee at the Congress of Berlin in 1878, which was organized to settle the first Balkan War. Berlin was dominated by the powers of Europe—Britain, France, Russia, Germany, and Austria-Hungary. The Ottoman Empire participated. Even though Bulgaria was the most important issue, no Bulgarian was permitted to speak officially. Representatives from Serbia, Romania, and Montenegro were allowed to address the congress, but not to participate formally in its deliberations. Greece, already recognized as an independent state, did attend but had no influence.[26]

The major powers at the congress recognized Serbia, Montenegro, and Romania as independent states and a smaller Bulgaria, one without access to the Mediterranean, as a tributary state of the Ottoman Empire. As a condition of international recognition, the major powers insisted that the new states accept minority rights—more precisely, religious equality. For instance, Article XXVII of the Treaty of Berlin of 1878 stated that "In Montenegro the difference of religious creeds and confessions shall not be alleged against any person as a ground for exclusion or incapacity in matters relating to the enjoyment of civil and political rights, admission to public employments, functions, and honours, or the exercise of the various professions and industries in any locality whatsoever. The freedom and outward exercise of all forms of worship shall be assured to all persons belonging to Montenegro, as well as to foreigners, and no hindrance shall be offered either to the hierarchical organization of the different communions, or to their relations with their spiritual chiefs."[27] Identical provisions were provided for Romania (Article XLIV), Bulgaria (Article V), and Serbia (Article XXXV).

In addition, the major powers also secured assurances from the Ottoman Empire itself regarding religious toleration. Article LXII provided for the following within the Ottoman Empire:

> In no part of the Ottoman Empire shall differences of religion be alleged against any person as a ground for exclusion or incapacity as regards the discharge of civil and political rights, admission to the public employments, functions and honours, or the exercise of the various professions and industries. All persons shall be admitted, without distinction of religion, to give evidence before the tribunals. The freedom and outward exercise of all forms of worship are assured to all, and no hindrance shall be offered either to the hierarchical organization of the various communions or to their relations with their spiritual chiefs. Ecclesiastics, pilgrims, and monks of all nationalities traveling in Turkey in Europe,

[26] Anderson 1966, 210–12.
[27] Treaty of Berlin 1878, 985–86, Article XXVII.

or in Turkey in Asia, shall enjoy the same rights, advantages, and privileges. . . .
The rights possessed by France are expressly reserved, and it is well understood
that no alterations can be made in the status quo in the Holy Places.[28]

The Porte also agreed to implement reforms related to the Armenians
and to "guarantee their security against the Circassians and Kurds." Turkey was to inform the powers of the steps it had taken and the powers
would "superintend their application." The Ottomans made this pledge
to secure the withdrawal of Russian forces from Armenian territory.[29]

These provisions of the Treaty of Berlin were entirely consistent with
existing European practices even though they were inconsistent with the
Westphalian model. The enumeration of rights for religious minorities,
especially when territory changed hands, as was the case in the creation of
new states out of the Ottoman Empire, had become a routine part of
European diplomacy after 1648. What was different about the Congress
of Berlin was that the enumeration of minority rights was the result of
intervention through coercion and imposition rather than invitation
through contracting. The would be rulers of Romania, Bulgaria, Montenegro, and Serbia were not, themselves, interested in religious toleration.
They accepted these arrangements only because it was the only way that
they could secure recognition as independent—or, in the case of Bulgaria,
tributary—states. The Ottoman Empire agreed to protect the Armenians
only to secure the removal of Russian troops form its territory, a clear
example of imposition.

The major powers insisted on provisions for religious toleration primarily because they were concerned with international stability. The Balkans
were a volatile area. Orthodox religious concerns had provided a pretext
for Russian intervention and Russian intervention in the Balkans and the
Ottoman Empire threatened British interests in the eastern Mediterranean. Austria-Hungary's anxiety about Slavic nationalism prompted its
demands for informal control of Bosnia and Herzegovina in 1878 and
formal incorporation in 1907. Bismarck was anxious to maintain Germany's alliance with Austria-Hungary and Russia, which could be, and ultimately was, destroyed by conflict in the Balkans.

In addition there were what would now be labeled humanitarian concerns. British public opinion had been agitated by reports of Turkish
atrocities against the Bulgarians; Gladstone's popularization of this issue
had helped to return him to the position of prime minister. Jewish groups
in the United States and Great Britain pressured their governments to
protest Romanian treatment of their coreligionists. Later in the century,

---

[28] Treaty of Berlin 1878, 996, Article LXII.
[29] Treaty of Berlin 1878, 996, Article LXI; Lewis 1995, 326; Mansfield 1991, 75, 81;
Macartney 1934, 167.

when it became evident that the situation for Jews in Romania was not much improved, American officials pressed Romania for reforms with the hope of limiting the flow of new emigrants.[30]

Imposition was possible only because there were large power asymmetries between the would-be rulers of the Balkan states and the major powers of Europe. Britain, France, Russia, Germany, and Austria-Hungary could extend international recognition and provide material resources and military support. Absent recognition, Balkan leaders could not be certain that they would have any kind of state to rule at all; with international legal sovereignty, albeit not Westphalian sovereignty, they secured both resources and legitimacy.

The efforts to secure minority rights in the Balkans in the nineteenth century failed. The treatment of Jews in Romania was particularly problematic. Articles XLIII and XLIV of the Treaty of Berlin conditioned recognition on acceptance of religious equality, and recognition was only extended in February 1880 after Romanian officials had publicly declared that a Jew could become a citizen. In practice, however, Romanian policy hardly changed. While the letter of the treaty was honored by making it possible for a non-Christian to obtain citizenship, this required an act of parliament for each individual Jew. Of the 269,000 Jews in Romania only 200 attained citizenship. Noncitizens had to pay for primary school and were excluded from professional schools in 1893, and secondary and higher education in 1898. Jews were prohibited from living in rural areas. By the beginning of the twentieth century, almost 90 percent of Romanian emigrants to the United States were Jewish.[31]

The attempt to secure Ottoman protection for the Armenians was also a dismal failure. There were a number of massacres, the first of which took place in 1894. Despite protests from the Western powers, including in 1909 the dispatch of two British warships to Messina, these depredations continued.[32]

Unlike the development of religious liberty in western Europe, the effort to secure minority rights in the Balkans was not undergirded by domestic political support. The Treaty of Berlin was an exercise in coercion and imposition rather than contracting. The would-be rulers of the new Balkan states would have preferred no restrictions on their treatment of religious minorities. Moreover, one major instrument of leverage available to the major powers, international recognition, was difficult to withdraw once it had been extended. Although the major powers did protest Romania's treatment of its Jewish population and Turkish treatment of

---

[30] Macartney 1934, 169, 281; Fouques-Duparc 1922, 112; Pearson 1983, 98.

[31] Fouques-Duparc 1922, 98–112; Jelavich and Jelavich 1977, 178; Pearson 1983, 98.

[32] Macartney 1934, 167, 170.

the Armenians, they were unwilling to apply more forceful economic or military pressure.

Although the effort to assure minority rights in the Balkans failed, the exercise was still inconsistent with the Westphalian model. Actors in new states were not left to structure their own relationships between rulers and ruled. Power asymmetries and different preferences made them vulnerable to intervention. They accepted formal restraints on their own domestic autonomy to secure international recognition and the legitimacy and material resources that accompanied it.

The Versailles Settlement

International efforts to secure minority rights culminated at the Versailles meetings that settled the First World War. All of the new states that were created, or the polities that had their boundaries redrawn, signed agreements or made unilateral pledges regarding the protection of religious and ethnic minorities within their own boundaries. In most cases these actions were the result of coercion or imposition, but in a few instances rulers in the new states welcomed international agreements on minority rights. They invited constraints on their own autonomy either because they were committed to such values or because they believed that international accords would either ease their domestic minority problems or improve the condition of their coethnics living in other states. Unlike the Berlin settlements, the Versailles arrangements provided for elaborate monitoring and enforcement through the League of Nations and the International Court of Justice. Like the Berlin settlements, they failed.

The minority rights established after the First World War were set in peace treaties signed with Poland, Austria, Czechoslovakia, Yugoslavia, Bulgaria, and Romania in 1919, with Hungary and Greece in 1920, and with Turkey in 1923; in declarations made as a condition for admission to the League of Nations for Albania in 1921, Lithuania in 1922, Latvia and Estonia in 1923, and Iraq in 1932. There were also provisions for the treatment of minorities in the 1920 Convention between Poland and the Free City of Danzig, in the 1921 Convention on the Aaland Islands, in the 1922 Convention between Germany and Poland Relating to Upper Silesia, and in the 1924 Paris Convention Concerning the Territory of Memel.[33]

The protections were detailed and elaborate. The treaty with Poland was a model. Article 2 stated that "Poland undertakes to assure full and complete protection of life and liberty to all inhabitants of Poland without

---

[33] Lerner 1993, 83; Claude 1955, 16; D. Jones 1991, 45.

distinction of birth, nationality, language, race or religion." Poland granted citizenship rights to individuals habitually resident on or borne within its territory of parents habitually resident there, even if they were not presently living in Poland, a provision that reflected concern about Romanian exclusion of Jews from citizenship even after the Treaty of Berlin. Article 7 stipulated that "Differences of religion, creed or confession shall not prejudice any Polish national in matters relating to the enjoyment of civil or political rights, as for instance admission to public employments, functions and honours, or the exercise of professions and industries." Article 8 provided that, in areas where there was a considerable number of non-Polish speakers, they should be educated in primary school in their own language, although the teaching of Polish could be obligatory. Article 11 stated that Jews would not be obligated to perform any act that constituted a violation of their sabbath and that "Poland declares her intention to refrain from ordering or permitting elections, whether general or local, to be held on a Saturday."[34]

The minority treaties were embedded in national law. The treaties signed with Austria, Poland, Bulgaria, and Czechoslovakia made the provisions for minority protections basic constitutional guarantees as well as international obligations. The treaties provided that the laws related to the treatment of minorities would not be changed without the approval of a majority of the League Council.[35]

In addition monitoring and enforcement mechanisms were established within the League of Nations. Individuals, as well as government representatives, could submit a Minority Petition to the league where it was considered by the Minorities Section of the Secretariat. If the petition was accepted (there were only a few restrictions such as that the petition had to emanate from an authenticated source and could not contain violent language), it was then sent to the state against which the complaint had been lodged. If a state commented on the petition, its observations, along with the original complaint, were sent to the League Council. If the state remained silent, only the petition was forwarded. A state had to indicate within three weeks whether it would comment. The petition was then considered by an ad hoc minority committee of three members, the president of the council and two members appointed by him. The Minorities Secretariat provided information to the committee.

The committee usually tried to deal with cases by informally urging the offending state to change its practices. If a satisfactory resolution was

---

[34] Polish Minorities Treaty, reprinted in Macartney 1934, 502–6; See also A. Sharp 1979, 174; Fouques-Duparc 1922, 112.

[35] Bilder 1992, 64; Laponce 1960, 40; Lerner 1993, 85.

achieved, then the results were usually reported to the council. If not, the case was taken formally to the council, which could request further information. If there was no satisfactory response, the issue was submitted to a committee of jurists to decide if the state had violated its international obligations. The committee could ask that Permanent Court of International Justice for an advisory opinion.[36]

The enforcement procedures were not implemented vigorously, although the League of Nations did act on many complaints. Some victories were Pyrrhic. For instance, in 1921 in one of the few cases to go through the entire procedure, the league was petitioned concerning the Polish treatment of German settlers who had come to what was now Poland under the terms of the German colonization law of 1886, but had failed to secure clear title to their land. The ad hoc minority committee, consisting in this case of representatives from the Netherlands, Italy, and Japan, was unable to secure a settlement. The case was referred to the League Council in 1922. The Poles, ignoring the council's position, expelled the Germans. In September 1922 the case was referred to a Committee of Jurists. The Poles rejected the committee's finding. The council then voted to send the case to the Permanent Court of International Justice for an Advisory Opinion. The court ruled against Poland in September 1923. The council again pressed Poland for a settlement. The Poles agreed to pay compensation of 2.7 million zlotys, but did not allow the settlers to return.[37]

The provisions for the protection of minorities associated with the Versailles settlement and the League of Nations were justified in terms of both established norms and Woodrow Wilson's new concept of collective security. Clemenceau maintained that the minority provisions of the peace treaties were consistent with diplomatic precedent. In a covering note conveying the treaty to Poland for signature, he noted that:

> This Treaty does not constitute any fresh departure. It has for long been the established procedure of the public law of Europe that when a State is created, or even when large accessions of territory are made to an established State, the joint and formal recognition of the Great Powers should be accompanied by the requirement that such States should, in the form of a binding international Convention, undertake to comply with certain principles of Government. . . .
> In this connection I must also recall to your consideration the fact that it is to

---

[36] Janowsky 1945, 117–21; Claude 1955, 20–28. A distinct regime was established for Upper Silesia based on a bilateral agreement between Germany and Poland, the Geneva Convention of May 15, 1922. The enforcement mechanism resided with the signatories, not with third parties. Individuals had standing and could appeal to specific regional institutions but not the League of Nations. See Stone 1933, vii–viii.

[37] Janowsky 1945, 121–22, 125 n. 8.

the endeavours and sacrifices of the Powers in whose name I am addressing you that the Polish nation owes the recovery of its independence. It is by their decision that Polish sovereignty is being re-established over the territories in question, and that the inhabitants of these territories are being incorporated in the Polish nation. It is on the support which the resources of these Powers will afford to the League of Nations that the future Poland will to a large extent depend for the possession of these territories. There rests, therefore, upon these Powers an obligation, which they cannot evade, to secure in the most permanent and solemn form guarantees for certain essential rights which will afford to the inhabitants the necessary protection, whatever changes may take place in the internal constitution of the Polish State"[38]

At Versailles, Woodrow Wilson championed a second rationale for the international protection of minority rights. Wilson's vision for a new world order in 1918 was collective security: peace-loving states would join together to resist attacks by any aggressor. Only democratic states would make such commitments. The first guarantee of democracy was self-determination. Self-determination alone, however, could not resolve political tensions because in much of central Europe ethnic minorities were inextricably mingled with majority populations. If minorities were ill-treated they could not only cause disorder within their countries of residence but also threaten international peace and undermine collective security. The treaties sought to resolve this issue by providing minorities with security within existing states. Wilson stated at the Paris Peace Conference that "Nothing, I venture to say, is more likely, to disturb the peace of the world than the treatment which might in certain circumstances be meted out to minorities. And therefore, if the great powers are to guarantee the peace of the world in any sense, is it unjust that they should be satisfied that the proper and necessary guarantees have been given?"[39]

Despite historical precedent, a clearly articulated rationale, and monitoring and enforcement procedures, the Versailles effort failed in most countries. The settlement reflected the preferences of the victors. Because power asymmetries were high, they could intervene, impose their views with regard to minorities on the rulers or would-be rulers of weaker states. The disaffected rulers of target states pointed out from the outset that the regime was asymmetrical. The victors, especially the United States and Britain, accepted no provisions for the protection of minorities within their own societies, such as the Welsh and Irish in Britain, or blacks and Asians in the United States. Italy refused to accept any constraints on its treatment of minorities despite the fact that the peace settlement placed a

---

[38] Quoted in Macartney 1934, 238.
[39] Macartney 1934, 275, 278, 297. The quotation is from A. Sharp 1979, 175.

large number of German speakers in the South Tyrol within Italy's new borders. An Italian spokesman stated that as a great power Italy could not accept the kind of derogation of sovereignty implied by the minority clauses. The United States along with New Zealand, Canada, and Australia also blocked Japanese efforts to introduce a clause endorsing racial equality into the covenant of the league.[40]

Where minority treaties were the result of imposition or coercion, they faltered. From the outset rulers or would-be rulers from Romania, Yugoslavia, Poland, and elsewhere complained about the terms of the settlement. For instance, at the Versailles meeting, Bratianu, the prime minister of Romania argued that the minority treaty violated Romania's sovereignty as well as the principle of equality among states. He maintained that legitimating external intervention undermined stability in Romania and made reconciliation among groups more difficult. The Allies threatened to break diplomatic relations if Romania refused to sign a minority treaty and Romanian leaders acceded after a change in government, but minority protections were never effective.[41]

The experience of minority populations in Poland, whose treaty was a model for all others, was mixed at best. Provisions for separate Jewish schools were, for instance, never implemented. Anti-Semitic pogroms and campaigns were tolerated by public officials, who sought to freeze Jews out of the economic life of Poland. The emigration rate of Jews was five times that of Poles. Poland did, however, schedule national elections for Sunday, a policy consistent with allowing Jews to vote without violating their sabbath. Some of Poland's Slavic minorities were also repressed in part because they were seen as presenting a security threat. The Ruthenes (Ukrainians) were attacked by the Polish military in 1930; Byelorussian schools, societies, and newspapers were suppressed and a concentration camp was established at Beresa Kartuska.[42]

Only in states where there was domestic support were the minority regimes more successful; invitation was more effective than intervention. Countries with large external minorities and few internal minorities, Hungary being the most important example, were sympathetic to the treaties. Countries with large internal minorities and relatively small external minorities, such as Poland, Yugoslavia, and Romania, were opposed. The exception was Czechoslovakia, which supported the treaties even though it had a large proportion of internal minorities (about 35 percent of the

[40] Macartney 1934, 252; A. Sharp 1979, 181–83; 1991, 61; Janowsky 1945, 126–29; Claude 1955, 17, 32–33; Trachtenberg 1993, 27; Bilder 1992, 65–66.

[41] Bartsch 1995, 75–76; Esman 1995, 24; Garces 1995.

[42] Pearson 1983, 162–64, 188–89; Gutman 1989, 103–5.

population), both because of more liberal values and because the Czech leadership believed that minority guarantees would make appeals from Germany less compelling for the German population in the Sudetenland.[43]

By the mid-1930s the minorities regime was dead. Hitler had come to power in Germany. Poland formally renounced its minority treaty in 1934. The Polish foreign minister stated that "Pending the introduction of a general and uniform system for the protection of minorities, my Government is compelled to refuse, as from today, all cooperation with the international organizations in the matter of the supervision of the application by Poland of the system of minority protection. I need hardly say that the decision of the Polish Government is in no sense directed against the interests of the minorities. These interests are and will remain protected by the fundamental laws of Poland, which secure to minorities of language, race and religion free development and equality of treatment."[44]

In sum, the Versailles regime for minorities was a violation of the Westphalian model, which was achieved in most cases through coercion and imposition rather than contracting or conventions. The necessary condition for successful intervention is that the initiator remains in a position to make threats that are sufficiently credible to lead the rulers of the target state to continue to implement policies that they would otherwise abandon. The extension of recognition, of international legal sovereignty, was a salient resource in the immediate aftermath of the war when boundaries, identity, and leadership were all up for grabs, but it was difficult to withdraw recognition once it had been extended. Moreover, it quickly became evident that minority rights were not a salient issue for their initial supporters. The United States refused to join the League of Nations. By the mid 1920s it was evident that Britain was not anxious to pursue an active policy on the continent. France was more concerned about developing security relations with the smaller states on Germany's eastern and southern borders than with their treatment of their minority populations.

The Versailles regime was informed by principles that were antithetical to the Westphalian model. The victors defended democracy, self-determination, stability, and collective security, even if this meant compromising autonomy. Most of the smaller states of central and eastern Europe endorsed the norm of nonintervention and condemned the treaties as a violation of their sovereignty. Rulers in smaller states that supported the treaties, notably Hungary and Czechoslovakia, did so because the treaties would enhance the stability of their polity or protect their coethnics in

---

[43] Bartsch 1995, 74–79, 81–82, 84–85; Macartney 1934, 413–15; Robinson et al. 1943, 169.

[44] Quoted in Janowsky 1945, 127 n. 11.

other countries. Principles were in conflict. Outcomes were the result of power and interests. A logic of consequences dominated a logic of appropriateness and by the mid 1930s, with the rise of German power, only security mattered.

The Postwar World

In the aftermath of World War II efforts to protect minority rights were almost totally abandoned. Minority rights were not mentioned in the United Nations Universal Declaration of Human Rights of 1948 and were noted in only a small number of other UN accords, such as the Covenant on Civil and Political Rights and the Genocide Convention. Postwar regimes sought to protect human rights rather than minority rights. Both minority rights regimes (in which the protection of an individual is based on membership in a group that provides affective self-identity) and human rights regimes (in which protection is accorded because an individual is a human being or because the individual is classified as a member of a group, such as stateless persons, which does not provide affective self-identity) can violate the Westphalian model because the rules governing relations between rulers and ruled within a territory can be subject to external monitoring and even enforcement. (Human rights are discussed in Chapter 4.) The virtual abandonment of minority rights after the Second World War reflected the preferences and power of the United States and the general disillusionment with the interwar experience.

The United States emerged from World War II as the dominant power in the international system. Minority rights were not part of the American political heritage. American identity was grounded in the mutual acceptance of Lockeian political values, which ennobled the individual and emphasized democracy and capitalism.[45] Although there has been an ongoing American discussion about how much melting actually takes place in the melting pot, and whether ethnic affiliation should be recognized, American identity has always been based on political beliefs, not ascriptive characteristics. In 1943 Sumner Wells, the under secretary of state, argued that there should not be a need for the term racial or religious minority because the liberty of individuals should be protected under the law. During the UN debate on the drafting of the Universal Declaration of Human Rights, Eleanor Roosevelt, its chief author, argued that the declaration should not mention minorities.[46]

Minority rights were, however, addressed in agreements dealing with South Tyrol in 1946 and 1969, Trieste in 1954 and 1974, Austria in

---

[45] Hartz 1955.
[46] Sigler 1983, 67, 77.

1955, and Cyprus in 1960. After the First World War Italy had been given the South Tyrol, an area with some 250,000 people, 90 percent of whom were German-speaking. When the fascists took power in the early 1920s Mussolini's government systematically denationalized the South Tyrolese. Only Italian could be used as a language of instruction. German family names were Italianized. Immigration from other parts of Italy was encouraged.

After the Second World War Italy and Austria signed an agreement in which Italy agreed to provide a greater degree of autonomy to the South Tyrol and more protection for its German-speaking majority. The province of Bozen was given a special administrative status. German and Italian were given equal standing as languages. Both groups would be proportionately represented in public service, including the judiciary and administration. There would be separate German and Italian schools and parents would decide which their children would attend. This agreement, however, had limited impact because Italy frustrated some of its provisions. Further terms were negotiated in 1969. Border disputes in the area were not finally settled until 1992.[47]

A special statute attached to the London Treaty of October 1954 divided Trieste, which had been administered as the Free Territory of Trieste between 1947 and 1954, between Italy and Yugoslavia. The treaty stipulated that there should be equality between Italians and Yugoslavs in Trieste. Specific schools, which could not be closed without the approval of a mixed Italian Yugoslav committee, were designated to teach in one of the two languages. In some areas public documents and inscriptions were to be promulgated in both languages. A second agreement between Italy and Yugoslavia, the Treaty of Osimo, which was concluded in 1974, reaffirmed commitments regarding political and economic equality, schools, and public documents.[48]

The Austrian State Treaty of 1955 offered special protections for the Slovene and Croat minorities. In specific areas each was guaranteed elementary school instruction in its own language. Slovene or Croatian would be accepted as an official language along with German. The two groups were to participate in the cultural, administrative, and judicial systems on equal terms with Austrian nationals.[49]

When Britain gave up control of Cyprus in 1960 the Treaty of Guarantee between Cyprus, Greece, Turkey, and the United Kingdom provided for the protection of the Turkish minority. The United States, which was not a party to the treaty, as well as Britain, was anxious to reassure Turkey,

---

[47] Alcock 1979, 189–91; Hailbronner 1992, 126–27; Woodward 1995, 475 n. 17.

[48] Hailbronner 1992, 127; Laponce 1960, 38.

[49] Laponce 1960, 37.

a member of NATO. The Turkish Cypriotes, who were a minority, had to be represented at all levels of government and had veto power in several issue areas. Key constitutional provisions could not be amended at all and the amendment of some provisions required the approval of Turkey. Enoosis, unification with Greece, the preferred outcome of the Greek majority on Cyprus, was in effect prohibited. If there were violations, the signatories were to consult, but if an accord was not reached, each reserved the right to take action aimed at reestablishing the state of affairs specified by the treaty. When Greece's military rulers took control in 1974 and enosis was actively discussed, Turkey used the treaty to justify invasion and division of the island.[50]

In sum, minority rights almost disappeared from the postwar world. Nevertheless, in some specific circumstances—the South Tyrol, Trieste, Austria, and Cyprus—they were invoked. In all of these cases the Westphalian model was compromised. With the exception of Cyprus, these arrangements were contracts and they worked effectively. In Cyprus, the Greek majority accepted constraints in exchange for independence from Britain—a fragile arrangement, which disintegrated when Turkish military power was used to frustrate amalgamation with Greece.

Minority Rights after the Cold War

The end of the cold war was accompanied by, and in some cases caused, a renewal of ethnic strife. For Europe, developments in the former Yugoslavia were the most dismaying example. Almost fifty years after the defeat of Nazi Germany, ethnic cleansing became an acceptable practice for some rulers.

In 1992 the General Assembly passed the Declaration on the Rights of Persons Belonging to National or Ethnic, Religious, and Linguistic Minorities. It was the first post–World War II convention for which minorities were the primary concern. The declaration, which was passed by consensus in the General Assembly, states in part that the rights of minorities should be protected, that conditions for the promotion of identity should be encouraged, and that minorities have the right to participate in local decision-making procedures that affect them provided that such participation is compatible with national legislation.[51]

At a regional level, Europe was the area where minority rights issues received the most attention; the Conference and later Organization for Security and Cooperation in Europe (CSCE then OSCE) was the most important venue. Created at Helsinki in 1975, the CSCE was initially a

---

[50] Bilder 1992, 69–70; Platias 1986, 153–57.
[51] Thornberry 1993, 16–17, 29–30, 38–40.

contract between the Western and Soviet blocs in which the West recognized the borders of eastern Europe and the East accepted stipulations about human rights. Minority rights were mentioned only in passing. Principle VII of the Final Act of the Helsinki accord recognized the right of persons belonging to minorities to equality before the law and equal human rights. There were no provisions for enforcement.

Over time, however, minority rights became a more prominent item on the agenda of the CSCE, especially with the end of the cold war. The 1990 Copenhagen convention recognized the rights of national minorities, including the free use of their mother tongue in public and private and the incorporation of their history and culture into the school curriculum. Anti-Semitism and discrimination against the Roma (gypsies) were condemned. There were even some modest provisions for monitoring. The signatories agreed to provide within four weeks a written response to inquires made by another signatory.[52] The Charter of Paris for a New Europe concluded by the CSCE heads of state in 1991 contained extensive provisions regarding minority rights. The Office of the High Commissioner on National Minorities was established at the Helsinki summit in 1992, and the first high commissioner took office in January 1993. The high commissioner was given the mandate of providing early warning of minority issues that could affect peace and stability and reporting these concerns to the Council of Foreign Ministers and the Committee of Senior Officials. The office of the commissioner was the first independent high-ranking CSCE official, as opposed to simply being a government representative. The first report of the high commissioner dealt with the Russian minority in the Baltics and the Hungarian minority in Slovakia.[53]

Minority rights were explicitly included in the conditions for European Community recognition of the successor states of Yugoslavia. When fighting first broke out in Yugoslavia in 1990, the initial European response was to try to hold the country together. By the fall of 1991 this policy was unraveling in part because of Germany's support for the recognition of Slovenia and Croatia. On December 16, 1991, the foreign ministers of the European Community made acceptance of the Carrington Plan, formally the Treaty Provisions for the Convention (with the former republics of Yugoslavia), the prerequisite for recognition. Chapter 2 of the Carrington Plan stipulated that the republics would guarantee the right to life, to be free of torture, to liberty, to public hearings by an impartial tribunal, to freedom of thought, to peaceful assembly, and to marry and form a

---

[52] Conference on Security and Co-operation in Europe, Document of the Copenhagen Meeting of the Conference on the Human Dimension of the CSCE, 1990, in Brownlie 1992, 454–73.

[53] Bloed 1993, 95–96; Moravcsik 1994, 48–49.

family. These rights were to apply to all regardless of sex, race, color, language, religion, or minority status. The republics were to respect the rights of national and ethnic minorities elaborated in conventions adopted by the United Nations and the CSCE, including the then proposed United Nations Declaration on the Rights of Persons belonging to National or Ethnic, Religious, and Linguistic Minorities, and the proposed Convention for the Protection of Minorities of the European Commission. The republics were to protect the cultural rights of minorities, guarantee equal participation in public affairs, and assure that each individual could choose his or her ethnic identity. Members of minority groups were to be given the right to participate in the "government of the Republics concerning their affairs." In local areas where members of a minority formed a majority of the population they were to be given special status including a national emblem, an educational system that "respects the values and needs of that group," a legislative body, a regional police force, and a judiciary that reflect the composition of the population.[54] Such special areas were to be permanently demilitarized unless they were on an international border. The rights established in the convention were to be assured through national legislation.[55]

The republics were to agree to a permanent international body that would monitor these special areas. Disputes were to be taken to a newly established Court of Human Rights, which would consist of one member nominated by each of the Yugoslavian republics and an equal number plus one of nationals from European states who would be nominated by the Member States of the European Community. The members of the court "must either possess the qualifications required for appointment to high judicial office or be juriconsults of recognised competence."[56] No two members were to be from the same republic or European state. Court decisions were to be taken by majority vote.

In January of 1992, after the European Community had recognized Croatia and Slovenia, the EC Arbitration Commission (Badinter Commission) ruled that Slovenia and Macedonia had met the conditions specified in the Carrington Plan.[57] Croatia, after being pressured by the EC, also promised that it would fulfill the conditions. In May 1992, Croatia passed the Constitutional Law of Human Rights and Freedoms and the Rights of National and Ethnic Communities or Minorities in the Republic of Croatia. Many of the provisions of the law repeat word for word the text of the Carrington report. The law endorsed UN human rights accords,

---

[54] European Community 1991, chap. II, Articles 4 and 5c.
[55] Crawford 1996, 497.
[56] European Community 1991, chap. IV, Article 7.a.1.
[57] Woodward 1995, 190–91.

the final act of the CSCE, the Paris Charter on a New Europe, and other CSCE documents related to minority and human rights. Article 4 committed Croatia to assist national and ethnic minorities to establish relations with their parent country. According to Article 49, special status districts were designated where minorities were to be educated in their own language using a curriculum adequate to "present their history, culture and science if such a wish is expressed." Representatives from minorities totaling more than 8 percent of the population of the whole country were entitled to proportional representation in the Croatian Parliament, government, and supreme judicial bodies. Those with less than 8 percent were entitled to elect five representatives to the House of Representatives of the Croatian Parliament. Issues regarding minority and human rights were to be decided by the Court of Human Rights, which would be established by all of the states created out of the territory of the former Yugoslavia. In the interim a provisional Court of Human Rights was established consisting of a president and four members "who must possess the qualifications required for the appointment to high judicial office or be juriconsult of recognized competence," a verbatim appropriation of the language of the Carrington report. The president and two members were to be nominated by the European Community from citizens of its Members States and the other two members would be Croatian nationals nominated by Croatia.[58]

The commitment to protect the rights of ethnic minorities was hardly visible in the actual behavior of the former Yugoslav republics in the first years of their existence. Atrocities in Bosnia were brought to a halt only after the intervention of NATO forces, and the negotiation of a settlement under American auspices at an isolated Air Force base in Dayton, Ohio. Annex 6 of the Dayton accords signed in December 1995 related to human rights and committed the signatories—the Republic of Bosnia and Herzegovina, the Federation of Bosnia and Herzegovina, and the Republika Srpska—to honor the provisions of fifteen international and European human rights accords. It provided for the creation of an ombudsman for human rights who would have diplomatic immunity, would not be a citizen of any parts of the former Yugoslavia, and would initially be appointed to a five-year term by the Organization for Security and Cooperation in Europe, as well as a fourteen-member Chamber of Human Rights, four of whose members would be appointed by Bosnia and Herzegovina, two by the Republic of Srpska, and the other eight, none of whom would be citizens of the states that had been part of Yugoslavia, by the Committee of Ministers of the Council of Europe. Individuals could bring complaints to the chamber, whose decisions, taken by a majority vote, would be bind-

---

[58] Republic of Croatia 1992, Articles 4, 49, 18, and 60. Also see Crawford 1996, 497.

ing on the signatories. Nongovernmental organizations and international organizations were to be invited to Bosnia to monitor the implementation of the terms of the annex. After five years the chamber and the office of the ombudsman would pass to the control of Bosnia and Herzegovina, if all of the parties agreed.[59]

Serbia was recognized by the member states of the European Union in April 1996. As a condition of recognition, Belgrade agreed to the continuation of a working group on minority rights that was established at the London Conference of December 1995, which followed the Dayton Peace Agreement. The German foreign minister also stated that the level of international financial assistance for Serbia as well as cooperation with the European Union would depend on Serbia's policies regarding human and minority rights, the return of refugees, and the establishment of greater autonomy for the Albanian minority in Kosovo.[60]

The minority rights provisions for the former republics of Yugoslavia were adopted as a result of coercion. The would-be rulers of these new states did not want to be encumbered by such international obligations. They did not invite in external authority; they yielded to intervention. The commitments, which were a condition of recognition by the European Community in 1992, had limited domestic support but elaborate protection for minorities including the creation of special-status districts and the establishment of a Human Rights Court, the majority of whose judges were to come from Member States of the European Community. The Dayton accords in effect established an international court (the Chamber of Human Rights) in Bosnia that could make binding judgments on the signatory states. The Westphalian principle of nonintervention was hardly in evidence. The major powers wanted a resolution of the conflict in the former Yugoslavia and they were more than prepared to invent new institutional arrangements to accomplish this end. The results, as had been the case for earlier examples of coercion and imposition, were discouraging.

The rediscovery of minorities in the 1990s reflects changes in the distribution of power and interests. The cold war repressed minority rights. Neither the Soviet Union nor the United States was prepared to acknowledge minority rights issues in their own spheres of influence or challenge their rival. The collapse of the USSR contributed to the outbreak of ethnic hostility in the former Yugoslavia, Nagoro Karabakh, Rwanda, and elsewhere because the superpowers, or the only superpower that was left, the United States, was, in the absence of a Soviet threat, not willing to intervene to maintain a level of domestic stability that would discourage external intervention. In their attempts to manage ethnic conflict for both hu-

---

[59] United States, Department of State 1995.
[60] *Frankfurter Allgemeine Zeitung*, April 18, 1996, 1, 7.

manitarian and security reasons, the major powers invoked international guarantees of minority rights as an alternative to the principle of autonomy so central to the Westphalian model. Both the agreements reached in the context of the CSCE and the United Nations Declaration were conventions. Rulers have been willing, in the case of the CSCE perhaps even anxious, to make pledges to protect the rights of minorities. Their behavior, however, has not been contingent on that of other parties. The minority provisions associated with the recognition of Croatia and Slovenia, and Annex 6 of the Dayton accords, were examples of coercion. The would-be rulers of these new states would have preferred autonomy in the treatment of groups within their own territory but the major European powers insisted on minority protection as a condition of recognition.

CONCLUSIONS

International efforts to regulate relations between rulers and minority populations residing within the territory of their state have been an enduring aspect of international politics. Many major international agreements from Augsburg in 1555 to Dayton in 1995 have included provisions related to minority rights. Often these same agreements endorsed principles resonant of Westphalian sovereignty. Mutually inconsistent principles along with imperfect implementation, decoupling, are the hallmarks of organized hypocrisy.

The Peace of Augsburg originated the fully Westphalian *cuius regio, eius religio*, but even Augsburg included some provisions for religious toleration. The Peace of Westphalia endorsed the principle of Augsburg, but at the same time mandated religious toleration in the Holy Roman Empire, including provisions for consociational decision making with regard to religious issues in the imperial Diet and courts. The Vienna agreements at the end of the Napoleonic Wars included terms for the protection of Catholic minority rights in the Netherlands and Geneva and for the recognition of Polish institutions in Russia, Austria, and Prussia. The Versailles treaty and other arrangements associated with the conclusion of the First World War and the creation of the League of Nations established a regime for minorities that included the specification of minority rights in national constitutions, monitoring by the League Secretariat, the right of individual appeal to the league, and adjudication by the International Court of Justice. The 1995 Dayton accords provided for the creation of a tribunal, the Bosnian Human Rights Chamber, a majority of whose members would initially come from outside of Bosnia and other states of the former Yugoslavia, which could make binding decisions regarding the treatment of minorities.

Contracts, mutually contingent Pareto-improving arrangements, have been effective in protecting minority rights. Rulers have been motivated to sign such agreements by political necessity rather than principled commitment. (If they were committed to toleration in the first place, it is not likely that they would need to enter into contracts, although they might endorse conventions.) The Peace of Westphalia and subsequent arrangements among the major powers of Europe were designed to prevent sectarian strife that could lead to revolution, war, and chaos—not an attractive prospect for rulers who were more interested in keeping their corporeal heads than in preserving their incorporeal souls by repressing those they regarded as blasphemers. In these contractual arrangements, rulers invited external supervision of their domestic authority structures because this enhanced the likelihood of a politically stable outcome.

Minority rights protections achieved through coercion and imposition were less successful. The Versailles arrangements proved futile; nothing could more clearly demonstrate their failure than the Holocaust. Interventions to secure minority rights in the Balkans at Berlin in 1878, after the First World War, and following the breakup of Yugoslavia in 1991, all failed. The rulers or would-be rulers of the Balkan states accepted limitation on their Westphalian autonomy because they were faced with credible threats by more powerful states. At Berlin and Versailles, the major source of leverage available to the great powers of Europe was international recognition. Recognition was critical because it could enhance the international and domestic legitimacy of rulers and make it easier to enter into contracts that would provide financial and military resources. Likewise, the European Community made minority guarantees a condition of recognition for successor states of the former Yugoslavia. Once extended, however, recognition could not easily be withdrawn. With the exception of NATO intervention in the mid-1990s, the major powers were not willing to use military force. International guarantees of minority rights can be effective but only if they are self-enforcing, and they will only be self-enforcing if rulers are committed to such rights in the first place (in which case they might enter into conventions) or if they fear that the violation of minority rights would lead to retaliation against their own coreligionists or coethnics in other countries (the situation in post 1648 Europe), in which case they could enter into contracts.

Since the sixteenth century and even before, the principle of autonomy has been challenged by alternatives including minority rights. Westphalian sovereignty has been endorsed and ignored. Organized hypocrisy, not embeddedness or taken-for-grantedness, has characterized the Westphalian model.

CHAPTER 4

Rulers and Ruled: Human Rights

UNTIL THE CONCLUSION of the Second World War, human rights, which stipulated the rights of human beings in their status as individuals or as part of class that was not a source of basic identity (such as refugees), were less salient than minority rights. Before this time only the abolition of slavery and the slave trade in the nineteenth century and some International Labour Organization agreements in the interwar period emphasized human, as opposed to, minority rights. There are now, however, more than twenty United Nations human rights agreements as well as accords associated with specialized international organizations and with regional groups.

A number of observers have suggested that contemporary concerns with human rights are a revolutionary development in the international system. One writer maintains that there are two clusters of values at play in the contemporary environment—state autonomy and human rights—which can be in conflict. Another avers that human rights law is "revolutionary because it contradicts the notion of national sovereignty—that is, that a state can do as it pleases in its own jurisdiction."[1]

These observations are correct with regard to their emphasis on human rights as a relatively new development but incorrect in their disregard of the extent to which relations between rulers and ruled in one state have been an enduring concern of actors in others. The League of Nations regime for minority rights gave status to individuals as well as groups; it was not just the state, the traditional subject of international law, that could act. After the Second World War the focus on minority rights was supplanted by an emphasis on human rights, a reflection both of the failure of the interwar minorities regime and of the preferences of the leaders of the United States, the most powerful state in the postwar world and of western Europe as well. In the last decade of the twentieth century questions of minority rights again became more prominent because of changing configurations of power in the international system associated with the end of the cold war and turmoil resulting from ethnic and religious conflicts.

With the exception of the abolition of the slave trade in the nineteenth century, which was in part the result of coercion by Great Britain, and of

[1] Damrosch 1993, 93; Forsythe 1983, 4.

the use of economic sanctions, especially against South Africa, human rights have been associated with conventions. These engagements have been voluntary, the status quo ante has remained available, and behavior has not been contingent on the actions taken by other signatories. Conventions never violate a basic tenet of international legal sovereignty, which is that juridically independent territorial entities should not be subject to coercion.

Conventions can but do not necessarily compromise Westphalian sovereignty. By signing conventions rulers have extended invitations that have the potential for insinuating external authority within their own polities. Rulers could voluntarily enter into such accords with the full understanding that in so doing they might limit their own autonomy by altering domestic views about legitimate behavior, authorizing external monitoring of internal practices, or creating third-party adjudication procedures that give individual citizens, not just states, legal standing. Participation in conventions might also have unanticipated consequences in civil society and within the government; what were thought to be empty pledges might actually change domestic authority structures. Conventions might, however, have no impact on domestic autonomy; invitations might be simply pro forma. An international pledge, for instance, to eschew torture might change neither the behavior of rulers nor the attitudes of groups in civil societies. Whether a convention affects Westphalian sovereignty at all is an empirical question.

In the postwar world rulers signed human rights accords for a variety of different reasons. In some instances rulers endorsed human rights conventions not because they had the intention or even ability to implement their precepts, but because such agreements were part of a cognitive script that defined appropriate behavior for a modern state in the late twentieth century. Signing, however, was decoupled from actual practice. In other cases rulers wanted to increase the probability that their commitment to human rights within their own polity would not be reversed by their successors. This was true for the policy makers who initiated and sustained the European human rights regime. In the case of the Soviet bloc, rulers might have seen participation as a ploy that could be used to increase support in third countries.

SLAVERY AND THE SLAVE TRADE

Slavery is a practice that has become universally unacceptable, yet into the nineteenth century it was routinely practiced in many different parts of the globe. The abolition of slavery and the slave trade was the result both of conventions among like-minded rulers who wanted an end to the practice of human servitude and contracts and coercion in which rulers in more powerful states, especially Britain, acted to alter the treatment of individuals in other states. For largely ideational rather than material reasons, Britain in the nineteenth century committed itself to end the practice of slavery. Britain enforced and monitored the international regime, which it had itself created through a series of international treaties. Ending slavery was more important than honoring the principle of autonomy and nonintervention.

Britain outlawed slavery for its own flag vessels in 1807. During the Napoleonic Wars, slave ships from enemy states were captured. Slaves on these ships were set free, usually in Sierra Leone. By 1815 Britain, Russia, Austria, Prussia, France, the Netherlands, Sweden, and the United States had agreed to prohibit the transatlantic slave trade. In 1817 Spain also agreed to abolish the slave trade north of the equator and in 1820 to abolish it completely. These were conventions that reflected the preferences of rulers in the signatory states.[2]

Despite these commitments, the slave trade was so lucrative that large numbers of Africans continued to be transported across the Atlantic. The major effort to enforce the ban on slaving was undertaken by Britain. Between 1818 and 1820 Britain signed treaties with a number of European countries that gave British warships the right to search and seize vessels suspected of engaging in the slave trade.[3]

Brazil and Portugal were the most recalcitrant slave-trading countries. Brazilian agriculture was heavily dependent on slave labor. Immediately after abolishing the slave trade for British shipping in 1807, Britain began to put pressure on Portugal, whose colonies in Africa and South America were both a major source of and point of sale for slaves. Portugal at first rejected British initiatives. However, when France invaded Portugal in late 1807, the Portuguese royal family was forced to flee to Brazil under British protection. In 1810 Portugal signed a commercial treaty with Britain that provided in part that Portugal would cooperate in gradually abolishing the slave trade. Britain conceded to Portugal the right to continue slave trading within its African territories. In 1815 Portugal signed an agreement with Britain agreeing to stop slave trading north of the equator, a commitment of limited consequence since most of Portugal's trade between Africa and Brazil was south of the equator.

In 1839 Britain unilaterally authorized its navy to board and seize suspected slavers that were flying the Portuguese flag. This came after long and unsuccessful efforts to sign a bilateral treaty with Portugal authorizing such seizures. The slaves were to be released in the nearest British port, the disposition of the ships was to be decided by British admiralty

[2] Ray 1989, 409; Bethell 1970, 10, 11–15, 20.
[3] Bethell 1970, 20, 26.

courts, and the crews of such ships were to be returned to their own countries for trial.[4]

Britain focused its attention on Brazil after its independence in 1822. In exchange for recognition by Britain in 1826, Brazil agreed to abolish the slave trade by 1830 despite strong opposition from many members of its parliament. The treaty stipulated that the slave trade would be treated as piracy after that date, providing Britain with legal grounds for seizing slave-trading ships on the high seas. Despite the agreement, slave trading continued between Brazil and Africa, even growing in the 1830s beyond what it had been before the treaty was signed.[5]

Confronted with the continuation of the slave trade some twenty years after it should have been abolished under the 1826 treaty, Britain acted unilaterally. Slaving had already been declared piracy, giving British ships the right to board and seize suspected vessels on the high seas. In 1850, British warships entered Brazilian ports and seized and burned a number of ships that were suspected of engaging in the transport of slaves. During these operations the British were fired upon from Brazilian forts. It is difficult to imagine a less ambiguous violation of the norm of nonintervention.[6]

These pressures were effective. Confronted with British naval power and the antipathy of other advanced states, Brazil passed and enforced legislation to end the slave trade. One Brazilian leader speaking to the Brazilian Chamber of Deputies in 1850 recognized that Brazil was the only country actively resisting the antislave regime and stated that "With the whole of the civilised world now opposed to the slave trade, and with a powerful nation like Britain intent on ending it once and for all, Can we resist the torrent? I think not."[7]

The abolition of the slave trade was a triumph for human rights and freedom made possible in large measure by the commitment and power of Great Britain. Britain took the lead in initiating a series of international treaties in the early part of the nineteenth century that committed states to abolishing the slave trade. Brazil was the most important defector from this system, failing to enforce its own treaty obligations. Britain used naval power, including entry into Brazilian territorial waters and the destruction of Brazilian ships, to compel Brazil to change its policies. Britain's commitment to ending international commerce in human beings triumphed over nonintervention.

[4] Ibid., 7–9, 13, 164.
[5] Ibid., 60–61 and chap. 3.
[6] Ibid., chap. 12.
[7] Quoted in Bethell 1970, 338.

Unlike issues related to religious toleration or the treatment of minorities, Britain's behavior cannot be explained in terms of specific economic, political, or security interests. The economic consequences of the abolition of slavery for Britain and its colonies were ambivalent at best, because British plantations in the Caribbean were heavily dependent on slave labor. Rather, British action was strongly motivated by the values and commitments of important parts of its domestic population. The British government was pressured by antislavery groups that based their opposition on religious doctrine, not economic self-interests or national security.

Slavery did not, however, disappear in the nineteenth century. Slavery was an issue for both the League of Nations and the United Nations. A 1926 league convention outlawed slavery and the slave trade and provided that disputes between states were to be referred to the International Court of Justice or, if the parties were not signatories to the Statute of the Court, to a mutually acceptable arbitration body as specified under the 1907 Convention for the Pacific Settlement of International Disputes. States could, however, declare that some of their territories were not subject to the convention. The 1956 Supplementary Convention on the Abolition of Slavery, the Slave Trade, and Institutions and Practices Similar to Slavery, endorsed by more than one hundred countries, obligated the signatories to end debt bondage and serfdom, to eliminate the practice of allowing a parent to give a child under eighteen for labor service, and to prohibit marriage arrangements in which a woman is given without choice in exchange for material payments or is inherited by another person if her husband dies. Signatories could not choose to exclude some of the territories under their control. Disputes were to be referred to the International Court of Justice.[8] These agreements, like other human rights accords that will be discussed here, were conventions that did not involve contingent behavior. Their efficacy depended critically on the support that they received from domestic groups and institutions.

THE TWENTIETH CENTURY

The focus on individual human rights is a phenomenon of the twentieth century. International human rights agreements have proliferated since the Second World War. These agreements have usually taken the form of conventions in which rulers make commitments regarding their relations with their subjects (individuals within their territorial jurisdiction) that are not contingent on the behavior of other signatories. Signatories have extended invitations, sometimes empty, that can implicate external au-

---

[8] Texts in Brownlie 1992, 52–63.

thority in domestic institutional structures. The monitoring and enforcement provisions of human rights conventions have varied widely from what amount to nothing more than pledges that do not have the status of a formal treaty, such as the Universal Declaration on Human Rights, to arrangements that include third-party monitoring and judicial review that can be initiated by private parties, notably the European human rights regime.

At the international level, human rights were first recognized in various conventions of the International Labour Organization (ILO), which was established after the First World War in response to the fear that domestic social upheaval could lead to international disorder. Individual member states can, but are not obligated, to endorse these conventions. The objective of the ILO was to promote labor relations that would enhance domestic political stability. Most ILO conventions deal with work-related issues including health and safety standards, the right to organize, the abolition of forced labor, and nondiscrimination. In recent years ILO conventions have sometimes gone further afield. In 1989, for instance, the Convention Concerning Indigenous and Tribal Peoples in Independent Countries was opened for signature. It provides for equal rights for indigenous peoples, respect and promotion of their cultural rights, nondiscrimination, the right to decide their own spiritual, cultural, social, and economic priorities, and consideration by national courts of indigenous penal practices. This convention had, however, only been ratified by a small number of states by the early 1990s.

The ILO has modest monitoring provisions. Each signatory to a convention is obliged to submit a report to the ILO's Committee of Experts on the Application of Conventions and Recommendations. These experts can offer comments. More significantly, under the tripartite structure of the ILO (government, labor, management) both workers' and employers' organizations can bring a complaint to the ILO Governing Body. By signing ILO conventions, rulers might or might not be altering their domestic authority structures depending on whether participation changed domestic attitudes or policies.[9]

During the first part of the twentieth century, however, the ILO was exceptional in the attention that it paid to human rights. Only after 1945 did human rights become a more salient issue. The minority rights regime of the interwar period was regarded as a failure, which had even been exploited by the Nazi regime (for instance, in its demands at Munich) to promote its own racist agenda. The dominant power in the postwar world,

---

[9] Brownlie 1992, 246–316, for the texts of ILO conventions.

the United States, was committed to individual rights.[10] The modal American solution for ethnic conflict was the melting pot, not the legitimation of separate political group identities. American leaders opposed including minority rights in the Charter of the United Nations and the Universal Declaration of Human Rights.[11]

Accords concerned with the rights of individuals or classes of individuals have proliferated since 1945. As of 1993 the United Nations listed twenty-five such instruments. Another compendium records forty-seven compacts including those associated with regional organizations and specialized agencies.[12] These conventions cover a wide range of issues including genocide, torture, slavery, refugees, stateless persons, women's rights, racial discrimination, children's rights, and forced labor. In some instances, human rights agreements specify general principles, but in others they are very precise.

There are several broad agreements that dignify human rights. The preamble to the Charter of the United Nations reaffirms fundamental human rights, the dignity of the individual, and the equality of men and women. The Universal Declaration of Human Rights was adopted by the UN General Assembly in 1948 after three years of debate. The declaration specifies personal rights such as protection against racial, sexual, or religious discrimination; legal rights such as the presumption of innocence and equality before the law; civil liberties such as freedom of religion, opinion, movement, association, and residence including the right to leave any country and "to seek and enjoy in other countries asylum from persecution"; family rights including the right to marriage, equal rights for both spouses in marriage, and full consent to marriage; subsistence rights such as the right to food; economic rights such as the right to own property, to work, to enjoy "periodic holidays with pay," and to social security; social and cultural rights such as the right to an education including the admonition that "elementary education shall be compulsory," and that "higher education shall be equally accessible to all on the basis of merit"; and political rights such as universal suffrage. The declaration was designed to provide substance for Article 55 of the charter which states in part that the United Nations shall promote "universal respect for, and observance of human rights and fundamental freedoms for all without distinction as to race, sex, language, or religion."[13]

Two covenants dealing with social and economic, and civil and political rights were passed in 1966. While these generally endorsed and elaborated

[10] Hartz 1955, 54.

[11] Sigler 1983, 67–77; Donnelly 1989, 21.

[12] United Nations 1994; Brownlie 1992.

[13] United Nations 1948, Articles 14, 24, 25, and 55.

the Universal Declaration, there were exceptions such as the absence of any mention of the right to private property and the addition of the right of self-determination.[14]

Human rights conventions on specific issues can be detailed and ambitious. For instance, the 1953 Convention on the Political Rights of Women, which has been ratified by more than 100 countries, provides for equal voting rights for women and equal rights to hold office.[15] The 1979 Convention on the Elimination of All Forms of Discrimination against Women, which has been ratified by more than 120 states, obligates parties to take all legal measures necessary to assure the equality of men and women, to "modify the social and cultural patterns of conduct of men and women," to provide equal access to education, to take measures to assure "the same opportunities to participate actively in sports and physical education," to assure equal work opportunities including promotion and job security, to introduce paid maternity leave, and to offer adequate prenatal and postnatal care including "free services where necessary."[16] The 1951 Convention Relating to the Status of Refugees, endorsed by more than 120 states, provides that each signatory will not discriminate among refugees on the basis of race, religion, or country of origin; will provide freedom of religion equal to that provided for nationals; and will allow refugees access to its legal system.

The enforcement and monitoring mechanisms for these agreements vary enormously. Some, such as the Universal Declaration of Human Rights, the 1960 United Nations Declaration on the Granting of Independence to Colonial Countries and Peoples, the 1981 Declaration on All Forms of Intolerance and Discrimination based on Religion or Belief, have no monitoring or enforcement provisions. At best, such conventions can specify salient objectives and express good intentions. The only mechanism through which such conventions could infringe on autonomy would be to alter the conceptions of legitimate practices that were held by groups within a state.

Other conventions—for example, those on slavery, the status of refugees, political rights of women, the prevention and punishment of the crime of genocide—provide that disputes can be referred to the International Court of Justice but only by one of the signatories. Such referrals would violate the Westphalian model since the court would constitute an external source of authority, but they would be perfectly consistent with international legal conceptions of sovereignty since cases could only

---

[14] Forsythe 1983, 8–9.

[15] Brownlie 1992, 106–8; United Nations 1994, 10.

[16] See Brownlie 1992, 106–8, for Convention on the Elimination of All Forms of Discrimination against Women, Articles 5.a, 10.f, and 13.2.

be heard by the International Court if the contending states had agreed to its jurisdiction. No human rights cases have, however, been referred to the court.

A number of conventions, such as those on racial discrimination, apartheid, torture and other degrading forms of punishment, and the rights of the child provide for the creation of expert committees to which signatories are obligated to make regular reports. In addition some committees can undertake investigations unless a state explicitly excludes such actions when it ratifies the convention. The state must, however, usually be informed and given the opportunity to participate in any inquiry. In some conventions signatories have the option of authorizing the expert committee to hear complaints from individuals.

Aside from specific United Nations conventions, the United Nations Commission on Human Rights was authorized by a 1970 resolution of the Economic and Social Committee to investigate reliable complaints about gross violations of human rights. The members of the commission are instructed by state delegates, not independent experts. There are, however, stringent restrictions on what the commission can do. It cannot investigate specific violations. Its activities must be confidential until they are concluded. For much of its history the commission only examined the behavior of pariah states, including South Africa, Israel, and Chile under Pinochet. The commission also reviews the reports that parties to the International Covenant on Civil and Political Rights are obligated to submit every two years, but it does not formally evaluate them, and some of the reports have been superficial.[17]

None of the United Nations human rights accords violate the international legal concept of sovereignty. They are all conventions that are entered into voluntarily and in which the behavior of one signatory is not contingent on that of others. The accords can, but do not necessarily, compromise Westphalian sovereignty by providing external legitimation for certain domestic practices involving relations between rulers and ruled.

The European Convention for the Protection of Human Rights and Fundamental Freedoms, which was signed in 1950 and entered into force in 1953, and its subsequent protocols, provides the most far-reaching example of infringements on the Westphalian model. Signatories commit themselves to the rule of law, the abolition of torture, slavery, and forced labor, the assumption of innocence in criminal cases, the right to counsel, to freedom of religion, to freedom of expression, to nondiscrimination, to emigrate, free elections by secret ballot, and the abolition of the death penalty except for acts committed in time or threat of war.

[17] Forsythe 1983, 46; Donnelly 1989, 208–9.

The European human rights regime has elaborate monitoring and enforcement procedures. The convention created the European Commission on Human Rights and the European Court of Human Rights. The commission is composed of experts who act in their individual capacity. (Each member state nominates three experts, one of whom is then elected from each country by all of the members). The commission can receive complaints from individuals and nongovernmental organizations, if the member has recognized its competence to do so, as well as from states. (Recognizing the standing of individuals is a departure from conventional international legal concepts, but this standing is still the result of voluntary choices by states.) If the commission pursues a complaint, it issues a report. If the issue is not satisfactorily resolved within three months after the report is issued, either the commission or the state involved can refer the issue to the European Court of Human Rights whose decisions are binding on member states. Since 1990 individuals as well as member states and the commission can bring a case directly to the court. Over time almost all of the signatories of the convention have recognized the competence of the commission to receive complaints from nonstate actors and the authority of the court. The commission can also send its recommendation to the Committee of Ministers, which can make binding decisions based on a two-thirds majority vote.[18]

Between 1953 and 1990 the commission received 15,457 petitions, almost all from individuals. About 95 percent were declared inadmissible, but 96 resulted in friendly settlements, 430 led to a commission report, and 251 led to judgments by the court. The number of petitions and court rulings has grown over time, especially since the 1970s. Decisions by the commission and the court including friendly settlements reached before adjudication have involved criminal procedure, penal codes, the treatment of prisoners, vagrancy, the rights of illegitimate children, expropriation policies, the care of the mentally ill, wiretapping, press censorship, interrogatory techniques, and homosexuality. There have been five instances in which states have brought complaints against another state. In four of these the complainants had ethnic ties with the individuals who were allegedly being abused. In the fifth, a number of smaller European states—the Netherlands, Norway, Denmark, and Sweden—filed a petition against the Greek military regime. Confronted with expulsion, Greece withdrew from the Council of Europe after an investigation by the European Human Rights Commission found against the military regime.[19]

---

[18] See Brownlie 1992, 326–62, for the text of the convention and protocols.

[19] Moravcsik 1994, 45–47; Moravcsik 1998, 20; Sikkink 1993; Forsythe 1983, 52, 57, 59; Donnelly 1992, 82–83; Forsythe 1989, 19.

There are other European human rights accords, although their scope and monitoring and enforcement provisions are less extensive than those associated with the European Human Rights Convention. By the early 1990s fifteen states had ratified the European Convention for the Prevention of Torture. The provisions of the convention parallel those of the UN Convention against Torture but the European document requires that signatories allow visits by the committee established by the convention to any site within their territory where individuals are deprived of their liberty. The committee, which consists of one individual serving in his or her private capacity from each member state, is elected by majority vote of the ministers of the Council of Europe from a list of three submitted by each signatory. The committee must notify a member state of a visit. The committee is, however, free to move anywhere within or without prison facilities and to interview privately anyone believed to have relevant information. Limitations on the committee's visits can only be made on the grounds of national defense, public safety, serious disorders, the medical condition of a person, or the need for an urgent interrogation. The committee first submits a report to the concerned state. If the state does not rectify conditions that violate the convention, the committee may, by a two-thirds vote, make a public statement.[20]

The European Social Charter has been ratified by twenty states. The charter endorses the right to work, to just conditions of work, to fair remuneration, to collective bargaining, to social security, and to protection for mothers and children. The signatories are committed to supporting high levels of employment, free employment services, vocational guidance, minimum two-week vacations with pay, a weekly rest period, higher pay rates for overtime, specialized services for disabled persons, the reunion of families of foreign migrant workers, and limiting employment for those below fifteen years of age. Members are obligated to submit reports every other year. These reports are reviewed by a seven-member Committee of Experts, which is appointed by the Committee of Ministers.[21] For the most part the signatories were already committed to the objectives stipulated in the charter. It could only compromise Westphalian sovereignty by exercising some marginal constraint on the policy choices available to signatory states.

Human rights have also been included in agreements reached within the Conference on Security and Cooperation in Europe (CSCE, now the Organization for Security and Cooperation in Europe, OSCE). The Final Act of the Helsinki Conference on Security and Cooperation in Europe

---

[20] See Brownlie 1992, 383–90, for Council of Europe, The European Convention for the Prevention of Torture and Inhuman or Degrading Treatment or Punishment, 1987.

[21] Brownlie 1992, 363–82, for Council of Europe, European Social Charter, 1961.

was signed in 1975 by thirty-five states. It was not a legally binding treaty but reflected the view by both the West and the Soviet bloc that the patterns of interaction that characterized the cold war could be stabilized. The rulers of the Soviet Union saw the Helsinki accords as legitimating their dominance of eastern Europe and facilitating technological and economic cooperation. Policy makers in the West, especially those from western Europe, pressed for the inclusion of human rights principles.

The Helsinki accords, like many other international agreements, endorsed principles that both legitimated and undermined Westphalian sovereignty. The agreement was divided into three sections or baskets: Basket I dealt with security issues, Basket II with economic and technological cooperation, and Basket III with human rights. Principle VI of the Declaration on Principles Guiding Relations between Participating States endorsed nonintervention, while Principle VII endorsed human rights including freedom of thought, conscience, and religion. Helsinki also endorsed sovereign equality, inviolability of frontiers, peaceful settlement of disputes, self-determination of peoples, and cooperation among states. There were no provisions for enforcement or monitoring.[22]

There have been a number of CSCE and OSCE conferences since Helsinki that have produced documents endorsing human rights (as well as the minority rights noted in Chapter 3). The accords signed at the conclusion of the Vienna meetings in 1989 included more extensive commitments to human rights such as protection against arbitrary arrest, degrading treatment, harsh detention, and torture. There were detailed stipulations regarding freedom of religion but no consensus on capital punishment, visas, and compulsory military service. The pact reached at Copenhagen in 1990 endorsed the right to a prompt trial, to peaceful assembly, and to participate in nongovernmental organizations committed to human rights, including "unhindered access with similar bodies within and outside their countries and with international organizations." The signatories agreed to bring their national laws into conformity with the provisions of various CSCE pacts. Countries that signed the Optional Protocol assented to provide a response within four weeks to questions raised by another state.[23]

Latin America is the other region that has developed a highly elaborated human rights regime, although one that has been in practice less consequential than its European counterpart. In 1948 the Organization of American States (OAS) approved the American Declaration of the Rights and Duties of Man, which endorsed the right to life, liberty, and security,

---

[22] Vincent 1986, 66–70; for text of the Helsinki Final Act, see Brownlie 1992, 391–449.

[23] See Brownlie 1992, 454–73, for the text of the Copenhagen Agreement; the quotation is from p. 461, Article II. 10.4. Also see Moravcsik 1994, 48.

to equality before the law, to freedom of religion, to establish a family, to preservation of health through sanitary and social services "to the extent permitted by public and community resources," to work, to leisure, to social security, to peaceful assembly, and to the presumption of innocence until proven guilty. The declaration also specified a list of responsibilities for individuals, including protecting minor children, voting, and obeying the law. The declaration does not provide for any enforcement or monitoring mechanisms.[24]

The American Convention on Human Rights, which has been ratified by more than twenty states has many parallels with the European convention. The convention, signed in 1969, endorses a standard list of rights including the abolition of slavery and torture, the presumption of innocence, the provision of legal counsel, and freedom of religion. In addition it provides that "usury and any other form of exploitation of man by man shall be prohibited by law," and that "Any propaganda for war and any advocacy of national, racial, or religious hatred that constitute incitement to lawless violence or to any similar illegal action against any person or group of persons . . . shall be considered as offenses punishable by law.[25] The convention also bans any extension of the death penalty to new crimes, although it does not prohibit it outright.

Unlike the Inter-American Declaration, the convention specifies enforcement and monitoring mechanisms. Signatories are committed to introduce any domestic legislation necessary to implement the convention. The convention established the Inter-American Commission on Human Rights and the Inter-American Court of Human Rights, each with seven members. Members of the commission, who serve in their individual capacity, are elected by the General Assembly of the OAS from a list of candidates submitted by member states who can nominate three persons, at least one of whom must not be a national of the nominating state. The commission can only pursue a complaint if its competence has been recognized by the signatory state and if domestic remedies have been exhausted. Individuals, groups, and states can bring complaints to the commission provided that the state has recognized the commission's competence. If a friendly settlement between the state and the complainant is not reached, then the commission prepares a report and recommendations which are transmitted to the concerned states. If the matter is not settled within three months, the commission can publish its report. If the commission's procedures are exhausted, the case can be taken to the Inter-American

---

[24] See Brownlie 1992, 487–94, for the text of American Declaration of the Rights and Duties of Man, 1948. The quotation is from Article XI.

[25] See Brownlie 1992, 495–520, for the American Convention on Human Rights, 1969, Articles 21.3 and 13.5.

Court of Human Rights whose judges are nominated and elected by the signatory states. If a state fails to comply with a ruling of the Court, the court can bring the issue to the Assembly of the OAS.[26]

In 1988 the OAS completed the Additional Protocol to the American Convention on Human Rights in the Area of Economic, Social, and Cultural Rights, which included commitments to full-employment policies, levels of remuneration that could provide decent living conditions, stability of employment, paid vacations, special facilities for the handicapped and elderly, and the provision of primary health care. States were to submit periodic reports to the OAS. Individuals could petition the Inter-American Human Rights Commission regarding economic, social, and cultural rights, if the commission's competence had been recognized by the relevant state.[27]

In some ways the formal powers of human rights institutions, the commission and the court, are greater than their European counterparts. The human rights regimes in Latin America have, however, been less effective. The commission issued critical reports about violations of human rights in Nicaragua under the Somoza regime and in Chile under Pinochet, which had little or no effect. Rulers in Latin American states endorsed human rights agreements but often failed to abide by them. Domestic factors that made the European human rights regime so effective, including support from groups in civil society and institutional structures, especially the courts, were less consequential in Latin America.[28]

Human Rights Conventions and National Autonomy

The human rights accords endorsed by the members of universal and regional organizations have been conventions, voluntary, Pareto-improving agreements in which behavior in one signatory has not been contingent on that in others. Human rights agreements have never violated international legal sovereignty, which stipulates that juridically independent territorial entities have the right to free choice. The very fact that rulers could freely sign such agreements is an affirmation of their international legal sovereignty, of the fact that they are recognized by other states as competent to enter into international accords.

Some of these compacts have, however, violated the Westphalian model; others have not. By extending invitations to external sources of legitimacy, rulers have sometimes compromised their domestic autonomy. Autonomy has been conceded by creating authoritative supranational institutions

---

[26] Donnelly 1989, 215; Vincent 1986, 95.
[27] Text of the protocol in Brownlie 1992, 521–30.
[28] Forsythe 1983, 53.

and, more obliquely, by altering conceptions of legitimate behavior among groups within civil society and the state. A human rights accord can violate Westphalian sovereignty if it has enforcement procedures. The European human rights regime is the best, and perhaps only, example. The decisions of the European Court of Human Rights are binding on signatories, although actual enforcement must still rest with police and courts of national states. Individuals can, and have, brought complaints against their own governments, which have led to policy changes. The existence of a transnational judicial body whose decisions are directly applicable in more than twenty states cannot be comprehended in terms of the Westphalian model. By joining the regime, European states have invited external authority structures into their domestic polities.

Human rights conventions may also compromise Westphalian sovereignty by changing relationships of authority and legitimacy within a state. The ability of any ruler, or government, to determine the grounds for domestic legitimacy will depend to some extent on external forces. No government can insulate itself from foreign influence. For instance, international nongovernmental organizations like Amnesty International try to change the practices and policies of governments as does the Catholic Church. Such private actors are not violating Westphalian autonomy; they make no claim to authoritative decision making. When a government, however, invites external legitimation of its own practices and institutions by signing a human rights convention, it might indirectly compromise its autonomy by altering conceptions of appropriate political authority held by actors in civil society, who may then press for the reorganization of domestic structures.

One example of such a phenomenon was the impact of the Helsinki Final Act on the activities of human rights groups in eastern Europe. Daniel Thomas has shown that this agreement, even though it lacked the status of a treaty and had no monitoring or enforcement provisions, changed political behavior in the Soviet bloc countries. Before Helsinki human rights protests in eastern Europe were made by isolated individuals; after Helsinki organized groups, Helsinki watch committees, became much more salient. The most active groups were in Poland and Czechoslovakia. Helsinki watch groups in Poland were later active in Solidarity. In the Soviet Union groups were established in Leningrad, Moscow, Armenia, Georgia, Lithuania, and the Ukraine. The Helsinki watch committees based their protests against government policy in eastern Europe on both their national constitutions and the Helsinki accords.

Why would Helsinki, an agreement that was not even a legally binding treaty, matter? In eastern Europe the accord provided a signal that facilitated organized resistance to Communist repression. Groups could be created more easily because the Helsinki accords provided a focal point.

Links with Western human rights organizations increased. The greater the level of formal organization and the larger the number of activists, the more embarrassing repression would be, and the more it would alienate more passive citizens in the Soviet bloc. Perhaps the most interesting example of the Helsinki agreement as a signal occurred in East Germany, which had no Helsinki watch group, but where 100,000 applied for emigration permits in 1976, justifying their action by referring to Basket III. Hence an international accord altered conceptions of legitimate behavior within the state. Rulers did not have complete autonomy because of international initiatives that they had themselves endorsed, even though they had not expected their invitations to external sources of authority to be consequential.[29]

If human rights conventions have some provisions for monitoring and reporting, they may also affect domestic concepts of legitimacy by mandating procedures that change the attitudes and behavior of both government officials and private citizens. The modal form of monitoring is a national report to a committee of experts. By themselves, such reports do not constitute a violation of the Westphalian model. A repressive regime could submit a pro forma document that would have no impact on domestic autonomy. But if a report mobilizes domestic opinion, either within or without the government, the monitoring functions of an international commitment could be indirectly consequential for national structures of authority. A government, for instance, that has obligated itself to report on the status of women could catalyze the formation of women's rights groups in its own society, and such groups could successfully press for a change in state practices. An international accord could reinforce particular norms, and these could change national concepts of authority and legitimacy.

The extent to which human rights conventions compromise the Westphalian model is critically dependent on the domestic base of support for such values. Andrew Moravcsik has pointed out that both shaming, which alters authority structures by mobilizing public opinion within a state, and co-optation, which alters authority structures by mobilizing ties between domestic and external actors, depend upon the existence of attitudes or organizations that are sympathetic to human rights in the first place. Without such domestic support, a human rights convention can simply be an empty invitation, or even cynical gesture, which has no consequences for the ability of rulers to exclude external authority from their territory.[30]

Interventions by major powers, such as mandating minority rights, always compromise the Westphalian model: domestic authority structures

---

[29] D. Thomas forthcoming; Moravcsik 1994, 48; J. Sharp 1984, 168; Donnelly 1995, 137.
[30] Moravcsik 1994, 52–55.

are influenced or even dictated by foreign actors. The consequences of invitations, such as endorsing human rights conventions, are more ambiguous. Their impact, if it exists at all, may be indirect. Rulers who endorse internationally legitimated values, especially ones that they do not believe in, may find that what they thought was an empty gesture has altered concepts of legitimacy within their own polities and precipitated changes in domestic authority structures. The extent to which such a process actually occurs is an empirical question. Sometimes an invitation to external sources of legitimation is inconsequential. Sometimes rulers endorse principles in which they and their subjects already believe; a convention does not change domestic sentiments. In some cases, however, conventions, even though they are entered into voluntarily and even though they have no provisions for enforcement, can alter domestic authority structures by introducing external sources of legitimacy.

Motivations

Rulers have signed human rights accords for three reasons: to constrain future governments, to follow the script of modernity, and, in the case of the Soviet bloc, to attract supporters in third countries. First, rulers may want to bind their successors. They may be committed to the values embodied in a human rights convention, but are uncertain about the preferences of those that will rule after them. An international accord can make abrogating human rights commitments more costly by strengthening domestic groups that support the same values, providing links with international nongovernmental organizations that can mobilize officials in other countries, making shaming more effective and, if the regime has enforcement provisions, establishing procedures for legal actions against the state. The clearest example of using an international convention to lock in particular policy preferences occurred in Europe. The governing authorities in Europe in 1950 could not be sure that their commitment to democratic principles and human rights would last. The German experience in the interwar years—Weimar followed by the Third Reich—had shown how vulnerable such values could be. By formulating the European Convention on Human Rights and creating the European Commission on Human Rights and the European Court of Human Rights, the rulers of the early 1950s hoped to reduce the likelihood that their subjects would again be governed by murderous and repressive regimes. The most vigorous supporters of a strong human rights regime, one that would have supranational officials and an independent court that would provide access for individuals and not just states, were those governments that were most anxious to solidify their democratic commitments, notably Austria, Belgium, France, Germany, Iceland, Ireland, and Italy.

Political leaders who were confident about the embeddedness of democracy within their own polities, such as the United Kingdom, or that were not so fully committed to human rights, such as Turkey, were less enthusiastic about a strong regime.[31]

A second motivation for signing human rights conventions is that participation in such accords is part of the script of modernity. Formal endorsement, however, may have little to do with actual behavior. Decoupling is easier if the regime lacks monitoring and enforcement provisions, and if domestic support for human rights is weak. John Meyer and his colleagues have shown astonishing similarities in the formal policies of most countries across a wide range of issue areas including social security, women's rights, and education, despite enormous variation in the socioeconomic characteristics and national value systems, but the actual implementation of national legislation is inconsistent at best.[32]

For most of the postwar period there has not been a tight empirical relation between the number of human rights agreements that a state has signed and its human rights performance. In 1987 the correlation was .11.[33] It is easy to imagine that states with well-developed judicial systems might be more reluctant to sign agreements because they could have a direct impact on decisions in their national court system. Autocratic rulers, in contrast, could sign with less anxiety about domestic consequences. Signing an agreement does not mean that its provisions will be honored. Whatever motivations rulers have had for signing human rights conventions, the actual promotion of human rights does not appear to have been a decisive factor.

The interpretation that some rulers sign human rights accords because they view them as part of the script of modernity is also supported by the existence of regional human rights agreements in Africa and the Arab world, which have had only the most limited impact. The Permanent Arab Commission on Human Rights was established by the League of Arab States in 1968 but there has been no agreement on substantive norms and the commission has been inactive. The Arab Charter of Human Rights of 1971 has been ignored. The African Charter on Human and Peoples' Rights was adopted by the Organization of African Unity (OAU) in June 1981. The charter creates an African Commission on Human and Peoples' rights and even "envisions" complaints from individuals. There are no provisions even for regular reporting much less monitoring or enforcement.[34] Africa's human rights record has been problematic at best.

[31] Moravcsik 1998, 22.

[32] Finnemore 1996b; Meyer et al. 1997.

[33] Figures for human rights record from Freedom House; for ratifications from information in United Nations 1987.

[34] Donnelly 1989, 217–18.

The ratification by the Soviet Union of many human rights conventions cannot be explained so easily from a world culture perspective emphasizing scripts of modernity. For the Soviets, the Helsinki Final Act involved a trade-off in which the West recognized the status quo in eastern Europe, including borders and, less explicitly, regime type, in exchange for an eastern bloc endorsement of liberal human rights. The CSCE agreements did promote the development of human rights groups in eastern Europe. The Soviets had overestimated both the strength of their repressive apparatus and the degree of support that they enjoyed from subject populations. They had issued an invitation but they had not expected that the invitee, liberal conceptions of human rights, would actually show up within their own borders. The West used the Helsinki accord as a device to pressure the Soviet Union on human rights, rejecting the charge that this amounted to interference in the internal affairs of another state on the grounds that human rights were universally recognized and that noninterference referred only to efforts to dictate to other countries.

Aside from Helsinki, the Soviet bloc countries routinely ratified United Nations human rights agreements. As of September 1, 1987, the Soviet Union, Bulgaria, Czechoslovakia, and Romania had all ratified 14 out of the 22 extant United Nations human rights instruments, East Germany 16, and Poland 13. For the industrialized countries there was wide variation. The United States had ratified 6 conventions, Switzerland, 8; Italy and the United Kingdom, 15; France and West Germany, 16; Sweden, 18; and Norway, 19.[35] The Soviet bloc rulers were not following a script of modernity propagated by the West; they had their own script, Marxism-Leninism, with its own claims about universality and scientific validity. For the Soviets, endorsing human rights accords might have been seen as a way to enhance the image of eastern bloc countries among sympathetic populations in the West or as an instrument of propaganda, which Communist rulers thought would have little or no impact within their own countries.

Economic Sanctions

Human rights conventions are consistent with the international legal sovereignty, understood as the right of a state to enter into agreements voluntarily, but such accords may violate the Westphalian model if they compromise the domestic autonomy of the state. In contrast, the use of economic sanctions to alter the relationship between rulers and ruled violates both international legal and Westphalian sovereignty because the tar-

---

[35] Derived from information in United Nations 1987.

get state is being coerced with regard to issues associated with its domestic political structures.

Out of the 106 specific cases of economic sanctions during the twentieth century presented by Hufbauer, Schott, and Elliot, 17 involved efforts to protect human rights. (Sixteen others were attempts to change the character of the domestic regime of the target by either removing the ruler or changing the institutional structure.) Collective sanctions against South Africa to end apartheid, which were first endorsed by the United Nations in 1962, are the most prominent example. Between 1970 and 1990 the United States imposed sanctions against more than a dozen countries for human rights violations.[36] In all of these cases the target, even if it did not comply with the sanctions, was worse off than it had been because it could not, at the same time, both avoid sanctions and maintain its ex ante policies. Either it suffered sanctions, at least for some period of time, or it had to change its policies.

The use of economic and other sanctions to end apartheid in South Africa is a rare example of coercion in the area of human rights that accomplished its objectives. Apartheid had no international defenders. African states opposed South African policies but had little economic leverage.[37] The frontline African states could not make credible threats against the South African economy because the implementation of any such threats, would have been more damaging to the initiators than the target. The OECD countries could make credible threats, although such policies were domestically contentious especially in the United States and Great Britain. In 1977 Europe espoused a Code of Conduct for investors in South Africa designed to normalize relations between firms and black workers, but it was ineffective because implementation was uneven. In 1985 Europe adopted a number of initiatives including limiting some oil sales, an embargo on military exports, the end of military cooperation, and discouraging sporting contacts. Britain and Germany, however, blocked more ambitious trade sanctions.[38]

The United States first pressured South Africa in 1963 when it imposed a voluntary arms embargo and some restrictions in Exim Bank loans. In 1979 the Carter administration extended controls by banning the sale of all goods to the military and police. In 1985 Reagan, responding to pressure from Congress, forbid the import of Krugerrands and ended the export of most nuclear technology. In 1986 Congress overrode a presidential veto and imposed additional sanctions including a prohibition on new investment, loans to the South African government, and the export of

[36] Hufbauer et al. 1990.

[37] Frazer 1994.

[38] Moravcsik 1994, 39.

computers.[39] As a result of both external and internal pressures, the apartheid regime was abandoned by many of its own supporters and Nelson Mandela became the president of South Africa. This transition was an extraordinary accomplishment, and one that took place with little bloodshed. But it was not consistent with Westphalian or international legal sovereignty. The pressure on South Africa was a denial of the right of its rulers to establish a race-based regime within their country.

CONCLUSIONS

Many contemporary observers have seen human rights as an issue area in which conventional notions of sovereignty have been compromised. They are right. Some human rights conventions are inconsistent with Westphalian sovereignty. Coercive practices, such as economic sanctions to promote human rights, violate international legal sovereignty as well. Before the last half of the twentieth century human rights had never been a particularly salient international issue.

Seeing human rights developments since the Second World War as a fundamental break with the past is, however, historically misleading. Understood more generally as a problem of the relations between rulers and ruled, human rights are but one more incarnation of a long-standing concern in the international system. From issues of religious toleration that were prominent in the sixteenth and seventeenth centuries (and even earlier with regard to European concerns about Christians in the Ottoman Empire), through minority rights in the nineteenth and early twentieth centuries and human rights in the late twentieth century, national autonomy has been persistently challenged. Rulers have intervened in the internal affairs of other states through coercion and imposition and invited the insinuation of external authority in their own polities through contracting and conventions. The minorities regime established under the League of Nations was more firmly institutionalized than any of the universal human rights regimes that have existed since the Second World War; it included the right of individuals to bring complaints against their own governments, a formal appeals process to the league, and the possibility of rulings by the International Court of Justice.

The issue of human rights, like minority rights and religious toleration, is an example of the fact that Westphalian sovereignty has always been characterized by organized hypocrisy. In some cases, such as religious toleration in Europe and some bilateral minority rights accords in the twentieth century, autonomy has been compromised by contracts. Coercion or imposition has, however, been the more typical modality for trying to es-

---

[39] Moravcsik 1994, 39; Martin 1995, chap. 4.

tablish minority rights. More powerful states, often concerned primarily with the international instability that could result from minority unrest, have intervened to force rulers in target states to change their domestic authority structures. Absent national support for such regimes, however, they have failed. Human rights accords in the late twentieth century have, in contrast, been conventions. With the exception of the European regime, compliance and enforcement mechanisms have been weak. Nevertheless, some of these conventions have infringed domestic autonomy by inviting external sources of legitimacy that have strengthened the positions of sympathetic national actors and changed domestic conceptions of appropriate policy.

Westphalian sovereignty has never been a foregone conclusion. In western Europe, the area that generated the notion of Westphalian sovereignty, most rulers have never enjoyed full autonomy with regard to the treatment of their own subjects. The issue of human rights is but the latest example of a long-standing tension between autonomy and international attempts to regulate relations between rulers and ruled.

CHAPTER 5

Sovereign Lending

INTERNATIONAL BORROWING by rulers has been a pervasive aspect of the European international system since the Middle Ages and of the global system since the nineteenth century. Rulers, whether of medieval monarchies or modern democracies, have often been unable to fund state expenditures from taxes and domestic borrowing. Indeed, despite all of the recent attention to financial globalization (an element of interdependence sovereignty), sovereign lending was more important in the past, especially prior to the nineteenth century, than it is at present. Rulers have relied on foreign lenders including other states, foreign bankers with varying degrees of closeness to their own governments, and international financial institutions such as the World Bank and the International Monetary Fund. The terms agreed to by sovereign debtors have often involved not just a promise to repay, but also measures that compromise their domestic autonomy. Sovereign lending has almost always been conducted through contracts, Pareto-improving, mutually contingent arrangements, some of which have included invitations that concede Westphalian sovereignty by accepting conditions involving changes in domestic authority structures.

Sovereign borrowing poses unique problems for creditors. In lending between private parties within the same national system, it is possible to appeal to third-party enforcement, usually a court system, if the borrower fails to repay. Lenders can also seek collateral that can be, again with legal authorization, seized if the borrower defaults. Third-party enforcement is more problematic for loans to rulers, both international and domestic.[1] No authoritative judicial system can adjudicate disputes between sovereign borrowers and international lenders. Collateral is hard to come by. A foreign lender can always withhold future funds, but for a ruler confronted with short-term political pressure and the accompanying need for immediately available financial resources, default may be more attractive than honoring foreign obligations.

Lenders are well aware of their limited alternatives should a sovereign borrower default. One approach is to charge high interest rates to compensate for the risks inherent in extending credit to rulers who are not subject

---

[1] For a discussion of the development of institutional mechanisms that increased the confidence of domestic lenders in England, see North and Weingast 1989. For a more general treatment, see Broz 1998.

to third-party enforcement. During the Renaissance, private international bankers did charge high interests rates and sovereigns did default, although financiers sometimes also sought control over specific sources of revenue as well, a device similar to contemporary arrangements. This regime was, paradoxically, often more consistent with the Westphalian model than more recent practices.

High interest rates and frequent defaults, however, are not the best outcome for either borrowers or lenders. Rulers would prefer lower interest rates, but they can only secure such terms if they can in some way tie their own hands—that is, limit their discretion so that potential providers of capital have more confidence that they will be repaid. One strategy is for borrowers to violate their own domestic autonomy by inviting lenders to exercise some authority over fiscal, and sometimes other, activities within their own borders. International sovereign lending in the nineteenth and twentieth centuries, especially to weaker states, has frequently been conducted through contractual arrangements in which borrowing rulers compromise their domestic autonomy in exchange for foreign capital. Both parties are better off as a result of these contracts; otherwise they would not be concluded, since the status quo ante is still available. The borrower secures capital, and the lender secures either economic benefits (the loan is fully amortized) or political gains (the borrower accepts policy or institutional changes that are preferred by the lender independent of debt repayment).

Sovereign lending has also resulted in violations of the Westphalian model through coercion and imposition. When borrowers have defaulted, lenders have sometimes seized control of sources of revenue. In gunboat diplomacy more powerful rulers have simply taken over the customhouses (a major source of revenue) of debtors by threatening or actually using force. In other situations, lenders have negotiated coercive ex post arrangements following defaults, which have given them authoritative control over major revenue sources including state monopolies and customs duties. Borrowers were worse off as a result of these arrangements; they would have preferred to default without giving up state revenue. Coercion and imposition were more prevalent before the First World War and have always involved power asymmetries.

Contractual violations of the Westphalian model have characterized the sovereign borrowing of rulers in weaker states throughout the nineteenth and twentieth centuries. Since the 1950s international financial institutions, such as the World Bank and the International Monetary Fund, have engaged in conditionality, a practice that makes their loans contingent not just on repayment (which would be totally consistent with the Westphalian model) but on changes in the domestic policies and sometimes even institutions of would-be borrowers. Conditionality is consistent with international legal sovereignty, but it can compromise domestic autonomy. By signing standby agreements with international financial institutions, rulers can extend invitations to external sources of legitimacy. Sovereign lending provides another illustration that the Westphalian model is organized hypocrisy, a set of principles constantly under challenge by alternative norms or overridden by material or security interests.

THE RISKS OF SOVEREIGN LENDING

Lenders who cherish peace of mind should not provide loans to rulers. International lending has occurred in Europe for at least eight centuries and so have defaults. There was substantial international lending during the Renaissance by transnational commercial and banking houses, often organized by families, that were based in major trading cities. These banks periodically suffered sovereign defaults. Nevertheless, they continued to lend to rulers. Courts were a major outlet for the luxury goods these same families traded. Making sales could require making loans, but there was no third-party enforcement and bankers could not always assess the risks. These early financial institutions were on their own.[2]

Defaults were not unusual. Edward III of England repudiated his debts in 1339 precipitating a financial crisis in Italy and leading to the first clearly recognizable business cycle in Europe. The king of France went bankrupt in 1598, 1648, and 1661. After borrowing heavily to pay for the wars of the sixteenth century, Spain repudiated its debts in 1557. Revolutionary France suspended its payments on foreign obligations in 1793 and annulled two-thirds of its domestic and foreign debt in 1797.[3]

Debt repudiations were tempting for rulers. External pressures were relentless. War required foreign borrowing because the sources of domestic revenues were limited. For Britain, military expenditures accounted for between 61 and 74 percent of public spending during the major wars of the eighteenth century. During the Great Northern War, Peter the Great spent 90 percent of Russia's revenues on the military. In the last years of the ancien regime, France spent about 25 percent of revenues on the military. Institutional limitations made it difficult to collect taxes and efforts to change what were regarded as legitimate traditional practices were a cause of major revolts in France (the Fronde), England, and Spain (Catalonia).[4] Rulers in early modern Europe were compelled to borrow and sorely tempted to default.

[2] Cohen 1986, 84–90, 103; Fox 1971, 60–61; Mattingly 1955, 59.
[3] McNeill 1982, 72; Brewer 1989, 23; Tilly 1990a, 79; Riley 1980, 198.
[4] Brewer 1989, 40, 137; Tilly 1990a, 89; Jouvenel 1957, 186–87.

The first steps in breaking this cycle of borrowing, high interest rates, and default took place in Holland in the sixteenth century and Britain at the end of the seventeenth century, with the development of a deeper international capital market in Amsterdam and a system of institutional checks and balances in Britain. The creation of the Bank of England, primarily as a device for providing transparent information about royal borrowing, made it possible for the British government to secure lower interest rates and contributed to Britain's ultimate military triumph over France, which was unable to introduce institutional reforms before the Revolution. Britain was also able to develop more efficient systems of tax collection than its rivals.[5]

After the Napoleonic Wars defaults declined and even disappeared, especially among states with more developed economies and more sophisticated domestic institutions that were able to constrain rulers. Since 1815 many countries have always paid their foreign debts including the European states, with the exception of Germany and Spain; the Arab states; the east Asian states, with the exception of the Philippines; China in the 1930s; and Japan between 1941 and 1952.[6]

The risks of sovereign lending, however, did not disappear after the Napoleonic Wars. The institutional structures of many states in less developed areas have not been adequate to place checks on sovereigns that would provide lenders with confidence that they would be repaid. Sources of revenue for weaker states have been subject to external shocks, such as vacillations in raw materials prices, over which rulers have no control. Leaders with fragile political bases and high discount rates on future revenues have found default an attractive option.

Moreover, over the past two centuries, lending to sovereigns has increasingly been conducted by governments and international financial institutions, and private bankers have become more closely associated with states. Not just transnational bankers but also state officials have determined which loans should be made and what measures, including the use of force, should be used to compel debtors to honor their obligations. The wealth and financial stability achieved by the major European powers in the nineteenth century provided capital that could be used as an instrument of statecraft, a policy option not available to the rulers of these countries when they were themselves dependent on foreign loans.

Increasingly, sovereign lending to weaker states involved transgressions against domestic autonomy. More powerful states were, at times, simply concerned with whether they would be repaid, and they used ex ante insti-

---

[5] Tilly 1990a, 90; Landes 1979, 10–11; North and Weingast 1989; Brewer 1989, 91–100.

[6] Lindert and Morton 1989, 43.

tutional reforms, or ex post coercion, to make sure that they received their money. In some instances loans were part of a bargain involving security arrangements that were perfectly consistent with Westphalian sovereignty. But loans were also used to secure changes in personnel, policies, and even institutional structures in borrowing states, a practice inconsistent with Westphalian precepts.

There have been several waves of sovereign lending since the end of the Napoleonic wars. They have all followed a cyclical pattern, with a period of rapid expansion of loans followed by defaults, and then a sharp decline. The first wave occurred in the 1820s with loans to the newly independent Latin American countries. Greece also received international funding when it was recognized as an independent state in 1832. Lending was also high in the 1850s, late 1860s and early 1870s, late 1880s, from 1904 to 1914, the late 1920s, and 1974 to 1982. Defaults or refundings have been frequent. Most Latin American countries defaulted during the first part of the nineteenth century, as did a number of states of the United States in the 1830s and 1840s and during Reconstruction, and Latin American and eastern Mediterranean countries in the last part of the nineteenth century. At the end of the nineteenth century Argentina, Brazil, and Colombia either defaulted or refunded their loans, as did Mexico during the Mexican Revolution and Russia after the Bolshevik Revolution. All of the Latin America states, much of eastern Europe, Turkey, and China defaulted during the 1930s. In the late 1970s and 1980s Latin American, eastern European, and African states failed to meet their original loan terms.[7] Lending to sovereigns is often not the most secure of enterprises, but it can be a vehicle through which the domestic autonomy of weaker polities is compromised.

LENDING IN THE NINETEENTH CENTURY

During the nineteenth century, economic growth, administrative sophistication, and political development made major European powers more financially self-sufficient. The successor states of the Ottoman, Spanish, and Portuguese empires were dependent on international loans. The inescapable problem of sovereign lending remained: in the absence of third-party enforcement how could creditors be assured that lenders would honor their obligations? Moreover, the temptation to use loans to secure more general political and security objectives grew along with power asymmetries among states.

European creditors frequently violated the autonomy of lending countries in the Balkans and Latin America. The arrangements associated with

---

[7] Marichal 1989, 43–60; Lindert and Morton 1989, 41–43.

sovereign lending in the nineteenth century were inconsistent with the Westphalian model. The relationship between private creditors and rulers in their home countries became more intimate because lending was tied to larger strategic and political objectives, such as cementing international alliances. A large proportion of international loans in the nineteenth century went to sovereign or near sovereign borrowers such as railways; about 70 percent of British and more than 50 percent of French and German credits at the beginning of the twentieth century were extended to such borrowers.[8]

The autonomy of borrowing states was compromised in two ways. First, rulers in borrowing states signed *contracts* that included invitations giving lenders some control over domestic fiscal activities, including the collection and allocation of tax revenue. Rulers in borrowing countries would have preferred terms that did not include such invitations, but their actions were still voluntary: capital with a loss of domestic autonomy was better than the status quo of no capital at all. These invitations gave foreign actors authoritative control over certain state functions. Second, if borrowers defaulted, then rulers in creditor countries could intervene using *coercion*, or in some cases *imposition*, to seize direct control of revenue sources, such as custom houses. More powerful states that were also nineteenth-century borrowers, notably the United States, were, in contrast, perfectly able to defend their Westphalian sovereignty.

Greece

When Greece was recognized as an independent state in 1832, its constitutional structure, personnel, and policies were imposed by the rulers of France, Britain, and Russia. The Greek leadership was too weak and divided to resist. Its options were nonexistence or the acceptance of the terms dictated by the major powers.

The dependence of Greece was particularly vivid in the area of finance. The government's sources of revenue were shaky. Even before independence, the revolutionary leaders had entered into international contractual agreements with private bankers that would have, had they been implemented, undermined the autonomy of any Greek state. The Greek revolutionary government secured its first loan in 1824. The interest rate was high—Greece was obligated to repay 800,000 pounds but secured only 348,000. To obtain this loan from private bankers, the revolutionary authorities assigned all of their revenues from customs, fisheries, and salt. The pledge written on the face of the bonds read: "To the payment of the

---

[8] Cohen 1986, 97.

annuities are appropriated all the revenues of Greece. The whole of the national property of Greece is hereby pledged to the holders of all obligations granted in virtue of this loan."[9] A second loan was floated in 1825. The revolutionary regime received 816,000 pounds and was obligated to repay two million pounds. The bankers demanded not just a general pledge but the designation of the proceeds from specific national lands. As reflected in the very high interest rates, these commitments on the part of the Greek revolutionary government were deeply problematic since it was not clear what the government controlled or that it would succeed in defeating the Turks. At the end of the 1825 negotiations, the lenders arrogated to themselves the right to create a board of control, which supervised the actual expenditure of the funds. The board authorized the building of several naval vessels, most of which never left England because they provided the lenders with collateral. Greece defaulted on these loans of independence, and they were not finally settled until 1878. The British government refused to intervene on behalf of the lenders, who did not receive anything from the funds that were provided to Greece when its independence was formally recognized in 1832.[10]

In 1832 the new Greek government signed an agreement with the representatives of Russia, France, and Britain. Greece received a loan of 60 million francs to be issued in installments. Greece pledged "the first revenues of the State in such a manner that the actual receipts of the Greek treasury shall be devoted, first of all, to the payment of the said interest and sinking fund, and shall not be employed for any other purpose, until those payments on account of the instalments of the loan raised under the guarantee of the three Courts, shall have been completely secured for the current year." In fact, the Greek government quickly found itself in arrears and did not devote its revenue first to the repayment of the 60-million-franc loan. In 1838 the entire finances of Greece were placed under a French administrator.[11]

At the conclusion of the Crimean War, France and Britain, which had occupied the port of Piraeus, proposed the establishment of a financial commission that would have direct powers over Greek finances. The Russians, however, protested, and Britain and France settled for a commission of inquiry with advisory powers, an example of the need for great-power consensus in situations involving coercion or imposition.[12]

[9] Quoted in Levandis 1944, 15 n. 70.

[10] Levandis 1944, chap. 1.

[11] Jelavich and Jelavich 1977, 75; Levandis 1944, 36, 53 (the quotation is from p. 36).

[12] Levandis 1944, 51.

Greece did not contract any substantial new loans from 1832 through 1878. In the next decade, however, external debts ballooned. Greece committed certain specific revenues, such as the customs at Athens, Piraeus, Patras, and Zante, and the revenues from the state monopolies on salt, petroleum, matches, playing cards, and cigarette paper, to retire these obligations. The loan of 1887 gave the lenders the right to organize a company that would supervise the revenues assigned for the loan. Greece, however, steadfastly resisted additional foreign controls during the mid-1890s.[13]

In 1898 after a disastrous war with Turkey over Crete, Greece's financial situation collapsed. It was unable to service its foreign debt or to pay the war indemnity that was being demanded by Turkey. France, and especially Germany, along with private creditors pressed for an international commission of control. Greece acceded when it became clear that it was the only way to secure new funding that could be used to ensure the withdrawal of Turkish troops. The terms for the establishment of a control commission were written into the provisional peace treaty.

The commission consisted of one representative appointed by each major power (Austria-Hungary, Italy, Germany, France, Russia, and Britain), even though Austria, Russia, and Italy held very little Greek debt. The commission could unilaterally assert control over the sources of revenue needed to fund the war indemnity and the consolidated foreign debt, such as state monopolies on salt, petroleum, matches, playing cards, and cigarette paper, tobacco duties, and the customs revenues of Piraeus. The commission also imposed other limits on Greek fiscal autonomy including control of public borrowing and a reduction in the money supply.

Disputes that might arise between the commission and agencies of the Greek government were to be settled by mandatory arbitration. The decision of the arbitration panel was final. The members of the commission were given the same standing as diplomats. With the exception of the Egyptian Caisse de la Dette, the financial commission established for Greece in 1897 was the only one composed of official representatives of foreign governments. At least one member of the Greek Parliament argued that the establishment of the control commission suspended the independence of Greece.[14]

The arrangements worked out in 1898 between representatives of Britain, France, Germany, Russia, Italy, and Austria-Hungary were presented to the Greek government as a fait accompli. The refusal to authorize would have left Greece not only destitute but also with part of its territory occupied by Turkish troops. The bargaining leverage of the Greek government was very limited. The transgressing of Greece's autonomy associated with

[13] Levandis 1944, 67; Feis 1965, 286.
[14] Levandis 1944, 97–115; Feis 1965, 287.

the Consolidation Loan of 1898 and the establishment of a foreign control commission was the result of a contract in which Greece secured revenues but only at the cost of domestic autonomy. Greece was better off with the contract than without, but its limited resources made it impossible to protect domestic autonomy.

The Ottoman Empire

Turkey suffered a similar but not quite so extreme fate as Greece. During the last quarter of the nineteenth century its autonomy was compromised by creditor control of more than one-quarter of state revenue. Turkey accepted these violations of its domestic autonomy because of its need for foreign capital. The bargaining position of the Ottoman Empire, however, was always better than that of Greece. The empire was a player in the European military balance. Its bureaucratic apparatus never totally collapsed. Turkey escaped direct foreign administration of its revenues, but did have to accept an external agency, the Council of the Debt, controlled by foreign creditors, ostensibly private but with close ties to their home governments.

By 1850 Turkey's financial situation was precarious. It could not match European technological progress or raise sufficient revenue to maintain the military strength needed to defend its borders. Turkey had to import arms and naval vessels. It was unable to mass-produce hand guns with rifled barrels or construct steam-propelled, iron-clad ships. Further domestic extractions through taxes, currency debasement, or failure to pay officials threatened domestic stability.[15]

The Ottoman Empire took its first foreign loan in 1854 after the Crimean War had begun. The loan was supported, but not guaranteed, by the British. The British and the French governments did guarantee the interest on additional loans made in 1855 because they were anxious to bolster the empire's ability to resist Russia. In exchange for the guarantee, the British and French insisted that the loan be used for war purposes and demanded the appointment of two commissioners to oversee the expenditure of the funds. A loan in 1858 provided that the bondholders could superintend the collection of the customs of Constantinople, which had been pledged as security. The bondholders, however, lacked the bureaucratic capacity to implement this and a similar provision in a loan concluded in 1862. The empire secured about a dozen more loans before it became bankrupt in 1875 and was forced to reduce payments. By that time over half of its revenues were committed to the debt.[16]

[15] Owen 1981, 100, 117.
[16] Owen 1981, 101; Blaisdell 1929, 28–30, 37–38, 44–45; Pamuk 1987, 59.

External pressures, the Crimean War, and then the first Balkan wars had been unrelenting. There was no easy path to domestic reform. The choices for the rulers of the Ottoman Empire were difficult. In 1875 they could have rejected further compromises of their state's domestic autonomy, but only at the cost of losing access to international capital markets.

In 1881, to secure additional loans, the sultan issued the Decree of Muharrem establishing the Council of the Public Debt, which was controlled by foreign bondholders. For the Turks, the Decree of Muharrem was a way to avoid placing Turkish finances directly under the control of official representatives of the European powers, an option that had been proposed at the Congress of Berlin in 1878, although the Porte did officially convey the decree to the major European powers. The decree ceded irrevocably to the council, until the debt was liquidated, revenue from the salt and tobacco monopolies, the stamp and spirits tax, the fish tax, and the silk tithe in certain districts. The bondholders were also to get certain potential increases from customs duties and the tax on shops. The Bulgaria tribute, the surplus of Cyprus revenues, and the revenue from Eastern Rumelia were also ceded to the council. The council could, with the consent of the government, initiate measures that would improve more general economic conditions since a more prosperous Turkey would mean higher revenue collections. The council promoted the export of salt (the tax of which it controlled) to India and introduced new technologies for the silk and wine industries. The council facilitated the development of railways in the Ottoman Empire by acting as a collection agent for the receipts that the government had committed to pay subsidies to foreign companies.[17]

The members of the council—two from France, one each from Germany, Austria, Italy, and the Ottoman Empire itself, and one from Britain and Holland together—were selected by either bondholders or banks or, in the case of Italy, by the Chamber of Commerce of Rome. The council established the Administration of the Public Debt, which was staffed by Turks and had, in 1912, more employees than the Ministry of Finance. The Ottoman government had the right to send a commissioner of its own to the meetings of the Administration of the Public Debt and to examine its books, but could not interfere in its operations. Disagreements between the government and the council were to be resolved by an arbitration panel of four with two appointed by the council and two by the government, with a fifth selected by the arbitrators if necessary. The Decree of Muharrem was not modified until 1903 and then only modestly.[18]

[17] Blaisdell 1929, 108–20, 124–30; Feis 1965, 332–41.
[18] Blaisdell 1929, 90–107; Feis 1965, 332–41; Mansfield 1991; Lewis 1995, 298–99.

In 1905 as the empire's situation deteriorated still further, the major European powers forced the Porte to accept a financial commission for Macedonia, whose members were appointed by the six major European powers. The Europeans based their action on provisions for reform in the Treaty of Berlin which had not been carried out. The Porte initially refused to recognize the commission, but the European states not only sent their delegates to Macedonia, they also occupied the islands of Mytilene and Lemnos. In 1907 the Porte and the European powers agreed that customs duties, whose magnitude was limited by treaties that the Porte had signed with the European powers, would be raised by 3 percent to cover the budgetary needs of Macedonia. The additional revenue was to be administered by the Council of the Public Debt, which now found itself acting directly as an agent of the major powers. The council was not finally disbanded until after the First World War.[19]

The creation of the Council of the Public Debt was the result of a contract between the Porte and its foreign bondholders and, through these bondholders, indirectly with the major powers of Europe excepting Russia. The contract did provide the Ottoman government with continued access to foreign capital markets, but it also included an invitation that compromised domestic autonomy. The council controlled more than a quarter of the empire's revenue and also promoted certain sectors of the economy. In 1907 the council began to act as an official agent of foreign powers when it was designated to collect and disburse additional customs duties. European rivalries and size, however, enabled Turkey to escape the onus of direct control by foreign governments of its finances with the exception of some issues associated with Macedonia.

Egypt

Egypt suffered a worse fate than Greece or the Ottoman Empire, of which it was formally a part. A financial crisis beginning in the mid-1870s led to increased foreign involvement, a nationalist reaction, and then British occupation in 1882. Military force was used to impose on Egypt and its nominal Ottoman overloads a British protectorate that included financial control.

Egypt began foreign borrowing in the 1850s largely to finance public works projects. By the early 1870s about 70 percent of Egyptian revenue was being used to service the debt, half of which was owed to foreigners. In 1876 Egypt's access to new loans was closed as a result of the crisis in Turkey, and its rulers announced that they would suspend interest

[19] Blaisdell 1929, 156–76.

payments for three months. This was taken by creditors as a declaration of bankruptcy.[20]

To secure additional loans Egypt's ruler concluded a contract with his European creditors, which compromised his domestic autonomy. The khedive Ismail issued a decree establishing the Caisse de la Dette in 1876. The caisse was designated as the agent to administer the funds that were committed to paying off Egypt's loans. The directors were appointed by Britain, France, Italy, Austria, and later Russia, but they could be dismissed by the khedive. The powers of the caisse were limited to disbursing funds that were provided by the Egyptian treasury.[21]

This arrangement, however, collapsed. Nationalist resentment grew against the appointment of foreigners to official positions (an Englishman as the minister of public works and a Frenchman as the minister of finance, as well as five hundred Europeans in lesser official positions), and the draining of revenues to pay off the foreign debt. The khedive then dismissed the foreigners and announced a partial default.[22]

Britain and France, the major European powers with the most at stake in Egypt because of investments and the Suez Canal, responded decisively. They pressured the Ottoman sultan to remove Ismail and replace him with his more compliant son Tewfik. They encouraged the Egyptian government to appoint two European controller generals who, along with the Caisse de la Dette, essentially controlled Egypt's finances. In 1880 they persuaded Tewfik and his prime minister to promulgate the Law of Liquidation, which gave the Debt Commission direct control of 60 percent of Egypt's revenue, which could then be used to pay off foreign obligations. The commission could also veto all changes in taxation and fiscal policy.[23]

The measures established by the Law of Liquidation undermined the legitimacy of Tewfik, who was increasingly seen as a puppet of Christian powers. The Egyptian army, led by a nationalist Colonel Arabi, forced ministerial changes in September 1881 and an anti-foreign cabinet came to power in February 1882. The new ministers demanded greater control over finances. In July 1882 the British fleet bombarded shore batteries that were being constructed in Alexandria, touching off riots against Europeans throughout the country and threatening violence against the Suez Canal. In August the British invaded, defeated the Egyptian army, captured Arabi, and took control of the country.[24]

---

[20] Owen 1981, 125–28; Gallagher and Robinson 1961, 81.

[21] Marlowe 1975, 217; Gallagher and Robinson 1961, 84; Owen 1981, 130–34.

[22] Mansfield 1971, 14.

[23] Gallagher and Robinson 1961, 85–86; Mansfield 1971, 11, 14–15; Lindert and Morton 1989.

[24] Gallagher and Robinson 1961, 86, 98, 112–14, 120.

Hence Egypt's debt led to direct European control. Egypt's leaders first reached contractual arrangements with the Europeans, but these failed to produce a stable outcome because the demands for repayment were so great that they undermined the domestic support for Ismail. The European powers then resorted to imposition, securing the sultan's backing in replacing Ismail with Tewfik. In 1882 Britain, the dominant naval power in the area, invaded and began an occupation that was to last until after the Second World War.

Other Balkan States

The smaller states of the Balkans also experienced compromises of the Westphalian model as a result of sovereign lending, although these were less severe than the experiences of Greece and Egypt. In return for the consolidation loan of 1895, Serbia created a monopolies commission, which was charged with overseeing the revenue from the tobacco, salt, and petroleum monopolies controlled by the state, liquor taxes, some stamp taxes, and some railway and customs revenues. Receipts were committed to paying off foreign loans. They did not flow into the Serbian treasury. The monopolies commission was composed of four Serbians and two representatives of foreign bondholders, one German and one French. In April 1877 Russia signed two conventions with Romania, one of which provided for Russian control of the Romanian railways, including revenue collection.[25]

Despite financial difficulties Bulgaria fared better than some of its neighbors because it was able to take advantage of rivalries among the major powers. The French secured indirect control over tobacco taxes in 1902 but were reluctant to push further in the face of domestic opposition in Bulgaria lest Germany secure greater influence. In the spring of 1914 Bulgarian leaders successfully resisted German demands for direct control over finances because of support received from France and Russia.[26]

In sum, the successor states of the Ottoman Empire, and the Ottoman Empire itself, suffered from compromised autonomy as a result of sovereign borrowing. In some cases, notably the Ottoman Empire, external private lenders assumed direct control over some revenue collection. Where power asymmetries were greater, as was the case for Greece at the end of the nineteenth century and Egypt in the 1880s, foreign states directly controlled financial activity. Bulgaria, despite financial difficulties maintained more autonomy because its rulers were able to play the major powers off against each other.

[25] Feis 1965, 266–68; Anderson 1966, 194.
[26] Feis 1965, 275–79.

South America and the Caribbean

The successor states of the Spanish, Portuguese, and (in the case of Haiti) French empires in the Western Hemisphere were the other set of weak states in the nineteenth century. Many of these countries had their domestic autonomy compromised by the home countries of their creditors when they defaulted on foreign obligations. These transgressions of the Westphalian model usually occurred as a result of coercion or imposition; more powerful states intervened using military force to secure control of the most important sources of state revenue. Occasionally autonomy was also compromised through contractual arrangements: rulers in borrowing countries entered into agreements because they believed that they were better off with less autonomy and continued access to international capital markets than they would have been if they had maintained full autonomy but were cut off from future lending.

The history of Latin American debt has been characterized by high levels of borrowing in specific time periods followed by widespread defaults. Increased borrowing was the result of economic booms in the advanced economies, which increased the availability of capital. Contractions in the economies of these same countries led to increased capital costs and financial crises for Latin American borrowers. Latin American states entered the international capital market shortly after independence. There were major defaults in the late 1820s, 1873, 1890, and 1931.[27]

Borrowing began in the early 1820s. Between 1825 and 1828 all of the Latin American countries with the exception of Brazil defaulted. The defaults were precipitated by a financial crisis that began in England. In 1826 English banks began calling in their loans. Banks in Berlin, Frankfurt, Rome, Bologna, and Vienna failed because of their ties with the English institutions. British loans dried up and new mining ventures in Latin America failed. Foreign obligations could not be honored. It took thirty years to renegotiate the defaulted debt.[28]

Some mid-nineteenth-century defaults led to episodes in which the domestic autonomy of borrowing states was compromised through the use of military coercion. In 1838 France occupied the Mexican port of Vera Cruz to force Mexico to honor claims of French nationals. In 1840 France established a naval blockade on the Rio de la Plata to pressure Argentina to pay $40,000 in claims. In 1861 France, Spain, and Britain seized Mexican ports and customs to enforce payments that had been suspended as a

---

[27] Marichal 1989, 4.
[28] Marichal 1989, 43–60.

result of civil unrest. Seizure of the Mexican government's main source of revenue was only one aspect of a larger set of developments that culminated with the installation of Maximilian, supported by a thirty-thousand-man French occupying force, as the emperor of Mexico.[29]

New lending began in Latin America in the 1850s, but flows declined with the global economic downturn of the 1870s. While Brazil, Argentina, and Chile honored their obligations, they were the exception. Honduras, the Dominican Republic, Costa Rica, Paraguay, Bolivia, Guatemala, Uruguay, Peru, Venezuela, Ecuador, and Mexico had all defaulted by 1876. Again, gunboat diplomacy was used. The British shelled a Honduran port in 1872 until Honduras agreed to pay its debts. The British seized control of Miskito province in Nicaragua, an area that included the eastern terminus of any transisthmus canal that might be built. Unlike the Ottoman Empire and Egypt, however, these defaults did not lead to elaborate efforts at new institution building or the deep penetration of domestic institutions. The strategic stakes in Latin America were less. Perhaps as important, the United States after the Civil War was in a better position to counter European probes.[30] The United States resisted European military encroachment in the Western Hemisphere but was not itself a significant source of capital for Latin American states.

In the decades following the Spanish American War, however, the United States compromised the autonomy of a number of smaller Central American and Caribbean states. Financial control was one element in a larger exercise of American dominion. American rulers had both economic interests and strategic concerns. Significant American investment in Central America and the Caribbean did not begin until the last decade of the nineteenth century. United Fruit's major expansion began around 1900. The first American investments in Haiti were for railway construction in 1910. U.S. leaders were also worried about European intervention and influence in the Western Hemisphere. This was an old concern, but by the first decade of the twentieth century the United States had the military and economic resources to act unilaterally rather than relying on the British navy to enforce the Monroe Doctrine. Roosevelt and Taft believed that the United States ought to be the major creditor for Central America, because the continued presence of European bankers coupled with unstable financial conditions was an invitation to European intervention.[31]

---

[29] Lindert and Morton 1989, 54–55; A. Thomas and Thomas 1956, 15; Marichal 1989, 66.

[30] LaFeber 1983, 28; Marichal 1989, 104–8.

[31] Munro 1964, 14–20, 162.

When the Dominican Republic threatened to default on its foreign loans in 1905, the United States acted decisively despite German, Italian, and Spanish commitments to their own creditors. Several European states landed troops to protect their citizens from civil unrest. On January 20, 1905, the United States and the Dominican Republic reached an agreement giving the United States the right to collect all customs revenue. Forty-five percent of revenues would be given to the Dominican government, the rest would be used to pay creditors. The United States would determine the validity of claims and the amount to be paid. In March, a retired U.S. Army officer designated by Roosevelt was appointed by presidential decree as the general receiver and collector of customs. The United States then renegotiated the Dominican debt, most of which was owed to Europeans. A formal treaty was ratified in 1907, stipulating that the United States would appoint a general receiver of Dominican customs who would pay $100,000 each month to the fiscal agent of the lenders. The Dominican Republic could not alter its tariffs or issue new bonds without the approval of the United States. The general receiver appointed other officials of the customs service.[32] American troops were sent into the Dominican Republic in 1911, partly justified by a threatened loan default.

The United States intervened in several other countries. Treaties were signed with Honduras and Nicaragua in 1911 providing for the appointment of an American as the controller general of customs. Both countries were in default on their foreign loans and were being pressured by European states. The United States Senate, however, refused to ratify the treaties. American bankers did refund the loans of these two countries, and in Nicaragua a customs receivership was established under an American nominated by the bondholders and approved by the secretary of state but acting as a private individual. After civil disorder the United States landed troops in Nicaragua in 1912.[33]

In sum, as a result of defaults on foreign loans a number of South American and Caribbean countries were subject to external coercion and imposition. With the exception of the French occupation of Mexico, the most extensive violations of the Westphalian model were imposed on the weakest states by the United States after the Spanish-American War. By 1900 American rulers were in a position to force the major European powers to recognize a sphere of influence in the Caribbean.

The target states had limited bargaining power. They lacked both economic and military resources and were often internally divided. With the assertion of an American sphere of influence it was more difficult to play

[32] Munro 1964, 95–125, 262–68.
[33] Munro 1964, 193–212; Langley 1989, 54, 59–61, 87.

off various creditor countries against each other. The Central America and Caribbean states were more vulnerable at the beginning of the twentieth century to imposition and coercion by the United States than was the case for the Balkan states after 1878. Both sets of countries were weak, but in the Balkans local rulers could sometimes take advantage of rivalries among the major powers. This option was not available to rulers in Latin America.

INTERNATIONAL FINANCIAL INSTITUTIONS

International financial institutions (IFIs) are a new organizational form that was initiated with the creation of the International Bank for Reconstruction and Development, commonly known as the World Bank, and the International Monetary Fund (IMF) at the end of the Second World War.[34] The so-called Bretton Woods twins were followed by regional development banks—the Inter-American Development Bank, the Asian Development Bank, the African Development Bank, and the European Bank for Reconstruction and Development. All of these institutions engage in sovereign lending. Moreover, the IMF in particular has become a kind of gatekeeper for private sovereign lending. The willingness of private banks to renegotiate international obligations to public borrowers has frequently been tied to the conclusion of agreements with the IMF.

In the post–World War II period, the agreements between international financial institutions and sovereign borrowers have taken the form of contracts rather than coercion or imposition. If the contract is rejected, the status quo is still an option, although not necessarily a very attractive one. The actions of borrowers and lenders have been mutually contingent. Unlike the nineteenth century, military pressure has not been part of the repertoire utilized by more powerful actors.

These contracts have, however, routinely contained invitations that violate the Westphalian model. The terms included in contractual arrangements between borrowing countries and IFIs have often involved detailed specifications of domestic economic behavior. The IMF, the World Bank, and other institutions have not simply been concerned with getting repaid. One of their central missions has been the restructuring of the domestic institutions and policies of borrowing states. In some instances IFI officials have occupied positions within the bureaucracies of states that have signed agreements. Some of the missions of IFIs are not so different from the bankers' committees that assumed control of state finances in the Balkans in the nineteenth century or the customs receivership established in Nicaragua. The ability of IFIs, and the major industrialized mar-

---

[34] The Bank for International Settlements, which was established in 1930, was not concerned with economic development.

ket economy states that support them, to secure contractual arrangements that include invitations that violate the Westphalian autonomy of borrowers reflects both the material resources and the technical expertise possessed by these institutions. They have been able to influence domestic authority structures not only because they can provide capital but also because, at least in some instances, their advice is regarded as authoritative due to the technical expertise which they possess.

The European Bank for Reconstruction and Development has gone further than any of its counterparts in including political and not just economic conditionality in its founding document. The opening paragraph of the Agreement Establishing the European Bank for Reconstruction and Development states that contracting parties should be "committed to the fundamental principles of multiparty democracy, the rule of law, respect for human rights and market economies." Chapter 1 of the agreement stipulates that the purpose of the bank is to foster the transition toward open market-oriented economies and to promote private and entrepreneurial initiative in the central and eastern European countries.

Other IFIs have charters that prohibit political conditionality. With end of the cold war, however, they too have become more expansive about the kinds of advice and conditions that might accompany their loans. At their annual meeting in 1996, the president of the World Bank and the managing director of the International Monetary Fund committed themselves to a more aggressive attack on corruption in Third World states, a position formally endorsed by the fund's executive directors. The IMF withheld loans to Kenya when its leaders failed to create an anti-corruption agency and dismissed a high-ranking official who had been battling against government dishonesty. The World Bank organized programs to help countries, including Latvia, Tanzania, Uganda, and Ukraine, to limit corruption. Bank officials dissuaded Romania from making a billion-dollar military purchase on the grounds that it would be inconsistent with good governance. The bank official coordinating these new policies stated that "You will see us giving a much higher profile to governance and corruption concerns in a selective way, delaying disbursements until we are satisfied, or suspending it altogether."[35] An IMF conditionality agreement signed with Indonesia in January 1998 not only specified macroeconomic targets but also stipulated an end to subsidies and government sponsored cartels for enterprises run by members of the president's family. The IMF announcement of the agreement stated that "All special tax, customs and credit privileges for the national car project will

---

[35] Kenya did relent and appoint the official but he became enmeshed in political controversy within a year, and questions were raised about his integrity. *Financial Times*, August 1, 1997, p. 4; *New York Times* August 11, 1997, p. A4.

be revoked, effective immediately." The project was run by the youngest son of President Suharto.[36]

In 1997 the theme of the World Bank's *World Development Report* was the state and the report was subtitled *The State in a Changing World*. Nothing could be more directly political. Earlier reports had focused on workers, the environment, and infrastructure, issues more narrowly associated with economic development. This report stated that the "clamor for greater government effectiveness has reached crisis proportions in many developing countries where the state has failed to deliver even such fundamental public goods as property rights, roads, and basic health and education." It describes the situation in sub-Saharan Africa as one in which there is an urgent priority to "rebuild state effectiveness through an overhaul of public institutions, reasserting the rule of law, and credible checks on abuse of state power." These very same governments are, of course, some of the World Bank's major clients. The reports goes on to specify fundamental tasks for the state including establishing a foundation of law, protecting the environment, and shielding the vulnerable, to chastise governments for spending too much on rich and middle-class students in universities while neglecting primary education, and to admonish them to manage ethnic and social differences. Executives are urged to limit their discretionary authority in order to contain opportunities for corruption.[37]

The extent to which IFIs could compromise the domestic autonomy of borrowing states was contested when the World Bank and the International Monetary Fund were established. The Americans, who represented the only country with significant amounts of capital at the end of the Second World War, advocated broad powers for these institutions. The British delegates, in particular Keynes, as well as emissaries from other countries were opposed to giving the bank and especially the IMF broad leeway, such as supervising central bank policies. It is hardly surprising that potential borrowers wanted liberal terms with IFIs prohibited from imposing significant conditions, while the major potential lender (even if the funds were channeled through the World Bank and the IMF), advocated more stringent requirements. American rulers wanted the World Bank and the IMF to have leverage so that these institutions could support a specific vision of how domestic polities and economies should be organized; U.S. leaders were not just concerned with debt repayment.

The use of conditionality, the principle that access to IMF resources were conditional on agreements by borrowing countries to alter their practices, was not specified in the Articles of Agreement, which left unclear whether the IMF could challenge a member's request to purchase foreign

---

[36] *New York Times*, January 16, 1998, A1, C5.
[37] World Bank 1997, 2, 14, 4, 8.

currency (borrow). Only in 1947 did the executive board decide that the fund had such authority. Conditionality was accepted in principle by the executive directors in 1950 to induce the United States, which essentially crippled the fund by ending its contributions when the Marshall Plan was initiated, to allow operations to begin again. The 1950 decision recognized that members could draw from their gold tranche (the first 25 percent of their quota) without restrictions. Drawing on higher tranches would, however, depend on the IMF's view of whether the country was acting to overcome its problems. Standby arrangements could be concluded covering future borrowing. Binding conditions for drawing above the first credit tranche began in 1958 when access for Paraguay was made conditional on a credit ceiling and on limiting public works expenditures. It was not, however, until 1969 that the Articles of Agreement were formally amended to provide for conditionality above the first credit tranche. The Americans ultimately prevailed because they had the money.[38]

In the late 1970s the attitudes about conditionality held by the developing countries were similar to the views that had been supported by the Europeans in the 1940s. Potential borrowers wanted to make access to the IMF more automatic. They failed, just as the Europeans had failed, because they lacked bargaining power. Rulers in Third World states needed international finance, sometimes desperately, because domestic saving was so low. Third World debtors would have preferred contractual arrangements that would have given them access to IMF resources without the need to make painful political choices that compromised their domestic autonomy. This was not, however, an available option. The holders of capital—by the 1970s the industrialized countries in general, not just the United States—routinized conditionality.

The standby agreements of the World Bank, the IMF, and other international financial institutions have dealt with a wide range of issues in borrowing countries. These have included monetary and financial policies, such as limits on credit expansion and ceilings on bank credit for parastatals; public sector policies, including freezing or reducing the number of government employees, ending salary indexation, capping or reducing subsidies on food, petroleum, and fertilizers, limiting government investment, reducing personal income tax, increasing payroll taxes, modifying corporate taxes, and raising excise taxes on beer and cigarettes; exchange rate and trade policies, including liberalizing the trading system and export promotion measures; and wages and prices policies, including increasing energy prices and wage restraint. A country entering into negoti-

---

[38] Dell 1981, 2–4, 8–11, 14; International Monetary Fund 1986, 51–53.

ations with the IMF could basically consider any aspect of its domestic economic policy open to discussion.[39]

The activities of IFIs have not been limited to specific policies; they have tried to influence institutions and personnel as well. The World Bank began as early as the 1950s to encourage the creation of agencies within national governments that would be insulated from domestic pressures and responsive to bank preferences. Many were energy authorities. The World Bank was also instrumental in creating planning agencies and cultivating technocrats. The resources provided by the bank, both material and ideological, could alter the balance of power within a government. Technocrats, most often economists trained in the West, shared the bank's fundamental intellectual stance, which was guided by neoclassical economics. The IMF had representatives in the central banks of some client states who had access to government records and files. The World Bank paid for foreign consultants to ministries of industry and other government agencies concerned with development. The bank had veto power over the choice of consultants.[40]

Accepting the conditions proposed by IFIs has often been painful for rulers in borrowing countries especially those in polities with centralized but weak states. Many African rulers, for instance, have relied on public corporations and import licenses as sources of patronage. They have exploited the agricultural sector in order to subsidize urban consumers who are more politically consequential. Structural adjustment programs, a standard package of reforms used by international financial institutions, have condemned such practices and have made loans conditional on disbanding of parastatals and adopting market-determined exchange rates in place of import licensing and overvalued fixed rates.[41]

The policies of the World Bank and the IMF have hardly been completely successful. Even the fund's own officials have been reserved about how well standby agreements have worked. In assessing the impact on

---

[39] See IMF 1986, 40, and table 12 for one discussion of the various measures included in standby agreements. A 1998 Letter of Intent from Uganda to the fund included commitments involving the sale of public enterprises, reductions in the number of employees at the Uganda Electricity Board, increasing public services for the poor, eliminating the differential between petroleum excise taxes in Uganda and Kenya, reductions in the sales tax on beer and soft drinks, installing seals on petroleum pumps to discourage smuggling, establishing a Large Taxpayer Unit to oversee the one hundred largest taxpayers in the country, contracting out the collection of customs to a private agency, reducing the number of ministries from twenty-two to seventeen, changing the retirement program for civil servants, and "strengthening good governance through transparency and accountability" as well as the usual macroeconomic issues such as money supply and exchange rate. Uganda 1998.

[40] Broad 1988, 26, 61, 73–75.

[41] Herbst 1990, 949–58; Bates, Brock, and Tiefenthaler 1991; Bates 1981.

public enterprises a paper by fund officials based on an examination of the operation of the Structural Adjustment Facility and Enhanced Structural Adjustment Facility in nineteen countries stated: "In retrospect, the World Bank and the IMF staff, as well as the authorities, have tended to underestimate the time required to design and implement reforms."[42] The ratio of the government deficit to GDP was reduced on average by only two percent. In fifteen of the nineteen countries, marketing boards, another target of fund and bank standby agreements, retained substantial monopoly power. Efforts to reform the banking system and limit credit to the public sector encountered difficulty; public enterprises continued to drain the public treasury. Exchange rate reforms were more successful. About half of the countries in the study made progress in controlling their foreign debt levels and experienced better domestic economic performance.

One major factor that distinguished the successful from the unsuccessful group was changes in the terms of trade. Countries that suffered a deterioration in export prices were generally not able to improve their external debt position or their domestic economic performance. In several countries political instability and declining terms of trade led to a reversal of reforms.[43]

In sum, since the early 1950s sovereign lending to developing countries has been governed by an international regime that violates the Westphalian model. Poorer countries have been able to secure significant amounts of capital but only if they agree to compromise their domestic autonomy. The kinds of conditions that are routinely included in such arrangements have reflected the values and preferences of the more powerful advanced market-oriented industrialized countries that have been embodied in the institutional norms of the major international financial institutions.

These arrangements have been contractual rather than coercive. The status quo ante has remained available to potential borrowers, and in some cases they have rejected the terms proffered by IFIs. The success of these contracts in accomplishing their own stated objectives has been limited in part because weak and poor countries are buffeted by external economic changes in terms of trade and interest rates over which they have no control and only a limited capacity to adjust. Moreover, the actual implementation of reform programs can be politically untenable because the power base of rulers in Third World states has sometimes been built on the rent-generating capacities of programs that interfere with market mechanisms—the very same mechanisms the officials of international financial institutions see as the key to economic development.

[42] Schadler et al., 1993, 13–14.
[43] Schadler et al., 1993, 13–14, 15, 16, 19, 39–41; Bates et al. 1991 also emphasizes the significance of changes in the terms of trade.

CONCLUSIONS

Sovereign lending poses inherent problems for creditors. Unlike financial transactions within a state, third-party adjudication is impossible. If loan agreements, including clauses associated with policy changes in borrowing countries as well as repayment, fail to create credible commitments, then mutually beneficial exchanges may never take place at all. At times lenders have simply been concerned about getting their money back, but since the Napoleonic Wars finance has also been an instrument of statecraft. Wealthier states have used international loans to promote their military, economic, and ideological objectives. In the latter part of the twentieth century international financial institutions, which have embodied the values of the more advanced capitalist states, have been more concerned with promoting particular domestic changes in borrowing countries than with being repaid.

The extent to which Westphalian principles have been transgressed depends on the relative bargaining power of the actors involved. The fiscal and tax authority of borrowers has only been directly taken over by officials of other countries when there have been large asymmetries in military power and when the creditor states could agree to a condominium or were prepared to recognize a sphere of influence. Egypt was occupied by the British who had enough naval power in the eastern Mediterranean to make good on their claim to establish a protectorate. Greece lost control of its finances after it was defeated by Turkey in 1898 and could only secure the evacuation of Turkish troops if it paid a war indemnity funded by the major western European powers. Several European states seized control of custom houses in Latin America during the nineteenth century. The United States was able to take control of the fiscal and other affairs of Cuba, the Dominican Republic, and other Caribbean and Central American states by the beginning of the twentieth century because it had the military power to establish an effective sphere of influence. These are all examples of intervention. The borrowing country would have preferred less intrusive measures; more powerful states did not offer the status quo ante as an option.

Most defaulting borrowers, even weak ones, however, have not sacrificed so much domestic autonomy. During the nineteenth century most Balkan states, including the Ottoman Empire, never lost control of their tax and fiscal affairs to representatives appointed by other states, although in some cases their revenues were controlled by mixed committees or officials appointed by bankers. The Balkan states were weak, but the major powers were divided. Britain was concerned about growing Russian influence. The Habsburgs feared ethnic unrest. France and Germany were military rivals. No one country could establish a sphere of influence and Balkan states, such as Bulgaria, could use great power rivalries to prevent direct control of their fiscal affairs even when they defaulted on their international loans.

Since the Second World War Westphalian principles have been extensively compromised by the standby agreements of international financial institutions. These have been contractual arrangements in which, in exchange for funding, borrowing countries have made commitments, many of which they have been unable to honor, to alter their domestic policies and institutions. Since 1950, the major objective of both international financial institutions and the wealthy market-oriented democratic states that have provided almost all of their funding has been to alter the domestic structures of borrowing countries. Initially these institutions focused on economic issues, but with the creation of the European Bank for Reconstruction and Development and the increased attention paid to good governance by other IFIs, political conditionality has become a legitimated practice. The more intrusive violations of autonomy associated with political conditionality occurred only after the collapse of the Soviet Union. During the cold war developing states had been able to play the West off against the East. With the collapse of Soviet power, the opportunities for balancing between the blocs disappeared, and the programs of international financial institutions became more ambitious. The ability of IFIs to secure invitations from borrowing countries that violate Westphalian autonomy has been a function not only of the capital that they can provide but also of the legitimacy that may be attributed to their recommendations because of the rational bureaucratic expertise that they embody.

More powerful states have not suffered a loss of domestic autonomy as a result of defaulting on their foreign debts, and their domestic institutional arrangements have not been a target of conditionality agreements with IFIs, although Russia, militarily strong but financially weak in the mid 1990s, may be something of an exception. Although many of the state governments of the United States defaulted in the nineteenth century, European lenders were not able to control the fiscal affairs of the United States. After the 1917 revolution, the Soviet Union defaulted on the huge loans that Russia had incurred before the First World War, an act that did not result in any loss of Westphalian sovereignty.[44] Loans that have been made by advanced industrialized countries from international financial institutions have not carried such stringent conditions as those imposed on poorer countries with more limited resources.

---

[44] Lindert and Morton 1989, 55–56.

In sum, since the beginning of the nineteenth century the principles that have governed sovereign lending to weaker states have been inconsistent with the principles that inform the Westphalian model. From the Greek loan of 1832 through the practices of the European Bank for Reconstruction and Development founded in 1990, creditors have routinely compromised the domestic autonomy of weaker lenders. In some instances, this has been accomplished through ex post coercion; in others, through ex ante contracting. As in the case of minority and human rights, sovereign lending is an area of international activity in which Westphalian sovereignty is best comprehended as an example of organized hypocrisy. The principles of Westphalia have been challenged by alternatives, and the outcome of such disagreements has been a function of the power and interests of rulers. Different preferences over outcomes and power asymmetries have resulted in violations of Westphalian sovereignty through both intervention and invitation.

CHAPTER 6

Constitutional Structures and New States in the Nineteenth Century

RULERS HAVE NOT limited their efforts to compromise the autonomy of their own and other polities to specific issues such as sovereign lending, minority rights, and human rights. They have also acted to alter basic constitutional structures. These efforts have usually taken place through coercion and imposition, although in some instances rulers or would-be rulers have contracted with their counterparts in more powerful states, and invited external influence on constitutional arrangements in their own polities. At the same time, however, there are many examples of basic state structures that are completely consistent with the Westphalian model. External actors have frequently been indifferent to developments in other states or have lacked the power to intervene effectively. Even in matters as fundamental as the constitutional order of a polity, the Westphalian model has been characterized by organized hypocrisy. Sometimes its governing principle, autonomy, has been honored, sometimes challenged, sometimes ignored by stronger powers.

The variation in the extent to which Westphalian norms have been honored does not imply that they are irrelevant or inconsequential. Because nonintervention is a widely understood social fact, it can facilitate the organization of political groups, both public and private. The idea of the Westphalian state is one factor among many that can influence the ability of leaders to resist coercion or secure more attractive contractual terms. A leader who would be deposed through internal revolt for accepting something less than a Westphalian state may be in a stronger bargaining position than one who could compromise Westphalian principles and still retain office. Well-understood norms like domestic autonomy can facilitate certain outcomes and impede others, but in the international environment they are never taken for granted, or constitutive in the sense that certain kinds of activities would be precluded if they were violated.

High power asymmetry is the necessary condition for effective intervention to alter the constitutional arrangements of a target state. The local population can revolt. Externally bolstered rulers are open to accusations of disloyalty. Policing is expensive.

Intervenors have only been successful when their initiatives have not been challenged by a major power rival. If a ruler in a weak state can find an external ally, power asymmetries can disappear. Without great power consensus achieved through either a condominium or mutual recognition of spheres of influence, intervention can be treacherous. Security has been the most common motivation for the rulers of major powers to intervene to alter the constitutional structures of target states.

This chapter and the one following examine two sets of contrasting cases: the Western Hemisphere as opposed to the Balkans in the nineteenth century, and the successor states of the European empires as opposed to eastern and western Europe during the cold war. All of the successor states to the Ottoman Empire were subject to some degree of external influence, usually through imposition or coercion, in the establishment of their domestic institutional arrangements. The major European powers worked in concert. Russia, which made several attempts to unilaterally secure its desired outcome, was frustrated by Britain, France, Austria, and Germany and had to join with them in Paris in 1856 after being defeated in the Crimean War, and at Berlin in 1878 after having failed to create a greater Bulgaria with access to the Aegean after the first Balkan Wars. The major powers had both military and economic resources. Russia, and especially Austria-Hungary, believed that their own security was connected with developments in the Balkans, as tragically proved to be the case in 1914. The other major powers were linked through a system of alliances. The major powers were anxious to influence domestic institutional structures in the new Balkan states. They worked in concert because they were unwilling to recognize a sphere of influence for any single power; no one power was strong enough to act unilaterally, and mutually agreed upon conditions for the recognition of the Balkan states were preferable to a hands-off policy that would have been consistent with the Westphalian model.

The situation developed very differently in the Western Hemisphere. There was no condominium. Britain and France fought throughout much of the eighteenth century, and, given divisions between Europe's two major naval powers, the leaders of the American colonies were able to lead a successful revolution and to determine their own domestic political institutions. The Spanish lost their empire because of the superior armed capability of the local population, and Portugal was unable to maintain control over Brazil. The major European powers did not have security interests in the Western Hemisphere in the nineteenth century, never agreed on a condominium, and were not able to establish spheres of influence. Until the latter part of the century the United States was too weak to effectively coerce other states or impose its preferences for constitutional structures; moreover, its rulers saw no need to do so provided that European powers were excluded. Until the end of the century, developments in most of the states of the Western Hemisphere conformed with the Westphalian model. Only after the United States became powerful enough to assert its own sphere of influence at the turn of the century were the constitutional structures of some Caribbean and Central American republics influenced, sometimes dictated, by American rulers.

In Europe after the Second World War, both the Soviet Union and the United States believed that the foreign policies of states would be influenced by their domestic institutional structures. Stalin did not trust democratic regimes in eastern Europe to adopt the Soviet Union's policy preferences. Once Stalin had asserted an effective sphere of influence over eastern Europe after the Second World War and imposed Communist regimes or coerced local rulers into accepting them, successive Soviet rulers were very reluctant to accept changes, even when nuclear weapons made the control of the satellite states less important for the protection of territorial integrity. Soviet leaders knew that the dismantling of Communist regimes in central Europe would raise questions about the stability of the regime in the Soviet Union itself, because the Communist Party legitimated its rule on the basis of Marxism-Leninism, a teleological ideology that could not accommodate capitalism replacing communism. Indeed, Gorbachev's acceptance of reforms in eastern Europe in the late 1980s did contribute to the disintegration of the Soviet Union.

Likewise the United States was not prepared to tolerate Communist institutions or Communist Party domination in the states of western Europe. Its security interests would be threatened if the Soviet Union dominated all of Europe. The United States, like the Soviet Union, was able to establish a sphere of influence over those areas of Europe that its military occupied in 1945. The Americans were in a better position to engage in contracting rather than coercion or imposition because they could ally with local leaders who shared their constitutional preferences.

In contrast, the dissolution of the European empires was not, with few exceptions, an issue that involved the security, the territorial and political integrity, of the colonial powers. Economic interests varied, but were often inconsequential; most colonies offered neither markets nor raw materials. None of the major colonial powers was able to establish a sphere of influence nor could all of the great powers agree on a condominium. Both the Soviet Union and the United States were opposed to colonialism. Almost all of the new states that emerged from the colonial empires after the Second World War were not only international legal sovereigns but also Westphalian sovereigns.

Ironically, the Westphalian model proved more apposite in Asia and Africa than it did in Europe. The rulers of the United States and the Soviet Union cared about the domestic structures of the European states and were willing to intervene to achieve their objectives. The rulers of Portugal, the Netherlands, France, and Britain were not indifferent to constitutional arrangements in their soon to be independent colonies. Their resources, however, were limited and, except in a small number of cases, their domestic constituencies were unwilling to support substantial military or economic outlays in the successor states of their empires. The Soviet Union and the United States were anxious to support their preferred constitutional arrangements in the Third World, but the competition between the superpowers precluded both spheres of influence in Africa and Asia and any condominium that included all of the major powers.

In both the nineteenth and the late twentieth centuries violations of the Westphalian model were endemic, but the model endured. Where power asymmetries were high, interests engaged, and either spheres of influence or a great-power condominium established, the Westphalian model was compromised. If any one of these three conditions was absent, rulers were able to maintain their autonomy with regard to constitutional arrangements. In contrast, international legal sovereignty was almost universally desired and secured.

THE SUCCESSOR STATES OF THE OTTOMAN EMPIRE

The Ottoman Empire, the dominant power on the western Eurasian land mass in the sixteenth century, crumbled during the nineteenth century, unable to match the industrial development and associated military might of Europe. It was a decomposition that the major powers could not ignore. The territorial boundaries and, more relevant for this study, the internal autonomy of every state that emerged from the Ottoman Empire in Europe was compromised by the major European powers, usually through imposition and coercion rather than contracting. In the most extreme instance, that of Greece, the Great Powers dictated the constitutional regime, delimited freedom of action in specific issue areas, and appointed central decision makers. In other cases, such as Serbia and Romania, local actors had more influence, and external imposition was limited to specific policies, notably minority rights. There is no example, however, of a Balkan state where domestic actors were able to choose their own fate completely—that is, where the basic constitutional structure, personnel, and specific institutions and policies exclusively reflected the preferences of the local population.

The Westphalian model is of limited value for understanding the end game of the Ottoman Empire. For the major European powers, there were three questions. What kind of regime would they create or recognize? What limitations would they impose in specific issue areas? What influence would they have over the selection of leaders? Superfluous to the debate was whether they would intervene. The rulers of Russia, Austria-Hungary, Germany, France, and Britain had the resources and motivation to make coercion or imposition both attractive and feasible. Moreover, they were usually able to act in concert and to avoid irreconcilably antagonist policies. The major exception was the Crimean War.

The power asymmetry was so great that none of the leaders of the successor states to the Ottoman Empire could hope to extricate himself entirely from coercion even if he could avoid outright imposition. Capability differentials were huge across a number of issue areas, particularly military and financial. If they were in agreement, the rulers of the major powers could credibly threaten any would-be Balkan rulers with a cutoff of international capital, denial of recognition, and, in some cases, military invasion.

Security concerns were the primary motivation for great-power intervention. Russia's rulers wanted to expand to the south and to secure access to the Mediterranean either through the Bosphorus and Dardenelles or a friendly port on the Aegean that might be controlled by a greater Bulgaria that would be under Russian tutelage. Britain's rulers feared Russian naval presence in the eastern Mediterranean. By the latter part of the nineteenth century, the leaders of Austria-Hungary were anxious about the growing impact of the newly independent Slavic states, especially Serbia, on their own restive Slavic population. In a number of successor states, financial obligations provided both a motivation and pretense for ongoing great-power influence over domestic political institutions. Finally, nonmaterial ideological motives were also expressed in some cases. Elements of the British population were concerned about the freedom of Greece in part because of sympathy for Greek nationalism and an appreciation for classical civilization. Russian leaders sometimes identified themselves as the defenders of the Slavs and the protectors of the Orthodox Church. All of the major powers were concerned about minority rights, sometimes because of concern with principle, sometimes because minority conflicts were viewed as potentially destabilizing.

Every successful instance of coercion or imposition by the rulers of the major powers took place through multilateral mechanisms. No great power could act unilaterally in face of opposition from others. The intervention in Greece was negotiated and carried out by Russia, England, and France. The settlements later in the century, especially the critical decisions taken at the Congress of Paris after the Crimean War in 1856 and the Congress of Berlin after the Balkan War in 1878, were all multilateral. Hence, the major powers had the motivation, the capability, and the ability to coordinate; these were the conditions that were necessary and sufficient to explain efforts at coercion and imposition that were inconsistent with the Westphalian model.

Greece

Greece was the first European state to secure its independence from the Ottoman Empire. The monarchical regime that emerged after a decade of war, the fiscal arrangements for the new state, the provisions for the protection of minorities, and the individuals who occupied major positions including the crown were all imposed by the major European powers. Developments in Greece did not conform with the Westphalian model.

The revolt in Greece began in 1821 and formally ended in 1832 with the establishment of an internationally recognized Greek state. From the outset, however, there were deep divisions among the rebels, which made them more susceptible than they would otherwise have been to external coercion.

In 1821 an assembly met at Epidaurus and established a government that, in January 1822, promulgated a constitution based on the French Directory, which gave power to a five-man committee. This government failed because of internal dissension. In 1827 a national assembly was held at Troezene, which established a presidential system. Two Britons were invited to head the military and naval forces. The president of this regime, Capodistrias, was assassinated in 1831 and replaced by a three-man committee. The internal strife among the Greeks enhanced the ability of the European powers to dictate their preferred outcome.[1]

The support of external powers—Britain, Russia, and France—was critical for the success of the Greek rebellion. In 1823 Britain recognized the Greek revolutionaries as belligerents, which meant that Greek ships would not be regarded as engaging in piracy. In 1824 Britain allowed the Greeks to float a loan in London, providing critical financial resources. Nevertheless, by the summer of 1827 the rebels were on the verge of defeat. In the fall of 1827 the British, French, and Russians established a naval blockade and, most critically, in October 1827 a fleet composed of ships from all three major powers destroyed the Turkish-Egyptian fleet at Navarino. Without this naval victory the Greek rebellion would have failed.[2]

The military situation of the Ottoman Empire was further undermined when it became involved in a war with Russia. By September 1829 Russian troops were on the Aegean and within forty miles of Constantinople. The other major powers feared that the Ottoman Empire would collapse. Russia sought a settlement, because its own resources were stretched, rather than pressing its military advantage. The Treaty of Adrianople, signed in September 1829, gave Russia some small territorial gains in Europe, larger

---

[1] Jelavich and Jelavich 1977, 45, 50–52; Anderson 1966, 74–75.

[2] Schwartzberg 1988, 294; Temperley 1966, 406–8; Jelavich and Jelavich 1977, 48–50; W. Miller 1936, 102–3; Stavrianos 1958, 286–87.

gains in Asia, and more supervision over administrative activities in Ottoman territories in the Balkans. Greece, then, was only able to free itself from Turkish rule with the support of the major European powers; in one of the last acts of the war, French troops drove the remnants of the Turkish army from the Morea.[3]

The strategic interests of Russia and Britain were the most obvious motivations for great-power involvement. The Russians wanted to expand to the south and increase their influence in the Balkans. Britain was concerned about growing Russian naval power in the eastern Mediterranean. All of the major European powers dreaded a total implosion of the Ottoman Empire, which would have dragged them into the Balkans in ways they could not control.

Russia was the most eager to become involved in Greece. Russia protested Ottoman efforts to suppress the uprising and claimed that it had a right to protect the Orthodox Church under the Treaty of Kutchuk-Kainardju of 1774. Russia had a long history of formal involvement with the Orthodox Church, whose Greek primate was in Constantinople.[4]

Initially, neither British nor Austrian rulers were anxious to provide the Greeks with support. Britain wanted a strong Ottoman Empire to prevent Russian penetration of the eastern Mediterranean. Austria, under Metternich, opposed revolt against legitimate authority. By 1826, however, the British were willing to contemplate some kind of joint action. They feared that continued Turkish depredations in Greece would provide Russia with a pretense for unilateral action. Britain wanted to prevent Greece from falling under Russian control and to frustrate Russian ambitions to dominate Constantinople and thereby secure for its fleet free access to the eastern Mediterranean and complete safety in the Black Sea.[5]

British leaders defended their involvement in Greece in more than strategic terms. They explicitly supported the national aspirations of the Greek rebels. The British governing class had been educated in the Greek classics. In his "Second Treatise" (1690) John Locke had argued that the Greeks had the right to overthrow their Turkish rulers if they had the power to do so. Byron's voyage to Greece and his death in Missolonghi increased popular support for the rebellion in England and elsewhere in Europe. More than a thousand volunteers came from Britain and several other European countries to support the Greeks.[6]

---

[3] Anderson 1966, 70–71.

[4] Schwartzberg 1988, 147.

[5] Temperley 1966, 320–21; Anderson 1966, 60–62; Jelavich and Jelavich 1977, 47; Schwarztberg 1988, 294.

[6] Schwartzberg 1988, 141, 145; Temperley 1966, 327–29; St. Clair 1972, appendix for data on European volunteers.

When fighting ended, the major concern of the European powers was to end strife and disorder. The Greeks were not able to present a cohesive political front. Piracy continued to plague commerce in the Aegean. The collapse of Greece could have led to Russian expansion to the south and precipitated a confrontation with Britain, which the rulers of both states wanted to avoid. By 1832 the traditional thrust and parry between Russia and Britain had been supplanted by a commitment by both states to policies designed to stabilize Greek political life.[7]

Regardless of their motivations, the rulers of the major powers did not simply limit their interest to securing independence for Greece, a pattern of behavior that would have been consistent with the Westphalian model. Quite the contrary. Between 1824 and 1832 they entered into several agreements about the constitutional structure, policies, and officeholders for a Greek political entity, as well as about territorial boundaries, an issue that is not relevant for conformity with the Westphalian model. Although the Greeks and Ottomans were sometimes asked to accept these agreements, they were never at the bargaining table.

In 1826 Britain and Russia signed a protocol at St. Petersburg in which they supported the establishment of Greece as a dependency of the Ottoman Empire. The Treaty of London concluded in July 1827 provided in part that Greece would be under the suzerainty of the Porte and would pay an annual tribute, but would enjoy complete freedom of internal administration. The treaty was signed by Britain, Russia, and France. Austria did not join because of Metternich's refusal to pressure the Ottomans, a legitimate conservative regime, and the Prussians took their lead from Austria. After the Treaty of London was signed, Britain, France, and Russia attempted to force the Greeks and Ottomans to end hostilities. The Ottomans, however, were in the stronger military position and refused mediation.[8]

Hence, through 1827 the major powers were engaged in discussions about altering the internal arrangements of the Ottoman Empire. They had not supported formal Greek independence but they had proposed creating an autonomous Greek entity with a defined territory. Turkey, the object of these discussions, was never at the conference table. There was no pretense of a contractual arrangement; the Great Powers wanted to coerce or impose a new domestic order on the Ottoman Empire, at least with respect to Greece.[9]

---

[7] See the numerous references to the need to establish stability in United Kingdom 1834, vol. 19, especally 41–54.

[8] Anderson 1966, 66, 67; Schwartzberg 1988, 154, 167; Temperley 1966, 390–91, 400.

[9] The Ottoman Empire was not formally accepted as a member of the European state system until the Treaty of Paris following the Crimean War, but the treatment of Turkey at Berlin in 1878, where the major European powers again defined the status of specific enti-

These more modest objectives for Greece were abandoned as the military situation changed. After the Battle of Navarino all of the major European powers came to accept that there would be an independent Greek state. But the kind of state would be determined by them and not by the Greeks.

The revolutionary leaders had chosen a republican structure at their own constitutional conventions in 1823 and 1827. But internal dissension coupled with military weakness made it impossible to reject the terms that were offered by the major powers. The Greeks, like the Ottomans, were never at the conference table, although by 1830 the president, Capodistrias, and the Greek senate had formally accepted the fact that the major powers would select a ruler for Greece. In a confidential memorandum of December 28, 1831, Canning, the British emissary in Constantinople, warned Capodistrias that the major powers could not remain indifferent spectators should their efforts to create a stable situation in Greece unravel.[10] For the Greek leaders the options were to accept the dictates of the major European states with regard to domestic structures or to forgo international legal sovereignty and the financial and military support that might accompany recognition.

In February 1830 Britain, France, and Russia signed three protocols in London regarding Greece. They insisted on religious equality to avoid sectarian strife. The protocols established that Greece would be a monarchy, a decision that ignored the preferences expressed by the provisional Greek governments during the 1820s. The allies designated Leopold of Saxe Coburg as king, set the boundaries of Greece, and provided for the right of emigration for Greeks and Turks. The Greek leader accepted these accords in April 1830. France, England, and Russia were to act as guarantors of the settlement.[11]

The appointment of Leopold, however, never came to fruition. Leopold made his acceptance by Greece a condition of his becoming king, something which the Great Powers rejected (no bow to Westphalia here, not even a curtsy). Leopold, fearing that he would be deeply unpopular in Greece, rejected the crown in May 1830.[12]

The major powers sought another candidate and settled on Prince Otho, the second son of the king of Bavaria. Their first criterion was that

---

ties—Bulgaria a tributary state, Montenegro independent—was little different than what had occurred in the 1820s.

[10] "Le gouvernement grec aux residens des trois cours en Grèce," "Le senat au president de la Grèce," and "Memoire confidentiel sur l'état de la Grèce, communique à Comte Augustin de Capodistrias par Son Excellence Sir Stratford Canning," in United Kingdom 1834, 19:6–7, 11.

[11] Dakin 1973, 281; Stavrianos 1958, 292–93.

[12] Dakin 1973, 275–88; Leopold got a better deal by becoming king of Belgium.

the new king not be closely connected to any of the royal houses of the major powers. His father negotiated with Britain, France, and Russia over Otho's title (king), extending the boundaries of Greece, a loan for the new government, the designation of officials, the provision of a 3,500-man military force, and even the terms under which Otho might assume the Bavarian crown should his elder brother die. Although his father urged that Otho by acclaimed by the people of Greece (a proposal that the three powers rejected on the grounds that Greece had given them unrestricted right to select a sovereign), the fact remains that the king of Bavaria, not the provisional government of Greece, was the interlocutor with Britain, France, and Russia in determining the constitutional structure, selection of personnel, and specific policies for the new regime.[13]

On May 7, 1832, a new convention was signed by France, Britain, and Russia on the one hand, and Bavaria on the other. The opening paragraph of the convention stated that the major powers were "exercising the power conveyed to them by the Greek Nation." Neither Greece nor the Porte was at the table. The powers agreed, however, to convert the February 1830 protocol, which specified that the new Greek state would be a monarchy, and which had been accepted by Greek decision makers and the Porte, into a definitive treaty to which the king of Greece would become a signatory (Article VI), although this promise was never fulfilled.

Article IV declared that Greece, "under the guarantee of the three Courts (Russia, France, and Britain), shall form a Monarchical and Independent State according to the 1830 protocol." Otho was offered the crown (by France, Britain, and Russia, not Greece). The terms of hereditary succession were suggested.[14]

Greece did not, in fact, have a native prime minister until 1837 and the king of Bavaria appointed and recalled officials at will during the 1830s. The existing military forces were disbanded, and only two thousand Greeks were allowed to join the armed forces. In the mid-1830s only about half of the soldiers in the Greek army were Greek. The regents established judicial and administrative procedures that ignored Greek tradition and were unsuitable for the primitive economic and social conditions they encountered.

---

[13] "Communication faire à la conference par le Plenipotentiaire Bavarois (Extrait): Points à regler entre le Plenipotentiaire Bavarois et les Plenipotentiaires des trois cours, relativement au choix de Son Altesse Royale Prince Otho de Baviere à la couronne de la Grèce," in United Kingdom 1834, 19:15–20; and the response of the powers "Projet de communication au Plenipotentiaire Bavarois (Confidentielle)," especially p. 31.

[14] The three major powers wanted Otho to renounce any claim to the Bavarian crown but the king of Bavaria refused to let his underage son (Otho was eighteen), take this step as a minor. See United Kingdom 1834, 19:41, 46, 47; and the final resolution in United Kingdom 1836, 20:281–82). The king of Bavaria was to appoint the three regents who would

Otho, a Catholic, became head of the Greek Orthodox Church. Once in power, he styled himself the absolute ruler of Greece, and refused to recognize formally constitutional limitations claiming that France, Britain, and Russia had bestowed a mandate on Bavaria. When Otho was overthrown by a military coup in 1862 and returned to Bavaria, the Great Powers insisted on the right to choose his successor. In 1863 the three powers, along with Greece, agreed that Greece would be a monarchical constitutional state and that Prince William (who ruled as George I), the youngest son of the king of Denmark, would be king. The agreement recognized the financial control given to France, Russia, and Britain by the 1832 treaty. A year later, however, a Greek constituent assembly did draw up a new constitution that limited royal prerogatives and provided for manhood suffrage and a unicameral legislature.[15]

Aside from specifying the constitutional structure of the new Greek state and designating the individuals who would hold authoritative offices (the king, the regents, and military officers), the convention of 1832 also delimited Greek fiscal autonomy. As discussed more fully in Chapter 5, Greece agreed to commit its revenues first to the refunding of a sixty-thousand-franc loan provided by France, Britain, and Russia. Because Greece was frequently in default on its international obligations, the terms of the loan provided a pretext for later foreign intervention.[16]

In sum, the creation of Greece offers a pellucid example of the Westphalian model as an example of organized hypocrisy. In conformity with Westphalian discourse, Britain, France, and Russia always claimed to be acting on the basis of powers given to them by the Greek provisional government or Greek nation, but the Greek leaders had little choice: internal affairs were in disarray, and the land and naval forces of the major powers were in command. Words and actions were decoupled; a logic of consequences prevailed over any logic of appropriateness. The major European powers toyed with alternative constitutional forms including some kind of tributary state within the Ottoman Empire throughout the mid 1820s, but concluded that an international legal sovereign was the only option after the Ottoman military losses. The central decision makers of France, Britain, and Russia, not those of Greece, selected Otho as king and provided for a government that was run by Bavarians. The condition that the revenues of Greece had to be committed first to the repayment

---

govern until Otho reached the age of twenty in June 1835, as well as military officers who would organize the Greek army.

[15] Stavrianos 1958, 293–95; Dontas 1966, 4; Dakin 1973, 315–16; Jelavich and Jelavich 1977, 68–72.

[16] Dontas 1966, 3.

of the sixty-thousand-franc loan was imposed on Greece in the convention of 1832, which was signed with Bavaria, not any representative of the Greek government. The Great Powers insisted that Greece accept religious toleration.

The asymmetry of power between Greece and the major powers was extreme not only because of aggregate capabilities but also because of domestic divisions within Greece. Russia would have preferred to dictate its own preferences to the Ottoman Empire, but it did not have the naval power to resist Britain, which opposed its unilateral initiatives. Great-power condominium was the most attractive strategy. If Greek leaders had rejected the conditions dictated by France, Russia, and Britain, they would not have been leaders of anything. Greece was given international legal, but not Westphalian, sovereignty. Only in the 1864, after Otho was overthrown, did Greece draft its own constitution, and even then the new king George I was nominated by the major powers.[17]

The Slavic States

The major powers of Europe were heavily involved in structuring the domestic affairs of all of the other states that emerged from the Ottoman Empire during the long nineteenth century—Serbia, Bulgaria, Montenegro, Albania, and Romania. These interventions occurred both before and after these states were accorded international legal sovereignty. Romania, Serbia, and Montenegro were formally recognized as independent states in the Treaty of Berlin of 1878. Bulgaria was recognized in 1908, Albania in 1912. Before they became international legal sovereigns, pressure was put on the Ottoman Empire to grant increasing levels of autonomy to these entities: the Porte was coerced into accepting changes in the basic institutional arrangements governing the Balkans even while this area was still formally part of the Ottoman Empire. All of the Slavic states had to accept some limitations on their internal autonomy with regard to the treatment of minorities, trade policies, and other economic matters in exchange for recognition. In the case of Bulgaria, basic constitutional structures and the ruler of the country were externally imposed.

As in the case of Greece, the major powers achieved a condominium. Russia probed for unilateral openings but was frustrated. Russian leaders were not prepared to risk intervention by their British, Austrian, and French counterparts.

Throughout the nineteenth century security issues were the focus of attention for the major powers. Economic and humanitarian considerations were less important. Britain feared Russian expansion in the eastern

---

[17] Jelavich and Jelavich 1977, 68–72, 80–83; W. Miller 1936, 273–74.

Mediterranean, an issue especially relevant for Bulgaria whose boundaries could have been extended to the Aegean. British public sentiment was enraged by press reports of Turkish massacres in 1876 after the Bulgarians revolted against Turkey. (Media coverage was slower than CNN, but not demonstrably less consequential.) The Habsburgs were concerned about the internal integrity of their empire with its large Slavic population. Russia probed not only for strategic advantage but also to actualize the ethos of pan-Slavism, which was one source of support for the czarist regime. All of the major powers worried about a collapse of the Ottoman Empire, a particular problem for Austrian and Russian leaders, who had conflicting interests in the Balkans but wanted, along with Germany, to preserve their *Dreikaiserbund* alliance of conservative states. These anxieties about instability in the Balkans were all too unhappily realized in the fateful summer of 1914.

In none of the Slavic countries, however, was the influence of the Great Powers as overwhelming as it had been in Greece, because even when there was severe factional strife (and there almost always was) the situation did not deteriorate into the kind of chaotic fragmentation that precluded effective indigenous leadership. Imposition of the sort that occurred with the establishment of the Bavarian regime in Greece would have encountered resistance in the other Balkan states. The major powers could coerce would-be Balkan rulers, but they could not impose outcomes.

BULGARIA

Bulgaria was the Balkan entity, and later state, most heavily influenced by coercion and imposition. Before the 1870s the Bulgarians had had only limited success in establishing their own autonomy within the Ottoman Empire. Bulgaria remained the Slavic area most closely under Ottoman control.[18]

Bulgaria secured greater autonomy but formally remained part of the Ottoman Empire as a result of the settlement that was reached at the Congress of Berlin in 1878. Its constitutional structure, leadership, and specific institutional arrangements were in part dictated by the rulers of the more powerful European states. The Ottoman Empire was compelled to accept these constraints on its own internal structures because it was militarily and financially too weak to resist. Indigenous Bulgaria leaders did not have enough domestic political support or resources to assure that their preferences, not those of the major powers, would determine Bulgaria's future.

---

[18] Jelavich and Jelavich 1977, chap. 9.

The events leading to Bulgaria's status as an autonomous principality, and to formal independence for the other states of the Balkans, began with a revolt of Christian peasants in Bosnia Herzegovina in 1875. Unrest spread, resulting in a war between the Turks and Serbia, Romania, and Montenegro (all part of the Ottoman Empire); in 1877 Russian intervention led to the defeat of Turkey. On March 3, 1878, representatives of Russia and the Ottoman Empire signed the Treaty of San Stefano, which, among other things, established a greater Bulgaria, with borders on the Aegean as well as the Black Sea, as an autonomous province of the Ottoman Empire. The Russians expected that this entity would be more or less under their control. The other major powers of Europe found this settlement unacceptable, as did Serbia and Greece, which received nothing. In the face of this opposition Russia, whose military resources were stretched thin and whose leaders feared internal unrest, agreed to a general conference at Berlin, which opened in June 1878.[19]

All of the major powers participated in the Congress of Berlin. Bulgaria was the most important issue at the Congress, but the Bulgarians were excluded from the meeting at the insistence of the Russians. Other representatives from the Balkans had no influence. The fate of the Slavic countries was to be determined by decisions that would be taken by the Great Powers of Europe, not by indigenous representatives from these areas.[20]

Bulgaria, although not the greater Bulgaria of the Treaty of San Stefano, was established by the first article of the Treaty of Berlin of 1878 as "an autonomous and tributary Principality under the suzerainty of His Imperial Majesty the Sultan; it will have a Christian Government and a national militia." Article III provided that the prince of Bulgaria would be freely elected by the population and confirmed by the Porte with the approval of the European powers. The prince, however, could not be from one of the major houses of Europe (Article IV). The Organic Law of the principality was to be drawn up by an assembly of Bulgarian notables. Although Bulgaria was still formally part of the Ottoman Empire, all Turkish troops had to be withdrawn. The Great Powers fixed the amount of tribute that Bulgaria was to pay to the Porte and the amount of Ottoman public debt that was to be assigned to Bulgaria.[21]

The treaty also established constraints on the economic independence of authorities within Bulgaria, whether Turkish or Bulgarian. The commerce of all of the signatory powers was to be treated equally. No transit duties were to be levied on goods passing through Bulgaria. Bulgaria, not

---

[19] Stavrianos 1958, 396–410; Jelavich and Jelavich 1977, 153.
[20] Anderson 1966, 210–12.
[21] Treaty of Berlin 1878, 975, 979; 980, Article XI.

the Porte, was to be responsible for existing contracts for railway construction with companies from the Western powers. Finally, Article V provided for religious toleration using the same language that was applied to Romania and Serbia (see Chapter 3).[22]

In addition to establishing major elements of the institutional structure of Bulgaria (although the actual constitution was formally left to a Bulgarian constituent assembly), the major powers also designated the new ruler of the country—Alexander of Battenberg. He fit the basic criterion, which was that the ruler not have clear ties to one specific ruling house. Alexander appointed a Russian general as the minister of war, although he was under no formal obligation to do this. All of the officers in the Bulgarian army from the rank of captain and above came, after 1878, from the Russian army.[23]

Bulgaria worked itself out from under these external impositions over the course of the next three decades. Despite his considerable popularity, the Russians forced Alexander to resign in 1886 and, at the same time, decapitated the Bulgarian army by withdrawing all Russian officers. The Bulgarians themselves then chose a new ruler, Ferdinand of Coburg, without the approval of the major powers, who did not accept Ferdinand's rule until 1896. In 1908 Bulgaria unilaterally declared its independence and was immediately recognized by Austria, which wanted Bulgarian support for its assumption of complete control of Bosnia Herzegovina. The Porte recognized Bulgarian independence after being paid an indemnity.[24]

An even more anomalous product of the Congress of Berlin was Eastern Rumelia, an area to the south of Bulgaria. Eastern Rumelia was created to preclude a larger Bulgaria. Article XIII of the treaty provided that Eastern Rumelia would remain under the political and military authority of the sultan "under conditions of autonomy." It was to have a Christian governor-general, who would be nominated by the Porte with the approval of the powers. The laws of the Ottoman Empire were to apply in Eastern Rumelia. According to Article XVIII, the administrative, judicial, and financial systems were to be established by a commission with representatives from the powers and in concert with the Porte. Different powers drafted different sections of Rumelia's Organic Statutes—the British the electoral laws, the Austrians the legal system, the Italians the financial system. The finance minister was German, the chief of gendarmes was British, the head of the militia was French; the officers of the militia were Russian or Russian-trained Bulgarians. In 1885 Eastern Rumelia leaders declared

---

[22] Treaty of Berlin 1878, 979–80, 978.
[23] Jelavich and Jelavich 1977, 161.
[24] Jelavich and Jelavich 1977, 167, 195; Stavrianos 1955, 432.

that they wanted to be part of Bulgaria. Although this violated the Treaty of Berlin, the Great Powers did not resist unification.[25]

The Bulgaria established at the Congress of Berlin was inconsistent with both Westphalian and international legal sovereignty. It was an autonomous principality paying tribute to Turkey but independent of its authority in most areas. The treaty imposed constraints both on the Ottoman Empire and on what the authorities in Bulgaria itself could do with regard to personnel (the person chosen as prince), to certain economic policies, and to the treatment of religious minorities. Eastern Rumelia was an even odder creation. Eventually Bulgaria did become a conventional international legal sovereign, but the form that it took in 1878 is a tribute to the imaginations of rulers attempting to reconcile their conflicting security concerns rather than the constraints arising from conventional forms of sovereignty. Neither Westphalian nor international legal sovereignty was taken for granted. Consequences mattered more than appropriateness.

ROMANIA

In Greece and Bulgaria basic constitutional structures, personnel, and policies were the result of coercion or imposition by the major powers. Romania suffered less from external imposition because it had an indigenous political structure, based upon the boyars or nobility, that could organize local political resources. Romania enjoyed considerable self-government within the Ottoman Empire even before the nineteenth century. Turkish prerogatives were explicitly limited to occupying certain strong points, appointing princes or governors, and receiving tribute. The extent of actual Ottoman control varied over time.[26]

When Turkish power began to wane, Russian pressure increased. Russian armies occupied Romania eight times for various periods from the beginning of the eighteenth century until 1853. At the end of the eighteenth century, the Ottomans recognized Russia as having a special position as protector of Romania (then Moldavia and Wallachia). In 1802 the sultan agreed that Muslims could not enter Moldavia and Wallachia except as merchants with special permission. The Ottoman-appointed ruler of the provinces could only be removed during his seven-year term with the approval of Russia. The Convention of Akkerman of 1826 between Russia and the Porte stated that the appointment and removal of the rulers (hospodars) of Wallachia and Moldavia had to be approved by both Russia and the Porte.

[25] Jelavich and Jelavich 1977, 163.
[26] Jelavich and Jelavich 1977, 10–11.

The Treaty of Adrianople of 1829 between the Porte and Russia stipulated that Ottoman troops would be removed from the left bank of the Danube and that land held by Ottoman subjects would be sold within eighteen months. Romania would establish a national militia. Adrianople left Russia as the most powerful force in Moldavia and Wallachia, even though they were still recognized as being part of the Ottoman Empire.

The treaty specified in some detail the internal institutional arrangements for the two provinces. Statutes were to be drawn up through a process that would include the Russian administrator, the Russian government, local boyars, and the Porte. The hospodar, who could prorogue the assembly but only with the approval of the Porte and Russia, was to be chosen by an assembly composed of boyars. Both the assembly and the hospodar could independently appeal to the Porte and to Russia, a situation that gave Russia many opportunities for intervention. In 1849, following a liberal revolt, Russia and the Porte agreed to jointly appoint the hospodars rather than having them elected by the boyars.[27]

Until the Crimean War, the major powers other than Russia were less concerned about Romania than they had been about Greece. Romania was geographically contiguous to Russia and did not offer an outlet to the Mediterranean. Greece mattered for British naval strategy; Romania did not.

Russian domination of developments in Romania ended with its defeat in the Crimean War. Henceforth, institutional structures in Romania, like those in the other Balkan states, were influenced or determined by a concert of the Great Powers. While formally leaving Wallachia and Moldavia as part of the Ottoman Empire, the Treaty of Paris, concluded in 1856, made Romania a quasi-autonomous entity. The Porte committed to guaranteeing freedom of worship, navigation, and commerce. A special commission appointed by the contracting parties was to transmit to the conference proposals for the future constitutional structure of the provinces, taking into consideration the views expressed by constituent assemblies that the Porte was obligated to call. These assemblies were to "represent most closely the interests of all classes of [Moldavian and Wallachian] society." The Final Agreement was to be ratified by the contracting parties as well as the Porte and would "constitute definitively the organization of those Provinces, placed thenceforward under the Collective Guarantee of all the signing Powers." The Treaty of Paris also provided that "No exclusive Protection shall be exercised over them (Moldavia and Wallachia) by any of the guaranteeing Powers. There shall be no separate interference in their internal affairs."[28]

---

[27] Jelavich and Jelavich, 1977, 86–98.
[28] Treaty of Paris 1856, Articles XXIV, XXV, and XXII.

Article XXVI authorized Wallachia and Moldavia to establish a national army. Article XXVII prohibited the Porte from engaging in armed intervention in the provinces without the previous agreement of the contracting powers. Existing privileges and immunities were to continue.[29] In the Treaty of Paris, the Westphalian model did not even receive a formal bow with respect to Ottoman control over Romania. With regard to international legal sovereignty, the provinces remained part of the empire, but Ottoman autonomy was severely constrained.

In 1858, working from the recommendation of the commission established by the Treaty of Paris, the major powers produced a new institutional structure for the two provinces. Moldavia and Wallachia were to remain under the suzerainty of the sultan. The hospodars were to be elected by a special assembly and approved by the sultan. Ignoring local sentiment, the powers rejected the unification of the two provinces.

Following a coup that overthrew the indigenous leader, Cuza, in 1866, Romania chose a foreign prince as ruler of the country, Charles of Hohenzollern-Sigmaringen. Although Romanian leaders consulted with Napoleon III and Bismarck before settling on Charles, his selection was a national initiative. The Romanians hoped that a foreign prince would provide them with a neutral leader. Charles's election was approved after the fact by the major powers including the Porte.[30] With regard to international legal sovereignty, however, Romania was still part of the Ottoman Empire.

Romanian leaders drafted a new constitution based on the Belgium constitution of 1831. The Porte granted the right to issue coinage and to have an army of thirty thousand. The prince remained, however, formally a vassal of the sultan. In 1870 Romania concluded treaties with a number of European states and established diplomatic agencies despite the fact that it did not have formal independence. From 1858 to 1878 Romania was recognized but not juridically autonomous. Romania declared its independence from Turkey in May 1877; a month before it had signed agreements with Russia providing for the free passage of Russian troops and for Russian control of Romanian railways.[31]

Romania, along with Serbia and Montenegro was recognized as an independent kingdom in the Treaty of Berlin of 1878. The treaty, however, imposed several constraints on Romania. As discussed at greater length in Chapter 3, recognition was accorded only on the condition that Romania accept provisions in its constitution for religious and ethnic equality.

---

[29] Treaty of Paris 1856, Articles XXIII–XXVII.

[30] Otetea 1985, 365–66; Georgescu 1984, 150–51.

[31] Anderson 1966, 194; Langer 1964, 126–27; Jelavich and Jelavich 1977, 114–16.

The treaty also imposed economic constraints on Romania. Like Serbia, Montenegro, and Bulgaria, Romania was prohibited from imposing transit duties.[32] More significantly, Romanian authority over the Danube, which was enclosed on both its banks by Romanian territory before flowing into the Black Sea, was limited. The European Commission of the Danube, which had been established after the Crimean War, was to continue to function and would have exclusive authority over the river from Galatz to the Black Sea, although Romania was given a seat on the commission. Article LII of the Treaty of Berlin provided that, to assure freedom of navigation, all forts along the lower Danube were to be razed and only light warships from states that were members of the Danube Commission were to be allowed on that section of the river. The commission was to exercise its functions as far as Galatz in "complete independence of the territorial authorities."[33]

Romania was forced to accept these provisions governing the Danube. Russia, which through its occupation of Bessarabia became a riverain state, excluded its section of the Danube from international control. Romania was not a signatory of the Treaty of Berlin. Its representatives did not participate in the deliberations. In Berlin, interests and power, not the norms of the Westphalian model, guided the creation of the institutional arrangements for the lower Danube.

In sum, from the Russian defeat of Turkey in 1829 until the Crimean War, the institutional arrangements for Moldavia and Wallachia were the result of intervention by Russia and then, after the war, by the other Great Powers as well. The local nobility, however, could never be ignored, and Romania drew up its own constitution, selected a foreign monarch, and signed treaties even when it was still formally part of the Ottoman Empire. When formal recognition came in the Treaty of Berlin, it was tied to the protection of minority rights and constraints on Romanian economic autonomy, especially with regard to the Danube.

SERBIA

Serbia, like Romania, experienced a number of institutional arrangements both before and after formal international recognition that were inconsistent with the Westphalian model. These arrangements reflected the power and interests of different actors including leaders in Serbia, the Ottoman Empire, and the major European powers. In 1815, after a series of revolts that had begun in 1804, Serbia won considerable autonomy within the Ottoman Empire. Both Serb and Ottoman judges were to sit on cases involving Serbs. Serbian officials were to collect taxes, and the country was

---

[32] Treaty of Berlin 1878, 993.
[33] Treaty of Berlin 1878, 994.

to be governed by a Serbian administrator. However, the agreement did not establish clear territorial boundaries for Serbia, nor did it remove all Ottoman officials.

In 1830 the Porte made Serbia an autonomous state within the empire. The right of hereditary rule was granted to Milos, who had become governor in 1815. (Milos was the founder of the Obrenovich dynasty, one of the two that defined factional divisions in Serbia during the nineteenth century; the other was the Karageorge.) The entire country was now ruled by ethnic Serbs, some of whom, however, came from the Habsburg Empire (where they had access to better education), a source of resentment among the local population. Ottoman landed property was taken with compensation to be paid by the Porte. In 1833 the Porte yielded additional land that had been recognized as Serbian in the Convention of Akkerman (1826) and the Treaty of Adrianople (1829), both between Russia and the Porte. In 1839 the Sultan issued the Turkish constitution for Serbia which provided for a council of seventeen members appointed by the prince. It was the basis of Serbian government until 1869. The de facto autonomy of Serbia was even greater than the de jure. While Milos implemented those Turkish decrees that he liked, he rejected others. For instance, the provision of the 1830 Ottoman declaration, which provided for an assembly and a council, was ignored by Milos.[34]

In the 1860s, after a period of unrest, the Serbian ruler, Prince Michael, was able to secure approval from the Serbian assembly for a new constitutional structure that made Serbia more like a constitutional monarchy. In 1861 Michael promulgated a law making all men between twenty and fifty subject to military service and establishing a ministry of war. Serbia created a national army of ninety thousand. Michael signed a series of bilateral treaties with Romania, Montenegro, Greece, and the Bulgarian revolutionary society, covering issues such as the allocation of territory between Greece and Serbia. All of this despite the fact that it, and the other signatories with the exception of Greece, were still formally part of the Ottoman Empire. In 1867 all that remained of Turkish rule was the Ottoman flag over the fortress in Belgrade and the annual tribute to the sultan. In 1869 a new constitution was promulgated without the approval of the sultan. It was prepared by a constituent assembly of five hundred delegates.[35]

In 1876, after the revolts in Bosnia and Herzegovina, and in Bulgaria, Serbia, with the private aid of Russian nationalists, attacked the Ottomans but was completely defeated. The major powers attempted to find some resolution that would satisfy both the Balkan states, still not recognized as international legal sovereigns, and the Ottoman Empire, but they failed.

[34] Jelavich and Jelavich 1977, 56–59.
[35] Jelavich and Jelavich 1977, 36–37, 55, 65–66; Stavrianos 1958, 395.

In April 1877, Russia declared war on the Ottomans after having secured Austrian neutrality by recognizing Austrian preeminence in Bosnia and Herzegovina.[36] Serbia was recognized as an independent state in the Treaty of San Stefano (March 1878), which ended the conflict between Russia and the empire, and in the Treaty of Berlin.

Thus, while Serbia was recognized as an independent state only in 1878, for the previous seven decades it had enjoyed increasing autonomy while still formally part of the Ottoman Empire. Serbia had promulgated its own constitution, raised a national army, and signed treaties with other entities in the Balkans. The violence that began in 1804 was an internal rebellion. The attack by the Serbian army on the Ottoman forces in 1876, unsuccessful though it may have been, became an international war.

The Serbs were not simply passive witnesses to their own fate, but the great powers especially Russia, were involved to one degree or another in every major development. The military success of the Serbs in their long struggle to win first autonomy and then independence was influenced, and at points even determined, by the decisions taken by the major European states. Before formal independence, the Ottoman Empire was coerced into changing its own domestic institutional arrangements to give Serbia ever greater levels of autonomy.

In 1804 the czar provided arms and officers to the rebellious Serbs and in 1806 induced the Serbian rebel leader, Karageorge, to fight with the Russians against the sultan (and Napoleon) in exchange for money, weapons, and medical and administrative support. (Unfortunately for the Serbs, three days after reaching agreement with them, the czar signed the Treaty of Tilsit ending, temporarily, his conflict with Napoleon, and Russian forces withdrew from Serbia.) The Convention of Akkerman of 1826 between Russia and the Ottoman Empire placed Serbia under Russian protection, although it was ignored by the Ottomans until their defeat in 1829 when the Porte accepted Serbian autonomy, with the Obrenovich dynasty recognized as having the right of hereditary rule. The constitution promulgated in 1838 was influenced by the Russians. The Treaty of Paris ending the Crimean War guaranteed the existing rights of Serbia, which was to have "Liberty of Worship, of Legislation, of Commerce, and of Navigation." Although the Porte could continue to maintain some garrisons in Serbia, armed intervention was prohibited without the previous agreement of the Contracting Parties. Hence, by 1856 according to international agreement, the Porte could not appoint officials, garrison troops, or even independently deploy forces in territory that was formally recog-

---

[36] Jelavich and Jelavich 1977, 143–49.

nized as part of the Ottoman Empire.[37] In 1862, after the Turkish garrison had fired canons into Belgrade for five hours, the Serbian ruler appealed to the Great Powers, and they pressured Turkey to abandon all but four of its fortresses in Serbia. The final outcome of the first Balkan Wars was determined by Russia's intervention against the Ottoman Empire.

Nevertheless, in Serbia, the influence of the major powers was never as extensive as it was in Greece or Bulgaria because the Serbs, despite the conflict between the Karageorge and Obrenovich dynasties (in 1817, for instance, Milos had his main rival, Karageorge, assassinated and sent his severed head to the sultan), developed more cohesive and coherent institutions and therefore the asymmetry of power between Serbia and the major powers was less. Although Serbia was riven with factional disputes, it did not suffer the same level of disorder that prevailed in Greece during the 1820s.

Developments in Serbia before 1878 are an example of coercion, not against the Serbs but rather against the Ottoman Empire. Absent external intervention, the empire would almost certainly have fallen apart, but the course of its disintegration would have been different. The various privileges accorded to Serbia were the result not only of the rebelliousness of the Serbs but also of the military might of Russia and the preferences of the other major powers. Several times in the nineteenth century, most notably 1829 and 1856, the Ottomans were compelled by the threat of military force by the major powers to accept changes in the constitutional status of Serbia.

The rulers of Serbia secured international legal sovereignty at the Congress of Berlin in 1878 only by compromising their Westphalian sovereignty. They were in a vulnerable position: Russia supported Bulgaria, and Austria-Hungary, whose rulers had assumed de facto control over Bosnia Herzegovina in an ultimately futile effort to contain the ethnic nationalism that threatened the Habsburg Empire, became Serbia's major supporter. Like the other new Balkan states, Serbia had to make a commitment to religious toleration. Serbia's rulers accepted a number of economic conditions that were intended to increase its economic dependence on Austria including the establishment of rail links, limitations on transit duties, and ultimately a customs union with the Habsburg Empire. Between 1884 and 1892, 87 percent of Serbia's exports and 66 percent of its imports were exchanged with Austria.[38]

---

[37] Stavrianos 1958, 246–55; Jelavich and Jelavich 1977, 55–59; Treaty of Paris 1856, 954, Articles XXVIII, XVIII, and XXIX.

[38] Treaty of Paris 1856; Stavrianos 1958, 449; Treaty of Berlin 1878, Articles XXXV and XXXVII–XXXVIII.

In sum, domestic institutional structures and policies within Serbia were influenced by external powers both while Serbia was part of the Ottoman Empire and after its rulers secured international recognition. Foreign coercion and Serbian resistance compelled the Ottomans to alter domestic institutional arrangements for Serbia before 1878. At Berlin the major powers made Serbian constraints on the treatment of religious minorities and economic initiatives a condition for the extension of international legal sovereignty. Still, in Serbia, unlike Greece, the basic constitutional structure of the country (some form of monarchy) was indigeneous, and the individuals holding critical positions were Serbs. Serbia, like Romania, had a lengthy history of quasi independence within the Ottoman Empire and indigenous leaders who could mobilize domestic support.

MONTENEGRO AND ALBANIA

Two other states also emerged from the wreck of the Ottoman Empire: Montenegro and Albania. Montenegro was recognized as an independent state in the Treaty of Berlin of 1878. Like Romania, Serbia, and Bulgaria the treaty stipulated toleration and civic equality for minorities. There were also provisions in Article XXIX prohibiting Montenegro from having ships of war and requiring its officials to come to an agreement with Austria-Hungary regarding the construction and maintenance of roads and railways.

Albania was the last state to secure its independence from Turkey. Most Albanians had converted to Islam and the indigenous population would have preferred some kind of status within the Ottoman Empire. By 1912 this was no longer an option because the Christian Balkan states were driving Turkey out of Europe. Albanian leaders declared their independence in November 1912 because they feared being swallowed up by their Slavic neighbors and Greece. The major powers recognized Albanian independence in December 1912.[39]

The constitutional arrangements and most important personnel for the new state were imposed from the outside. Like Greece eighty years earlier, the internal situation in Albania was chaotic; there were no effective indigenous authority structures. In October 1913 the Great Powers established an International Control Commission. The commission, which had one Albanian member, presented the draft of a constitution in April 1914. Albania was to be neutral. Representatives to the National Assembly were to be elected from different districts and appointed by the prince. Albania would have a foreign monarch. A German prince, William of Wied, accepted the throne, but he left Albania permanently after the outbreak of the First World War and his government collapsed.[40]

---

[39] Jelavich and Jelavich 1977, 229.
[40] Jelavich and Jelavich 1977, 232–34.

In sum, during the nineteenth century the domestic institutional arrangements, personnel, or policies of the Ottoman Empire itself and its successor states—Greece, Serbia, Montenegro, Bulgaria, Romania, and Albania—were the targets of intervention by the major European powers. In Greece and Albania the major powers dictated the constitutional structures of the newly independent states as well as a number of specific policies, and chose major officeholders including the king. For most of the nineteenth century the empire was compelled to recognize the quasi independence of Bulgaria, Romania, and Serbia at least in part because of coercion, especially from Russia, which intervened militarily on several occasions. Romania, Montenegro, and Serbia were recognized as independent states in the Treaty of Berlin, but only with some restrictions on their economic and minority policies. Hence after the Napoleonic Wars the successor states to the Ottoman Empire, as well as the empire itself, never conformed with the Westphalian model. The major powers were always able to engage in coercion or imposition to secure at least formal acceptance of their preferred policies with regard to minorities and some economic issues and, in the case of Greece, Bulgaria, and Albania, were able to impose basic constitutional arrangements. Throughout the nineteenth century in the Balkans, the Westphalian model offers an example of organized hypocrisy. In contrast, the basic principle of international legal sovereignty—the recognition of juridically independent territorial entities—was generally adhered to, although even here there were exceptions, such as the recognition of Bulgaria from 1878 until 1908 when it was still formally a tributary state of the Ottoman Empire and the acceptance of emissaries from Romania before its formal juridical independence in 1878.

THE WESTERN HEMISPHERE

While developments in the Balkans often were at variance with the Westphalian model, this was not the case in the Western Hemisphere. The states that secured their independence from Britain, Spain, France, and Portugal at the end of the eighteenth and the first part of the nineteenth century were Westphalian as well as international legal sovereigns. Institutional structures, personnel, and policies were autochthonously generated. The European powers were not able to maintain their empires in the Western Hemisphere, nor were they able to influence the domestic political structures of the successor states. The difference between southeastern Europe and the Western Hemisphere reflected both capabilities and interests. No single power was able to establish a sphere of influence in the Western Hemisphere, until the United States asserted such prerogatives at the end of the nineteenth century. The major powers were also unable to act in concert as they had in the Balkans. Britain lost the Revolutionary

War to the thirteen colonies, which were aided by France. Spain was not able to defeat the armed forces that were mustered by regional leaders in Latin America. Brazil by the early part of the nineteenth century was stronger than Portugal. The United States, a regional power, opposed European incursions. No states in the Western Hemisphere were confronted with imposition and coercion with respect to their basic institutional structures until the United States intervened in Cuba after the Spanish-American War.

The United States

The first state to secure its freedom in the Western Hemisphere was the United States, which fought a revolutionary war with Britain and established a new form of polity based entirely upon the preferences of indigenous leaders. The Articles of Confederation, the Constitution, and George Washington had nothing to do with external imposition or coercion. While Britain had an interest in repressing the Americans, it was unable to prevail at least in part because the Revolutionary War became one more theater of operations in the conflict between Britain and France, which dominated international politics during the eighteenth century. Not only did the colonists pose a serious military challenge, but Britain could not count on other European powers to recognize its primacy in North America—just the opposite. The French intervened in the war because they wanted to weaken Britain. There was no hope of a European condominium that would either have suppressed the rebellion or coerced the Americans with regard to constitutional arrangements in the new state. The creation of the United States conforms with the Westphalian model: basic constitutional structures, personnel, and specific institutional arrangements were determined by the interests and political vision of American leaders.[41]

The Spanish and Portuguese Empires

The experience of Latin America was similar to that of the United States, and in sharp contrast with the successor states of the Ottoman Empire. In almost all cases the Spanish and Portuguese colonies secured their independence through armed rebellion and chose their own political institutions and personnel. The constitutional structures developed by the leaders of the newly independent states were their own invention and reflected

---

[41] Deudney 1995 for a discussion of the initial American constitutional arrangements including that which emerged from the constitution of 1787, which Deudney refers to as the Philadelphian system.

both the liberal thinking of the Enlightenment and conceptions associated with sovereignty and governance in Spain.[42] The freedom that Latin America's new rulers had to act independently reflected not only their ability to defeat their colonial rulers, but also the unwillingness of the United States and especially Britain to support any joint European effort to restore Spanish and Portuguese rule.

The revolutionaries were able to defeat Spanish forces throughout South America, albeit only after severe struggles and a number of setbacks, especially in the northern half of the continent. Spain itself was internally divided, experiencing several regime changes in the first two decades of the nineteenth century. Portugal was in no position to fight against Brazil, which declared its independence in 1822.

A joint effort to repress the South American revolutionaries might have worked, but given the conflicts among the major powers within Europe and the opposition of the United States, no such concert could have been constructed. During the Napoleonic Wars, Latin America was an extension of the conflict in Europe. When Napoleon occupied Spain in 1808, Britain supported autonomy for Spain's Western Hemisphere colonies. After 1815 the United States championed liberation movements and opposed European intervention. In 1822 the United States became the first country to recognize the independence of the new republics. When a conservative monarchical government was restored in Spain by French troops in 1823, both Britain and the United States feared that the Latin American revolutions might be thwarted and trade closed off to them.[43] The Monroe Doctrine, which depended on the British navy, implied that there would be no American participation in a condominium with the major European powers and no acceptance of European spheres of influence.

Argentina was the first South American country to establish at least de facto independence. A British invasion of Buenos Aires in 1807, part of the war against Napoleon's coalition, catalyzed effective organization and resistance in the local population and demonstrated the weakness of Spain. The Napoleonic victory in Spain in 1808 prompted local leaders in Argentina to establish their own regime, which pledged loyalty to the captive Spanish king. (Ferdinand VII was being held prisoner in France.) After Ferdinand had been restored to the throne at the conclusion of the Napoleonic Wars, however, these same leaders refused to accept Spanish rule and declared formal independence as the United Provinces of the Rio de la Plata in 1816. Efforts to find a European who might accept the position as king failed, and Argentina promulgated a republican constitution in 1819. Despite severe domestic conflicts, external actors never played a sig-

[42] Rodriguez 1998, 2–4.
[43] Kinsbruner 1994, 91–92.

nificant role in the creation of the Argentine polity; political institutions and personnel were indigenously determined. Argentina was a Westphalian sovereign.[44]

Peru declared its independence in 1821 when San Martin, moving north from Chile, occupied Lima. The Spanish authorities fled to the interior and were completely defeated in 1824. Again, the institutional structure established in Peru was the result of local preferences.[45]

Venezuela formally declared its independence in 1811 after a revolt by the Creole elite. The Spanish, however, recaptured the country in 1812 and fighting continued. Bolivar, not the most effective of leaders, was unable to secure control of the country until 1821. The constitution that was adopted in 1821 was a product of local preferences. It established a republic with a bicameral legislature and a powerful president.[46]

The elite in Colombia first moved toward greater autonomy in 1810, setting up a highly decentralized governmental structure, after the position of royalist supporters in Spain collapsed. When Ferdinand VII returned to the throne, he sent a large force to Latin America, which initially succeeded in reestablishing colonial control in Colombia. In 1819, however, Bolivar defeated the Spanish and a republic was established. Bolivar was elected president in 1821.[47]

By 1825 Chile, Ecuador, and Peru had all secured their independence after fighting Spanish troops. Paraguay had earlier broken away from the United Provinces of Rio de la Plata, establishing itself as an independent entity in 1811. Despite internecine conflicts, institutional structures were internally constructed. Thus, by 1825 all of the Spanish colonies in South America—save Uruguay, which secured its independence in 1828 after having been annexed by Brazil—had become independent. They had all fought wars of national liberation. In all cases the basic constitutional structure, personnel, and specific institutional arrangements were determined by local leaders.

Brazil secured independence through a different path. When Napoleon captured Portugal in 1807, the royal family fled to Brazil. In 1815 King Joao established Brazil as a kingdom coequal with Portugal. He did not return to Europe until 1821 when his throne was threatened, but he left his son, Dom Pedro, as regent in Brazil. When the Portuguese government attempted to return Brazil to its subservient colonial status, including the reimposition of highly restrictive tariffs in 1822, the local elite declared independence and Dom Pedro joined them. Fighting was light.

---

[44] Lynch 1973, 39–79.
[45] Kinsbruner 1994, 75–76.
[46] Rodriguez 1998, 120–22, 84–192, 221–22.
[47] Kinsbruner 1994, 76–95.

Portugal was in no position to resist, and the new state adopted a monarchical regime with Dom Pedro as king. Britain immediately supported Brazilian independence, seeking both the continuation of commercial contacts and the abolition of the slave trade. The governing structure established in Brazil reflected the choices of Brazil's Creole elite.[48]

In Mexico, Napoleon's capture of Spain in 1808 precipitated internal conflicts among the Creole elite, and an Indian revolt led by Father Hidalgo. None of these developments, however, generated independence movements. Initially the local Mexican elite simply wanted more effective home rule. The liberal coup in Spain in 1820 touched off a new revolt in Mexico, and independence was declared in 1821. Mexico first established a monarchical government, with the local General Iturbide crowned emperor in 1822, but only after Spain refused to recognize the new regime, much less provide a royal head. Opposition to Iturbide grew, and in 1824 the government was reorganized as a republic. Constitutional outcomes in Mexico were the result of struggles among indigenous forces.[49]

The Central American countries, with the exception of Panama, all declared their independence in 1821. They were briefly annexed by Mexico, but when the imperial government of Iturbide fell apart, they formed a loose confederation and then became the independent states of Guatemala, Honduras, Costa Rica, Nicaragua, and El Salvador. The only effort at external imposition, Mexico's attempt to annex Central America in the early 1820s, failed.[50]

In sum, there are no examples of external imposition or coercion in Latin America during the first part of the nineteenth century with regard to basic institutional structures, although, as Chapters 4 and 5 show, Britain did coerce Brazil to give up the slave trade, and most Latin American states compromised their autonomy, or had it compromised for them, as a result of defaults on international loans. The major powers, here including the United States, never formed a condominium. During the Napoleonic Wars Britain opposed French claims to Latin America based on the conquest of part of the Iberian Peninsula, and after the wars the United States and Britain preferred independent Latin American states rather than a return to Spanish and Portuguese colonialism. In the British case the motivations were commercial (access to Latin American markets) and ideological (the abolition of slavery, especially in Brazil); in the American case they were ideological (support for republican government), commercial, and security. Moreover, indigenous leaders in the New World, in both North and South America, were able to mobilize enough domestic sup-

[48] Skidmore and Smith 1989, 35–36.
[49] Kinsbruner 1994, 95–97; Rodriguez 1998, 206–13; Lynch 1973, 318–26.
[50] Kinsbruner 1994, 97–98.

port to defeat militarily their colonial overlords. The state structures that developed in the successor states of the Spanish and Portuguese empires in the New World were consistent with the Westphalian model.

Central America, the Caribbean, and the United States

Developments in the Western Hemisphere conformed with the Westphalian model for most of the nineteenth century, but the rising power of the United States altered this situation. By 1900, after facing down the British in a confrontation in Venezuela in 1895, the United States had commandeered a sphere of influence in Central America and the Caribbean. No other major power could challenge its initiatives or offer credible assistance to rulers who were the targets of American intervention. American officials became directly involved in the domestic affairs of a number of smaller neighboring states.

Cuba became independent with the help of the American military. Spain was decisively defeated in 1898 and driven out of the Western Hemisphere as well as the Philippines. The war resolution had contained the Teller amendment, which declared that the United States would not annex Cuba. In 1901, however, the Platt amendment, attached to the Military Appropriations Act, stipulated the conditions under which the U.S. military would withdraw from Cuba, including a prohibition on Cuban transfer of land to any power other than the United States, limitations on Cuba's treaty-making power, a grant of a naval base at Guantanamo Bay, and the right of the United States to intervene to preserve Cuban independence. Cuba reluctantly incorporated the terms of the Platt amendment into its constitution. The amendment was also part of a formal treaty between the United States and Cuba which was signed in May 1903 and ratified by both governments in 1904. Some Cuban leaders had tried to alter the wording legitimating American intervention, but they were not successful.[51]

In 1906 the leaders of Cuba precipitated American military action by resigning from office following a period of civil strife. William Howard Taft, who had headed an American mission of inquiry in 1905, became the provisional governor, and he was succeeded by another American.[52] Troops were sent again in 1912 when internal disorder threatened American economic interests.

Cuba, like some of the successor states of the Ottoman Empire, experienced imposition. The would-be rulers of Cuba had to accept American

---

[51] Munro 1964, 25–30, 36; Langley 1989, 21.
[52] Munro 1964, 128–40.

conditions to get American troops off the island. They did not have enough power to resist. The option to not accepting the Platt amendment would have been nonexistence.

In the 1904 State of the Union Message Roosevelt articulated what came to be known as the Roosevelt corollary. He said: "Chronic wrong-doing or an impotence which results in a general loosening of the ties of civilized society, may in America as elsewhere ultimately require intervention by some civilized nation, and in the Western Hemisphere the adherence of the United States to the Monroe Doctrine may force the United States, however reluctantly, in flagrant cases of such wrong-doing or impotence to the exercise of an international police power."[53] Brezhnev articulated a similar doctrine with regard to the Soviet right to intervene in eastern Europe some sixty-five years later. The Westphalian model did not guide American relations with its small southern neighbors in the first part of the twentieth century.

Cuba was not the only Caribbean or Central American state that experienced American imposition. In 1911 the president sent 750 marines into the Dominican Republic to stifle civil disorder and forced the resignation of the government by threatening to cut off the short-term loans on which it depended. The United States occupied the Dominican Republic again in 1916, after political unrest, and declared martial law. The American commanding officer appointed U.S. officials as ministers of war and marine and of the interior, and as commanding officers of the national guard. Elections were suspended in 1917 and the press was censored. The occupiers reorganized and expanded the educational system.[54]

American troops landed in Haiti eight times between 1867 and 1900. As a result of pressure from the United States, American banks were included in the scheme for customs receivership that was established for Haiti in 1909–10. In 1915, in the midst of civil disorder, American rulers again sent in troops and also chose the new president. From 1915 to 1929 U.S. military tribunals made rulings on political cases. A treaty that provided for American control of customs and construction of roads, as well as supervision of schools and the constabulary, was approved by the Haitian legislature under threat that American troops would remain in the country. American officials dissolved the Haitian legislature when it refused to approve a new American-sponsored constitution, which was then ratified by a referendum supervised by the U.S. military. In 1919 the marines killed more than three thousand Haitians who were fighting against American rule.[55]

[53] Quoted in Langley 1989, 29.
[54] Langley 1989, 77–85; Munro 1964, 262–68.
[55] Langley 1989, 69–77.

Central America was also a target of American intervention. The area was fraught with both domestic and international conflicts. American rulers wanted to control any transisthmian canal and to limit European challenges to American economic interests largely in agriculture and railways. The United States supported rebel groups in Panama after the government of Colombia rejected its proposals for American control over a zone around the proposed canal.[56] In Honduras in 1911, the United States forced out the president and chose his successor. In 1910 the United States intervened in the Nicaraguan civil war. A hundred marines remained in the country until 1925, a tangible demonstration of the American commitment to the government. In 1916 U.S. officials effectively selected the president, Chamorro, after securing the Bryan Chamorro Treaty (1914), which gave the United States control over any canal that might be constructed in that country.[57]

In sum, once the United States had effected a sphere of influence in the Caribbean and Central America, violations of Westphalian principles were abundant. American rulers sent in troops, collected taxes, and appointed heads of government.

CONCLUSIONS

In the long nineteenth century new states emerged in two areas: the Balkans and the Western Hemisphere. The would-be rulers of these political entities were almost universally interested in securing international legal sovereignty. Recognition was a valuable resource and it carried few costs. Only in very rare cases did rulers consider giving up international legal sovereignty. Nicaragua's legislature asked that the country be annexed to the United States in 1822 when it confronted an invasion from Mexico, but the request became moot when Mexican troops occupied the capital. In 1849 El Salvador, Nicaragua, and Honduras were again confronted with invasion, and Nicaragua's ambassador in London asked the U.S. minister if the three countries might be admitted to the Union. He was rebuffed.[58] These efforts at amalgamation with the United States, or any other power for that matter, were exceptional.

While international legal sovereignty was widely embraced, Westphalian sovereignty in the nineteenth century was more problematic. Intervention was extensive in the Balkans. During the first part of the century, the major powers coerced the Porte into accepting new institutional arrangements for its Balkan holdings. When Greece secured recognition in 1832

---

[56] Langley 1989, 35–38.
[57] LaFeber 1983, 45–50; Munro 1964, 184, 208.
[58] LaFeber 1983, 25.

and Albania in 1913, and when Bulgaria became a tributary state of the Ottoman Empire in 1878, the major powers of Europe played a decisive role in determining their basic constitutional arrangements. The rulers of Montenegro, Serbia, and Romania were better able to secure their autonomy at least with respect to their basic form of government if not with regard to minority rights and economic policies.

Imposition and coercion characterized the situation in the Balkans because the major states of Europe had the power and interest to act. Britain, Russia, and Austria-Hungary had important security interests. The Ottoman Empire was collapsing and suffered a series of military defeats. The leading European states were able to form a condominium that made it impossible for the new Balkan entities to play one external power off against another.

The situation in the Western Hemisphere was radically different, at least until the creation of an American sphere of influence at the turn of the century. With limited assistance from Britain, Bolivar, Martin, and other South American leaders were able to defeat the armies of Spain. Brazil, by the end of the Napoleonic Wars, was larger and more powerful than Portugal. The United States announced the Monroe Doctrine and rejected any condominium with the European powers. The new states of the Western Hemisphere, including most notably the United States itself, were international legal and Westphalian sovereigns. The contrast with the situation in the Balkans during the same period is vivid. It was not any difference in principles—the norm of nonintervention had been articulated by the end of the eighteenth century—but rather variations in power and interest that explain the contrasting outcomes in the two areas.

Westphalian sovereignty was hardly, however, embedded in the Western Hemisphere. The United States established a sphere of influence in Central America and the Caribbean after defeating Spain in the Spanish-American War. The United States then proceeded to violate Westphalian principles with abandon, using military force to alter basic constitutional structures and to select leaders in a number of countries.

Throughout the long nineteenth century Westphalian sovereignty was challenged by alternative principles including minority rights, fiscal responsibility international stability, and what would later be called good governance. All were used to justify imposition and coercion with regard to basic institutional arrangements in other states. The variations in outcome between the Balkans and Central America and the Caribbean, on the one hand, and South America, on the other, were not the result of different principles but rather of different distributions of power and interest. A logic of consequences prevailed over a logic of appropriateness.

CHAPTER 7

Constitutional Structures and
New States after 1945

IN THE LAST HALF of the twentieth century as in the nineteenth, states
that were newly created or transformed by war varied across regions to
the extent that they conformed with the Westphalian model. In Europe
violations of autonomy were extensive, especially after the Second World
War when the United States and the Soviet Union influenced or determined the constitutional structures of many states within their respective
spheres of influence. In contrast, the rulers of the states that emerged from
the European imperial empires in the Third World after 1945 were generally able to establish their own institutional arrangements. These states
had few resources, but they were able to act autonomously because the
stakes were low for the major powers whose rulers were unable to establish
a condominium and only rarely accepted claims to spheres of influence by
their rival. External involvement remained significant only in the former
French colonies in Africa.

The conclusion of the Second World War ushered in momentous
changes in the global order. The Soviet Union and the United States were
the only military superpowers. Even victorious Britain found its circumstances severely diminished. The other European colonial powers had limited resources. France was resurrected as a major participant in the postwar
settlement only because of support from Britain and the United States.
Italy, which had switched sides in the middle of the war, lacked political
coherence and economic vitality. Germany was prostrate. The small states
in central Europe had been conquered, occupied, or intimidated first by
Nazi Germany and then by the Soviet Union. The distribution of power
was hierarchical with the two superpowers at the pinnacle, both in possession of formidable military capabilities, both championing coherent and
universal ideologies, and both with economic resources, although in this
arena the United States was much better endowed.

In Europe, superpower rivalry, coupled with the establishment of
spheres of influence, led to extensive violations of Westphalian sovereignty
with regard to basic institutional arrangements. At the same time, however, international legal sovereignty was honored with few exceptions,
such as the Western recognition of governments in exile for the Baltic
states that had been absorbed by the Soviet Union, and the membership
of Byelorussia and the Ukraine in the United Nations. The Soviet Union

imposed Communist regimes on the states of central Europe, but they remained formally independent territorial entities that were internationally recognized. American rulers sought to promote the development of democratic capitalist regimes in western Europe. As opposed to their counterparts in the Soviet Union, they operated primarily through contracting rather than imposition or coercion. They supported public and private actors in Europe whose preferences were complementary to their own, or who were at least determined to oppose communism.

The rulers of the Soviet Union and the United States regarded Europe as critically important for the security of their polities. Russia and the Soviet Union had been invaded twice in the twentieth century from the west. In 1914 there was no buffer between Germany and Russia. In 1941, Hitler broke the Nazi-Soviet pact and attacked his supposed ally. Stalin wanted above all to make sure that the regimes that governed the small central European states were friendly to the Soviet Union. The military conclusion of the Second World War, with Soviet troops occupying many countries and the tacit albeit begrudging acceptance by American leaders of a Soviet sphere of influence, made it possible for Stalin to intervene and impose his preferred regimes.

The leaders of the United States were also concerned about the constitutional arrangements of the European states, especially those in the West. Once it became evident that the wartime alliance had broken down, American rulers were determined to establish or support domestic regimes in western Europe that would be sympathetic to their objectives. Soviet domination of western Europe would have made one of the two centers of world industrial power (East Asia was later to become a third) hostile to the United States, threatening American interests. American policy makers were able to identify and support actors in many European countries who were happy to extend invitations to influence the domestic institutional arrangements of their polity. American rulers were able to deploy not only economic and military resources, but they also embodied values that were accorded legitimacy by at least some groups in western Europe. Communism enjoyed some support from groups in eastern Europe (and western Europe as well), but without the military backing of the Soviet Union it is doubtful that Marxism-Leninism would have prevailed except in Yugoslavia.

In contrast, the states that emerged from the European colonial empires conformed, with the exception of francophone Africa, to the basic rules of Westphalian as well as international legal sovereignty. While the end of empire imperiled the conceptions of national greatness embraced by some elites in Europe, decolonization did not affect the territorial or political integrity of any of the home countries; indeed the costs of fighting to retain imperial control undermined regime stability in France and

Portugal. The economic value of most colonies was limited. The military security of the United States and the Soviet Union was not threatened by developments in the former colonial empires. Neither superpower was willing to recognize a sphere of influence for the other in Asia or Africa. Even with local allies with whom contracts might be concluded, the costs of involvement could be prohibitively high as the United States experienced in Vietnam and the Soviet Union in Afghanistan. Only in the Western Hemisphere was the United States able to act unilaterally, and even here, as Cuba so well demonstrated, American rulers did not have a free hand.

The variation in behavior with regard to Westphalian sovereignty in Europe, as opposed to Africa and Asia, cannot be explained from a sociological perspective that emphasizes the embedded character of norms. Autonomy, at least with regard to constitutional structures, was honored in the Third World but violated in Europe, despite the fact that the major actors were the same. The variation was a function of the difference in power and interest. In Europe, both the Soviet Union and the United States were deeply concerned about their own security, and they were able to establish mutually recognized spheres of influence. In Africa and Asia the stakes were less and neither superpower was willing to recognize a sphere of influence for the other, nor were they able to act in concert. Violations of Westphalian sovereignty in some specific issue areas, notably sovereign lending, were commonplace, but foreign efforts to influence basic constitutional orders through intervention or invitation occurred with any regularity only in francophone Africa.

DECOLONIZATION

The Second World War accelerated the end of European formal control of overseas territories, even though none of the colonial powers was on the losing side. The leaders of both the Soviet Union and the United States opposed overseas empires. For the Soviets, decolonization was a way to weaken the position of the Western powers. For American rulers decolonization would both open economic opportunities and conform with ideological values. For the European colonial powers the burdens of holding their empires were increasing. Across Asia and Africa, nationalist movements were growing. Japan had conquered areas of Southeast Asia, breaking the administrative control of France in Indochina, the Netherlands in Indonesia, and Britain in Malaya. The participation of Africans and Asians in European armies had raised national awareness. Individuals from colonized areas were more highly educated. Economically, many colonies were becoming less important. The norms of international legal sovereignty were not, as Chapter 8 elaborates, taken for granted, but they did facilitate some kinds of outcomes, and the would-be rulers of colonial areas seized upon them and demanded juridical independence and mutual recognition. Perhaps surprisingly, given the limited material capabilities commanded by many of these rulers, their polities often conformed with the Westphalian model as well largely because more powerful actors were disinclined to intervene or, often, even to pursue invitations.

The British Empire

Britain shed its empire in several waves. At the end of the eighteenth century it lost the thirteen colonies. During the nineteenth and first half of the twentieth centuries Britain was, however, able to exercise considerable influence over developments in Canada, South Africa, New Zealand, Australia, and, to a lesser extent, Ireland through a process of negotiation and contracting that led to Dominion status in the British Commonwealth as an alternative to the Westphalian state. After the Second World War Britain gave up its colonies in Africa and Asia. Its attempts to maintain influence by contracting with local leaders regarding constitutional arrangements were largely unsuccessful as were its efforts to nurture the Commonwealth as an alternative institutional form. In only a small number of cases, where the local elite needed and would not be delegitimated by support from the former colonial master, were British rulers able to engage in contractual arrangements that gave them significant influence over basic political structures. In other areas British rulers were able, at best, to affect only transitional arrangements. Short-term successes in securing preferred British options, such as membership in the Commonwealth or specific constitutional choices, were often quickly reversed or proved to be of little consequence. Britain had neither the capabilities nor the interest in committing the level of resources that might have been needed to maintain significant influence. The basic institutional structures of the successor states to the British Empire after the Second World War were indigenously generated, even though the autonomy of many of these states in specific issues areas, most notably sovereign lending, was later compromised.

British rulers wanted to conserve their influence in the Indian subcontinent and to control its material and human resources, but they were unable to do so because of the impact of the Second World War, their loss of power (as a result of the increasing organization by indigenous groups in India as well as a reduction in British military and economic capabilities), and American as well as Soviet opposition to colonialism. They were resigned to conceding self- government but believed, or hoped, that India as a Dominion would cooperate on issues of commerce and trade and would contribute to the defense of the empire.

British efforts to manage the course of political and institutional change in India began long before formal independence in 1947. Recognizing rising nationalist sentiment, Britain established a legislative assembly in New Delhi in 1919. The 1935 Government of India Act gave additional power to elected provincial leaders in an attempt to weaken the Indian National Congress, which under Gandhi's leadership had been engaged in campaigns of civil disobedience. The British kept taxes low, deferred to religious practices, and slowed the pace of social change. Their principal focus, however, was institutional and constitutional design. London insisted that India would attain independence only as a federation, after union of the decentralized British India and the autonomous princely states. Such an amalgamation would force nationalists in the Congress to deal with the conservative leaders of the princely states as well as with the provincial governments, the civil service, and the army, all of which would serve as a brake on any postindependence realignment. London would remain India's primary creditor and the guarantor of its security vis-à-vis China, Russia, or Japan. Whitehall also expected that dominion status would preclude the abrupt withdrawal of all British personnel.[1]

World War II and its aftermath shattered this scenario. When Britain went to war in 1939, India followed automatically as a dependency of the crown. There was no consultation with Indian leaders. To ensure India's contribution to the war effort, British rule tightened. The British tried, but without success, to entice the cooperation of the Congress by promising to facilitate complete independence immediately after the war. In the search for local leaders who would cooperate, they cultivated ties with the enemies of the Congress, especially Jinnah's Muslim League, which was dedicated to the creation of a separate Muslim state and opposed to the Congress's plans for a united India under a strong central government. The war intensified opposition from the Congress and weakened the colonial administration. By the end of the war, India had become Britain's creditor, and the army and civil service had been dramatically Indianized due to a shortage of British personnel.[2]

After the war British efforts to impose or contract for desired institutional structures in the Indian subcontinent unraveled. Britain tried but failed to secure agreement on a federal structure. Relations between the Congress and the League worsened. The danger of a full-scale rebellion, which Britain would not be able to control, grew. The Labour government, under intense domestic pressure to avoid huge outlays, announced on February 20, 1947, its intention to hand over power to a representative Indian government (or governments, implying the possibility of partition)

---

[1] Darwin 1988, 82–86.
[2] Darwin 1988, 87–88.

by the middle of 1948, a timetable accelerated by Lord Mountbatten. India did become a member of the Commonwealth, but refused to recognize the British sovereign as head of state and applied to enter as a republic. Indian leaders felt no obligation to support British foreign policy—indeed, just the opposite. India became a leader of the nonaligned movement and severely criticized Britain's Suez adventure in 1956.[3]

In Burma, Britain had even less influence over postcolonial developments than was the case on the Indian subcontinent. Britain's plans for a gradual transition to dominion status were rejected by indigenous leaders. Burma was conquered by Japan and declared an independent state in 1943. By the time Britain regained control in the summer of 1945, the apparatus of British rule had been destroyed; the economy was in ruins; the towns were devastated; and private nationalist armies roamed the countryside. The most important forces were those of Aung San, a general who turned against the Japanese after it became clear they would lose the war. The British promised Burma rapid movement toward complete self-government in 1943 and 1945. After the war Aung San demanded full independence. In 1946 there was a strike by the police and public servants. The British government was not willing to commit the resources that would have been necessary to rule without local support. The Cabinet decided to offer immediate de facto Dominion status, but Burmese leaders rejected this proposal after Aung San was assassinated in 1947. In October 1947 Britain signed an independence treaty in London, recognizing Burma as an independent state.[4]

In West Africa Britain's efforts to influence postcolonial developments also had only very limited success. By the mid-1950s the British were anxious to extricate themselves but they hoped to do so on terms that would maintain British influence and secure local stability. In the Gold Coast, Britain confronted a local political machine organized by Kwame Nkrumah whose party, the Convention People's Party (CPP), won several elections beginning in 1951. Nkrumah organized a number of successful strikes, boycotts, and demonstrations in the early 1950s, taking advantage of economic dislocation, dissatisfaction among ex-servicemen and elementary school leavers who could not find nonmanual employment, and antagonism between traditional rulers supported by the British and a more Westernized middle class. At least before independence Nkrumah needed British support and the British saw him as the best hope for an easy transition. Independence was granted in 1957 and Nkrumah accepted membership in the Commonwealth and the rules of the Sterling Area. This was a mutually acceptable arrangement. British influence, however,

[3] McIntyre 1977, 370; Cross 1968, 240–44.
[4] Darwin 1988, 98–100.

rapidly declined. Nkrumah cast himself primarily as a leader of the pan-African movement, visited Communist bloc countries, introduced preventive detention, and castigated British imperialism. When Ghana, like other West African states deteriorated into military rule, Britain played virtually no role.[5]

In Nigeria, British leaders sought a graceful transition in a country that was deeply divided by ethnic and regional tensions. They feared fragmentation along ethnic lines and expected, erroneously as it turned out, that they would continue to have influence in a united postindependence Nigeria. The initial constitutional arrangements provided for three regions, each of which was dominated by a different ethnic group and political party. The British successfully pressed for the inclusion of a bill of rights in the 1957 constitution, a policy that was designed to reassure the two hundred or so small ethnic groups in the country. Nigeria made some modest foreign-policy concessions to Britain in the period immediately after independence in 1960, especially in recognizing the Federation of Rhodesia and Nyasaland. Economic and political ties with Britain, however, quickly became more attenuated. After the civil war of the mid-1960s Britain had essentially no influence on domestic institutional structures, and Nigeria followed a tortured path that included lengthy periods of arbitrary and repressive military rule. Unhappy though these developments were for the peace and prosperity of the Nigerian population, they were the result of indigenous developments. The principle of autonomy was not violated.[6]

Likewise, in the rest of West Africa developments were consistent with the Westphalian model. In the Cameroons, which was a trusteeship territory administered by France and Britain, the British Cameroons chose unification with the French part of the country in a UN-sponsored plebiscite in 1962. The French Cameroons had been granted independence in 1960. Sierre Leone and the Gambia, both much smaller colonies, were granted independence in 1961 and 1965 respectively. Once the more important West African territories had become independent, the British had no inclination to resist demands from even their smallest holdings. Developments throughout British West Africa were consistent with the Westphalian model. Britain was anxious to leave. Local elites were initially willing to accept British suggestions in some areas. British influence rapidly declined.

In much of East Africa, Britain's interest in influencing the course of postindependent developments was also limited. The British were anxious

---

[5] Darwin 1988, 174–79; Cross 1968, 325–27; Watson 1971, 151–56; Holland 1985, 212–20.

[6] Darwin 1988, 179–83, 303–4.

to get out of Somaliland, which had no strategic or economic significance, and were pleased when it merged with the former Italian trust territory. Britain granted independence to Tanganyika in 1961 even after its efforts to sponsor a more multiracial system were rejected by the electorate. Tanganyika did join the Commonwealth but withdrew in 1965 because of Britain's policy toward the white rebellion in Rhodesia. British officers dominated the army until 1964 when a military revolt, which forced Julius Nyerere, the country's leader, to call on British forces, led him to swiftly Africanize. Britain played a role in negotiating the 1962 constitutional provisions that led to a sharing of power in Uganda between different tribal groups, but this arrangement collapsed in 1966.

In Kenya and parts of central Africa the large white settler population posed a fundamental challenge. The whites wanted control. British leaders realized after the Second World War that stability was impossible without accommodation with the local population. They hoped to construct multiracial societies in Kenya and Rhodesia but ultimately failed. In Kenya in the 1950s the British jailed Jomo Kenyatta and unsuccessfully tried to repress the Kenya African Union, which he led. The Mau Mau movement galvanized some parts of the African population (and resulted in 95 European and 14,000 Kikuyu deaths), brought in British troops, and increased distrust between the white settlers and the British government. By the early 1960s divisions among various African ethnic groups were deep and the economy was deteriorating. British officials participated in all party negotiations for a postindependence constitutional structure, and helped to negotiate a federal structure and civil rights, which reassured the small tribal groups in the country, but the basic objective of British rulers was to get out without leaving too much of a mess. Continued control would have been costly and burdensome, and Harold Macmillan, the prime minister, wanted to project a new and more progressive image of the Conservative Party.[7]

During the 1950s Britain supported the Central African Federation, which joined Nyasaland, Southern Rhodesia, and Northern Rhodesia. This structure was a compromise with the white settlers who dominated Southern Rhodesia and wanted to further their already high level of autonomy from Britain. The federation gave whites political power far in excess of their numbers. Although it provided for some political protection for Africans and for the expansion of the franchise based on literacy and property ownership, the African populations, especially in Nyasaland and Northern Rhodesia, became increasingly restive. The British, searching for a new strategy, abandoned their support for the federation, and it was dissolved in 1963. Nyasaland became independent Malawi, and Northern

---

[7] Holland 1985, 236–48; Darwin 1988, 184–89, 262–69.

Rhodesia became independent Zambia in 1964, both with black majority rule. In Southern Rhodesia, where there were 300,000 whites, five times the number in Kenya, white nationalism proved more problematic for the British than African demands for independence. The white-dominated government of Southern Rhodesia declared unilateral independence in 1965. Britain did not coerce, impose, or even contract, although it did sponsor constitutional negotiations in 1979 and 1980 that led to the transition to an independent, internationally recognized, and African-ruled Zimbabwe in 1980.[8]

In southern Africa, Britain granted independence to the three High Commission Territories—Botswana, Lesotho, and Swaziland—in the late 1960s. The main concern of the indigenous leadership was to avoid annexation by South Africa, a goal that the British supported. There was no compromise of the constitutional structures, policies, or personnel of the successor regimes. Likewise, the Mauritius was granted independence in 1968, also with no real compromise of autonomy, although the new state did become a member of the Commonwealth.

Thus, in almost all of its former colonial territories including India, the largest and most important, Britain failed to influence significantly the constitutional structures of the postcolonial states. The indigenous leaders sometimes adopted British institutions, the most readily available script, although often these initial arrangements were short lived. There was little support in Britain for the use of military force to suppress nationalist rebellions. The Labour Party had not been sympathetic to Britain's imperial vision. At least some leaders of the Conservative Party, like Macmillan, wanted to establish a new identity. The United States opposed colonialism in general and feared that British resistance to nationalist movements would provide an opening for the Soviet Union, especially in Africa where events in the Congo and the Portuguese holdings alarmed American decision makers.

Only in a small number of cases, including Egypt in the 1920s and Jordan and Ceylon after the Second World War, did Britain engage in contractual arrangements that influenced basic institutional structures. The common characteristic of these three cases was the presence of a local elite that needed British support and would not be discredited by accepting it. In Egypt after the First World War the British were able to work out an institutional structure that satisfied their basic objectives, especially control of the Suez Canal, while at the same time limiting the costs of policing and administration. Under the Anglo-Egyptian Settlement of 1922 Britain agreed to end the protectorate, which had formally been established in 1914, and to cede control of domestic affairs, but it insisted

[8] Darwin 1988, 195–202, 269–78, 314–24; Ansprenger 1989, 184–97.

that Egypt recognize British rights of occupation, confirm Britain's advisory role in administration and finance, and grant it control of Egyptian foreign policy. As one colonial official quipped, "Why worry about the rind, if we can obtain the fruit?" The fruit in Egypt was "secure operation of the Suez canal passage, Egypt's anchorage within a British-orchestrated regional alliance and the efficient servicing of Egyptian foreign debts under negotiated terms."[9]

This settlement was stable for some three decades, through depression and war, but unraveled in the face of rising nationalist sentiments in the 1950s. The 1922 agreement, which had been restated in the 1936 Anglo-Egyptian Treaty, was abrogated in 1951. The monarchy, which had welcomed British support, was overthrown by a military coup in 1952 led by junior officers including Gamel Abdul Nasser, which had been catalyzed by widespread riots precipitated by British retaliation against Egyptian nationalist activity. Yielding to U.S. pressure, British rulers agreed in the autumn of 1954 to withdraw their troops from the canal zone, ending the "temporary occupation" begun in 1882. Nasser, however, reneged on the treaty and nationalized the Suez Canal in July 1956. In response, the British in October 1956 engineered an invasion by Israeli forces, followed a week later by troops from the United Kingdom and France. Amid widespread international condemnation and intense U.S. pressure (through its control of oil supplies and influence over the stability of sterling), Britain abandoned the operation, unilaterally withdrawing its troops by December.[10]

The failure of the Suez occupation of 1956 is an example of how difficult imposition is in the absence of great-power condominium or mutually recognized spheres of influence. The Americans were anxious about Soviet influence in the Arab world. The rulers of Britain, France, and Israel could not sustain their effort to overthrow the government of Egypt in the face of American opposition. Hence, Britain was able to direct constitutional arrangements in Egypt from 1922 until the mid 1950s, but only because it had a local interlocutor who welcomed British support.

After the Second World War Britain was able to influence constitutional arrangements in Jordan and Ceylon, again because a local elite needed and would not be delegitimated by external support. In Jordan, where the Palestine issue and the creation of a Jewish state confronted British rulers with nothing but uncomfortable choices, they were anxious to support a Hashemite monarchy. London moved quickly to cede formal independence in 1946. Abdallah was crowned king. British influence remained so extensive, especially in the military area, that the United States questioned

[9] Holland 1985, 17–18 (the quotation is from p. 18).
[10] Darwin 1988, 206–14.

Jordan's status and the Soviet Union was initially able to block Jordan's admission to the United Nations on the grounds that it was not sufficiently independent. Without strong British support, including a military alliance, Abdallah might not have been able to maintain his throne in the face of local opposition.[11]

In Ceylon, Britain was able to transfer power to conservative Sinhalese landowners who were fearful of India externally and of the Tamil and Indian minorities, as well as the Communist Party, domestically. The Communists had won 40 percent of the seats in the 1946 elections. Nationalist sentiments in Ceylon were weaker than in other parts of southern Asia. Unlike Burma, which was occupied during the war by the Japanese, the British had maintained control. Ceylon, which became independent in 1948, accepted membership in the Commonwealth. Constitutional arrangements were modeled on Westminister. The new government signed two agreements with Britain guaranteeing defense and foreign-policy cooperation. Britain secured extended control of a naval and an air base.[12]

In sum, the experiences of the states that emerged from British rule after the Second World War were for the most part consistent with the Westphalian model, even in cases where the new governments were hardly able to maintain their domestic sovereignty, understood as effective control over their own territory. The Westphalian model was not taken for granted; British rulers did attempt to engineer new institutional arrangements in the form of Dominion status within the Commonwealth, but this effort failed. Britain did not have the resources or inclination to resist nationalist forces. Domestic support for the empire was waning. The superpowers opposed colonialism.

The French Empire

Decolonization in the French empire began in the mid-1940s and ended with the conclusion of the Algerian war in 1962. In that interval some twenty-one French overseas territories gained independence, most in Africa (save the three successor states of Indochina). Only Haiti (1804), the Comoro Islands (1975), and Djibouti (1977) preceded or followed this burst of decolonization. France had limited success in designing the basic institutional structures of its former colonies but only in sub-Saharan Africa. In Indochina and Algeria, France was driven out by the armed resistance of indigenous groups. In Syria and Lebanon, mandates that France had been awarded after the First World War, local resistance and opposition from Britain and the United States ended French rule in the mid-

---

[11] Nevo 1996, 57–59; Wilson 1987, 145–48.
[12] Darwin 1988, 102–6.

1940s. In North Africa alone the variation in constitutional structures at independence is striking, with a monarchy in Morocco, a bourgeois oligarchy in Tunisia, and a socialist republic in Algeria. Only in sub-Saharan Africa, where local nationalist movements were weak and where the rulers of the newly independent states lacked resources, was France able to enter into contracts that gave it some influence over institutional arrangements, especially with regard to monetary affairs. France was also able to secure a privileged position in some specific issue areas, including military bases, access to raw materials, and trade regulations. As in the case of the British Commonwealth, however, French efforts to create an institutional form that would have provided an explicit alternative to Westphalian and international legal sovereignty, the French Community, failed as much because it was abandoned by de Gaulle as because it was resented by African rulers.

Before the Second World War France controlled two territories in the Middle East, Syria and Lebanon, which it held as mandates of the League of Nations. British and American forces occupied both in 1941, denying them to Vichy France and Nazi Germany, and gave the Free French formal authority. In 1941 the Free French representative in the region, in an effort to increase local support for France, declared that Syria and Lebanon would soon be independent and persuaded the provisional governments to restore the Syrian and Lebanese prewar constitutions and to hold elections. To the discomfort of the French, the elections were won by Lebanese nationalists who demanded immediate independence. In April 1945 De Gaulle sent three battalions to Syria and Lebanon in an effort to reassert French preeminence. The local population protested. A full-scale armed revolt broke out in Syria and hundreds of people were killed in Damascus and Homs after the French used artillery, mortar, and air strikes against Syrian nationalists. To restore order, the British with American support ordered all French units to return to their barracks. The French lacked the military strength to resist. The last French troops left Syria in April 1946 and in early 1947.[13] Lebanon and Syria became international legal sovereigns, founding members of the United Nations whose institutional structures were a result of developments that conformed with the Westphalian model.

In Indochina and North Africa, most emphatically in Vietnam and Algeria, French rule was ended by armed resistance from indigenous groups. During World War II France lost effective control of Indochina. French authorities were loyal to Vichy but governed only at the sufferance of the Japanese. In response to de Gaulle's appointment of a new French governor for the colony in 1945, the Japanese assumed direct control and en-

[13] Clayton 1994, 36–39; Betts 1991, 62.

couraged leaders in Vietnam, Laos, and Cambodia to declare independence. In Vietnam a civil war erupted and the Communists, led by Ho Chi Minh, seized Hanoi and declared Vietnam an independent state in September 1945. After a period in which the French and Vietnamese attempted to come to some mutual agreement, war broke out in 1946 in the northern part of the country. The French, attempting to reassert control by military force, killed as many as six thousand civilians in the first few days of fighting.[14]

Seeking some way to deal with rising nationalism, the French then attempted to develop the French Union as an alternative to international legal and Westphalian sovereignty, just as the British had attempted to use the Commonwealth and Dominion status in the same way. The Union would have given greater local autonomy to Vietnamese leaders but would have retained French control over foreign and defense policy and other major issues. Bao Dai, the Vietnamese emperor, signed an agreement promising adherence to the French Union in 1948 and France, in return, recognized Bao Dai as the leader of all of Vietnam. Boa Dai's rule depended on French support. Both Laos and Cambodia became full associate states of the French Union during 1949.[15]

French efforts to control events by developing an alternative to Westphalian and international legal sovereignty failed. The constitutional structures of the Indochinese states were determined by indigenous leaders. In 1954 the North Vietnamese surrounded the French garrison at Dien Bien Phu, prevented resupply from the air and forced the surrender of more than ten thousand French troops. The Americans, more anxious by the mid-1950s to defeat communism than to oppose colonialism, backed the French but refused to provide the air power that would have been needed to save France's military position. Support in France for continuing the war dissipated.[16]

The Paris accords of 1954 provided for a temporary boundary at the seventeenth parallel, free elections in the whole country, and withdrawal of North Vietnamese and French forces from Laos (although the French were allowed to keep two bases) and Cambodia, an example of a negotiated compromise of Westphalia, at least with regard to elections. The United States and the new government of South Vietnam, however, never signed. Monitoring provisions were weak. The elections were never held largely because it appeared that the North Vietnamese would win, by means of intimidation if necessary. Ho Chi Minh and his colleagues determined political institutions first in North Vietnam and later for the whole

---

[14] Betts 1991, 85–88; Clayton 1994, 20.
[15] Clayton 1994, 51.
[16] Clayton 1994, 69.

country, after the Americans withdrew and the South Vietnamese were overrun in 1975. Newly independent Vietnam was a fully Westphalian state.[17] Military power secured full autonomy. In the rest of Indochina, control spun out of American hands with the withdrawal of troops in the early 1970s.

In North Africa France faced a full-scale revolt in Algeria, where more than a million French nationals lived, as well as armed resistance in its two other dependencies in North Africa, Tunisia and Morocco, both of which were formally protectorates. Gabib Bourguiba, who led the nationalist movement in Tunisia, had been arrested twice by the French before the Second World War. After he returned in 1949, he attempted but failed to negotiate a mutually acceptable institutional structure and was placed under house arrest. Civil unrest and terrorist attacks followed. When Mendès-France, who was unsympathetic to colonialism, became premier in 1954, he reached a settlement with Bourguiba that provided for internal autonomy, but this was short-lived. Tunisian leaders continued to demand full independence. In 1956 France's rulers acceded, having decided that their military resources would be concentrated on holding Algeria. The domestic institutional structures of the new state reflected not external but indigenous preferences.[18]

In Morocco events unfolded in a similar fashion. The independence movement gained momentum after Roosevelt's January 1943 meeting with the sultan Mohammed Ben Yousef V at the Casablanca Conference. In January 1944 the Istiqlal (or Independence) Party was founded on a platform of national sovereignty and constitutional monarchy. For a decade after the conclusion of the Second World War, the French attempted to suppress the nationalist movement. At one point or another they outlawed the Istiqlal Party; exiled and deposed the sultan, who had led calls for independence; and cracked down on popular demonstrations. Bloody protests in 1955, however, compelled French officials to allow Mohammed V, by now a major nationalist hero, to return. Shortly thereafter France's leaders concluded that only by recognizing Morocco as an independent state could they hope to maintain any military presence or economic influence. Moroccan independence was recognized in March 1956 and Mohammed V converted the basic institutional arrangements from a sultanate to a kingdom in the following year. These were indigenous choices.[19]

France abandoned Morocco and Tunisia, hoping to hold on in Algeria, where the nationalist opposition was more intense and the domestic politi-

---

[17] Clayton 1994, 69–73, 77–78.
[18] Clayton 1994, 88–89; Betts 1991, 98–102.
[19] Betts 1991, 99–100; Clayton 1994, 93–103, 126; Hargreaves 1988, 151.

cal stakes higher because of the large settler population. Algerian leaders called for independence during the Second World War. Nationalists disrupted V-E celebrations in the western town of Setif, prompting a French response that led to thousands of deaths. Algerian nationalists launched an armed revolt on All Saints' Day in 1954: on November 1 the National Liberation Front (FLN) declared Algeria independent as its military arm, the National Liberation Army (ALN), attacked French troops.[20]

The war in Algeria became a central issue for French domestic politics. It was expensive. The left, both the Socialists and Communists, opposed colonialism. The Battle of Algiers, a bloody conflict, was condemned by many in France. The Fourth French Republic was immobilized. In May 1958 colons in Algeria seized government buildings. Sympathetic French paratroopers did nothing. A military coup was in the offing. On June 1, 1958, the National Assembly invited de Gaulle to return to power as premier. The Fourth French Republic came to an end.[21]

Under de Gaulle's leadership the military situation at first improved, and he sought a compromise solution in which Algeria would remain in some way associated with France, an alternative to the Westphalian model. The settlers, however, rejected efforts at compromise. In 1960 de Gaulle endorsed a referendum, which produced a vote in favor of Algerian independence in both France and Algeria and touched off an ultimately unsuccessful mutiny in part of the army and further terrorists activities by disaffected military officers and the colons.[22]

In 1962 French leaders entered into negotiations that led to an independent Algeria.[23] Though he sought a permanent guarantee for the French minority, de Gaulle accepted civic protections that were to last only three years, after which French nationals could choose to become Algerian citizens. Those transitional guarantees, which one analyst has judged "in practice valueless," included "full civic rights, political representation in proportion to their numbers, special safeguards in Algiers and Oran, special courts, dual nationality for three years, and a promise of no expropriation of property without indemnity."[24] These protections were in effect nullified by the frantic exodus of most French residents well before the three years had passed.

France also secured some concessions in specific policy areas as opposed to issues related to basic constitutional structures, but they were transitory. France received a fifteen-year lease for the Mers-el-Kebir air base but with-

---

[20] Clayton 1994, 119–20; Betts 1991, 97–98, 104–6.
[21] Clayton 1994, 134–43, 146–45; Betts 1991, 107–8.
[22] Betts 1991, 109–12; Clayton 1994, 162–67.
[23] Hargreaves 1988, 170.
[24] Clayton 1994, 173.

drew within six years. The Evian agreement provided for the continuation of French nuclear tests in the Sahara but domestic and international pressure forced an end to these trials after four years. French oil companies were given some modest advantages with regard to the exploitation of Algeria's hydrocarbon resources.[25]

Hence basic institutional structures in Algeria, like those in Tunisia and Morocco, were not significantly affected by the preferences of French leaders, although Algeria's rulers did make some concessions with regard to protections for French settlers and oil exploitation in the Sahara. It was not through lack of effort or imagination that France failed to compromise the Westphalian model in North Africa. Numerous alternatives were explored, but French leaders lacked the military resources and domestic and international support that would have been necessary to maintain French control or instantiate some alternative to the Westphalian model.

The successor states to the French Empire in sub-Saharan Africa were poor, sparsely populated, and of limited consequence for the international system. Independence movements were weak; in only a few places were they highly organized, much less armed.[26] Here France had greater success in compromising domestic autonomy.

In the later 1950s, de Gaulle advanced an institutional alternative to the Westphalian model, the French Community. The community would have given francophone Africa more local autonomy, but critical issue areas including foreign policy, monetary affairs, raw materials exploitation, justice, telecommunications, international transport, and higher education would have been effectively under French control. The president of the French Community would also have been the president of France; the community's council of ministers would have been chaired by the premier of France. In September 1958 all of the African territories in Africa save Guinea (whose leader, Sekou Toure, wanted full independence) voted to join the French Community rather than secure immediate independence and the total loss of French support.[27]

De Gaulle, however, abandoned the idea of the French Community shortly thereafter, judging that French interests would be better served in an Africa of independent states that relied on French resources than in a French Community within which France might have to bear unwanted burdens. The French Community was replaced by a set of contractual arrangements that gave France a privileged position in its former colonies, in some cases including stipulations regarding basic institutional arrange-

---

[25] Hargreaves 1988, 169–71; Betts 1991, 112–13; Clayton 1994, 170–75.

[26] Hargreaves 1979, 21; Hargreaves, 1988, 92–93, 140–42; Clayton 1994, 180; Chipman 1989, 97–98, 123–24; Betts 1991, 119–20.

[27] Chipman 1989, 103–7; Betts 1991, 123–25; Hargreaves 1988, 172–73.

ments, such as justice and monetary affairs, in exchange for military, economic, and technical support. France also secured base rights, priority in the purchase of raw materials, and special access for French products.[28]

France linked the independence and the cooperation agreements. To the leader of Gabon, for example, de Gaulle's Premier, Michel Debre, wrote on June 15, 1960: "We give independence on the condition that the state once independent engages itself to respect the cooperation agreements it first signs. There are two systems that come into play at the same time: Independence and cooperation agreements. . . . I will be obliged if you would please, in acknowledging receipt of this communication, confirm to me that on the proclamation of independence by the Republic of Gabon, the government of the Gabonese Republic will proceed to the signature of cooperation agreements."[29] Several states defied this direct linkage, but eventually leaders in all fourteen African colonies and Madagascar entered into contractual arrangements with France that lasted for at least a decade and in many cases for much longer, in part because African rulers relied on the French military to keep them in office.[30]

These contracts were departures from the Westphalian model, especially in their military and economic dimensions, but they were consistent with international legal sovereignty. The presence of French bases, the reliance on French troops to maintain internal order, the commitment of strategic raw materials to French use, and the linkage of national currencies to the French franc all compromised the autonomy of the new francophone African states. The rulers of these states were willing to extend an invitation that undermined their autonomy because of their reliance on French economic and military support.

In sum, the extent to which the successor states of the French empire conformed with the Westphalian model varied. In the Middle East the strength of local resistance movements coupled with British and American opposition to continued French rule led to fully autonomous regimes in Syria and Lebanon. In North Africa, confronted with fierce nationalist resistance, France lacked the resources either to impose or to contract for constraints on the basic institutional structures of Tunisia, Morocco, and Algeria, although in the last case some modest temporary concessions were secured regarding the rights of French settlers. In sub-Saharan Africa, however, France had greater leverage. Although de Gaulle abandoned efforts to create a French Community that would have offered an alternative

---

[28] Chipman 1989, 29, 86, 107; Hargreaves 1988, 172; Betts 1991, 123–26.
[29] Chipman 1989, 108.
[30] Chipman 1989, 107–9, 123–25, 128–29.

to Westphalian and international legal sovereignty, he was able to enter into contractual arrangements with the rulers of almost all of the newly independent francophone African states, agreements that in some cases allowed France to influence basic institutional structures, especially with regard to monetary and financial affairs.

Hence, postcolonial developments in the British and French successor states (and most of the successor states to other European empires as well) generally conform with the Westphalian model. Robert Jackson, one of the most interesting analysts of the English school, has pointed to this as evidence for the significance of international norms. The ex-colonial areas became states despite having limited resources and often limited control over their own domestic territory.[31] These states conformed not only with the international legal concept of sovereignty, since recognition meant that they could enter into agreements with other international actors, but to a large extent with the Westphalian model as well. In issue areas where their autonomy was compromised, as was the case in sovereign lending, it was not the result of the influence of the former colonial rulers. Both the British Commonwealth and the French Community failed to develop as alternatives to Westphalian and international legal sovereignty. Although there was a small number of exceptions, mostly in francophone Africa, the basic institutional structures of most of the new states were indigenously determined.

If the Third World is examined in isolation, events suggest that both international legal sovereignty and Westphalian sovereignty are embedded, although not taken for granted (because the British and French did conceive of and unsuccessfully try to implement alternatives). If, however, the geographic scope of analysis is extended to Europe, this conclusion cannot be sustained. In Europe the Westphalian model provides no understanding of the political structures that developed after the Second World War. The rulers of the United States, the Soviet Union, and many European states violated the principle of autonomy through conventions, contracting, coercion, and imposition.

Given that Westphalian principles were honored in some areas but violated in others, they cannot be embedded. Rather, the Westphalian model is an example of organized hypocrisy; it has been enduring, but it has not necessarily been constraining. Norms have been decoupled from behavior, which has been motivated by power or interest or guided by principles that have been inconsistent with Westphalian autonomy. In cases of contracting, the interests of rulers in different states were served by mutual agreements that violated autonomy, a situation that characterized Ameri-

---

[31] Jackson and Rosberg 1982, 2; Jackson 1990, 90.

can involvement in western Europe. In eastern Europe, differences in power and interests resulted in the Soviet use of imposition and coercion to establish preferred regime types. Looking at the decolonization experience alone gives a misleading picture of the extent to which the Westphalian model has been institutionalized.

EUROPE DURING THE COLD WAR

Europe was the focus of the political struggle between the Soviet Union and the United States after the Second World War. Their domestic political and economic structures were informed by radically different political ideologies. The rulers in both countries were determined to reproduce their preferred political structures in those states in Europe that fell within their respective spheres of influence. The Westphalian model was hardly worth a nod. In western Europe, the United States operated largely through contractual arrangements with sympathetic indigenous leaders, although in Germany its position as an occupying power provided it with opportunities for coercive leverage as well. In eastern Europe, the Soviet Union pursued a more complicated strategy, using imposition to establish and maintain Communist regimes, but later engaging in contractual relationships with Communist rulers in the satellite states who, nevertheless, remained dependent on the Soviet army for their survival.[32]

Unlike Africa and most of the rest of the colonial world, Europe mattered. It affected the economic and security objectives of the two major powers, and their ideological values as well. These powerful material interests and ideational concerns provided reasons for violating the Westphalian model. Both the Soviet Union and the United States sought to influence, indeed determine, the domestic authority structures of the states of both eastern and western Europe.

Violations of the Westphalian model did not, however, imply that the international legal concept of sovereignty was ignored or inconsequential. International legal sovereignty could serve the interests of the powerful even in situations where the rulers of the weaker state were given only the most limited autonomy, or policy discretion. International legal sovereignty provided a mechanism through which the rulers of the most powerful states could pursue their interests by engaging the support or compelling the acquiescence of their most compromised colleagues without at the same time bearing the direct costs of governance.[33] Providing a ruler with the right to enter into a contract, even if that ruler was deeply depen-

---

[32] Lake 1996, 1, also notes the difference between Soviet and American strategy.

[33] Lake (1996, 1999) has been particularly emphatic in noting the importance of governance costs as a factor in determining the strategies of powerful states.

dent on foreign support as was the case in most of eastern Europe, was more attractive for the strong than other institutional alternatives. For the rulers of weak states, having international legal sovereignty was better than not having it, even if the kinds of agreements that they could enter into, and indeed their ability to determine their own domestic regimes, were severely constrained.

At the conclusion of the war, Soviet troops occupied much of eastern Europe. Stalin had a number of options. He could annex territory to the Soviet Union, a step he took by taking parts of Germany, Poland, and Romania as he had done by making the Baltic states republics of the Union of Soviet Socialist Republics at the beginning of the war. Their international legal as well as their Westphalian sovereignty was crushed. Stalin could have created a supranational organization, a path that was not seriously pursued at all because annexation or compromised autonomy could satisfy Soviet objectives without the expense of constructing and monitoring a new institutional form.[34] He could have accepted the de facto as well as de jure autonomy of the rulers of eastern Europe as the Europeans later did in their ex-colonial holdings in most of Asia and Africa, but autonomy was unacceptable because the Soviet leaders believed that the security of the USSR could only be assured if the eastern European states were controlled by friendly governments, and only Communist governments could provide this assurance, and Communist governments could only be guaranteed by compromising Westphalia. Hence, Stalin accepted the international legal sovereignty of the eastern European states but violated their Westphalian sovereignty.

American options were more constrained; annexation was not a possibility because it would have been rejected by constituents on both sides of the Atlantic. U.S. rulers did, however, seek to influence the domestic political structures of the western European states. They also, much more vigorously than their Soviet counterparts, supported the creation of supranational institutions, beginning with the Organization for European Economic Cooperation (OEEC) in 1947. This process culminated with the signing of the Treaty of Rome in 1957, the first step in the creation of the European Union, an institutional form that compromises both the autonomy and territoriality of existing states. Supranationalism in western Europe was accomplished through self-enforcing contracts.

The Americans, like their Soviet counterparts, had no compunction about violating the autonomy of western European states to promote re-

---

[34] Alternative supranational institutions were not, however, entirely ignored. In 1945 Kardelj, one of the leaders of the Yugoslavian Communist Party suggested that the Soviet Union should think of Yugoslavia not as an independent country but as part of the "All-Union Communist Party." In the future Yugoslavia could become part of the USSR. See Brzezinski 1967, 39.

gimes that were consistent with their values and preferences. American rulers had a less arduous task than their Soviet counterparts because there was more support for democracy and capitalism in western Europe than there was for communism in eastern Europe. The Americans had the option of contracting; at least initially, the Soviets had to use coercion and imposition, although once Communist regimes were in place they too contracted with local rulers. Hence, in Europe, as opposed to the postcolonial world, violations of the Westphalian model were pervasive. Moreover, the Americans in alliance with many Europeans promoted supranational institutions that were inconsistent with Westphalian sovereignty.

The United States and Western Europe

At the conclusion of the war in Europe, American policy was far from set. Roosevelt and his successor, Harry Truman, hoped for cooperation with the Soviet Union. There was no domestic support for maintaining a large American force overseas, nor were the Americans prepared to provide much in the way of financial resources. The World Bank and the International Monetary Fund, for instance, had been created with only modest levels of capital in accord with the preferences of American leaders. Plans for deindustrializing Germany, pushed by Secretary of the Treasury Henry Morgenthau, had received widespread attention and support, but were opposed by many officials, especially in the State and War departments. As conflict with the Soviet Union grew, however, hardening into the cold war in the winter of 1947, a division brilliantly captured in Churchill's 1946 phrase that "an iron curtain" had descended across Europe, American policy makers formulated a coherent strategy for countering the Soviet threat and promoting American interests. They were determined to create democratic regimes that would respect private property and the free market, even if politicians also embraced social democracy. Through the Marshall Plan and other measures, they provided American support for European domestic actors who shared these goals. Above all they sought to block the expansion of communism in western Europe and to frustrate any Communist Party participation in governing coalitions. In Italy, France, Belgium, Norway, and Denmark the position of American decision makers was that only a cohesive government coalition could initiate effective government policy, and therefore receive American aid and participate in the Marshall Plan, and such a coalition could not include Communists.[35]

Hence, American interests were promoted by efforts to influence the domestic political structures of the states of western Europe, not just to alter the policies that the rulers of these states would pursue. (For the

[35] Poggiolini 1994, 131; Knapp 1981, 47; Duignan and Gann 1994, 40.

question of Westphalian sovereignty addressed in this study it is immaterial whether these goals were motivated by a desire to protect world capitalism and American business, which revisionist historians have emphasized, or antipathy to an assertive Communist movement and aggressive Soviet Union, which traditional analysts have focused on.) Had American policy been constrained by the Westphalian model, it would have been very different and so, for that matter, would the choices of many western European politicians. In a Westphalian world American rulers would have tried to change the foreign policies of other states not to influence their domestic structures. In an anarchic system, however, there was nothing to prevent American decision makers and their European counterparts from embracing strategies designed to promote particular institutional arrangements in the countries of western Europe.

Italy was a focus of American attention during the 1940s. Allied troops invaded southern Italy in 1943. The armistice that was signed in September of that year was close to an unconditional surrender. The Control Commission, run by the British and Americans, could veto any Italian government initiative. In 1944 Britain, for instance, rejected Carlo Sforza as foreign minister because it viewed him as unsympathetic to the monarchy, which Britain was supporting. The Italian government agreed to break relations with Germany, surrender war criminals to the allies, suppress fascist ideology, release political prisoners, and repeal racist legislation. Both the international legal sovereignty and the Westphalian sovereignty of Italy were compromised until a peace treaty was signed in 1947, hardly a surprising situation in a former enemy state now occupied by its conquerors.[36]

Even while fighting continued, the allies took a strong interest in the nature of the Italian government and institutions. They wanted individuals with whom they could deal and structures that were consistent with their preferences. By 1944 the objective of American rulers was to create a democratic government in Italy along the lines of the Anglo-Saxon model, although they did not have the resources simply to impose their most desired outcomes. American officials had to choose allies within Italy. They were unable to purge the civilian and military bureaucracies of fascist collaborators. The United States supported the Bonomi government because it was seen as most sympathetic to the U.S. position. Badoglio, the prime minister who took over after Mussolini was deposed, had been forced to resign in June 1944, as had the king, although the fate of the monarchy as an institution had not been decided. In 1944 the British and Americans were prepared to use military force should the Italian resistance in the south, which was dominated by Communists, attempt to overthrow

---

[36] J. Miller 1986, 57; Poggiolini 1994, 121–43.

the interim government although no such effort ever took place, and To-
gliatti, the Italian Communist leader, agreed to join the government after
returning from Moscow.[37]

When the war ended in Europe, however, the Americans had less interest and even less to offer Italy. American conservatives opposed foreign
aid. Business was unwilling to invest in a country that was still so unstable.
In 1946 a referendum, supported by the United States, abolished the monarchy. Neither the British nor the Americans intervened directly in the
voting. In elections for Parliament held at the same time, the Christian
Democrats won 207 seats; the Socialists, 115; the Communists, 104; and
the right-wing Uomo Qualunque, 30.[38]

American interest in Italy, however, was revived by the fear of communism, the break with the Soviet Union, and the possibility of a Communist
guerrilla victory in Greece. The Italian Communist Party was the most
powerful in western Europe and was able to spend substantial sums on
electoral campaigns. The Italian ambassador to the United States warned
of the possibility of a takeover, and the American ambassador in Italy ca-
bled that the forces of democracy and communism were precariously balanced and that American aid was critical. From 1947 to 1949 and even
into the 1950s, the United States, with its Italian allies, worked to marginalize the Communists, and to make Italy a full participant in the Marshall
Plan and the Atlantic Alliance, external commitments that were contingent on domestic political configurations. The United States provided
large amounts of assistance from 1947 to 1949.[39]

The Americans indicated in April 1947 that they were prepared to aid
Italy, but only if the Communists were excluded from the government.
With the development of the Marshall Plan and other initiatives, the
United States had something to offer. By May 1947 Secretary of State
George Marshall was alarmed by deteriorating conditions in Italy, which,
he believed, "would further increase Communist strength" and worsen
the "situation of moderate elements." Marshall asked the American ambassador "what pol and eco steps if any this Govt should and could take
towards strengthening democratic, pro-US forces. [*sic*]." He approved a
policy to support a Christian Democratic government in which "Communist participation is reduced to minimum," with trade and civil aviation
agreements, aid, Exim bank loans, the return of frozen Italian assets, and
assistance from the French and British. The Americans publicly endorsed
the Christian Democrats led by De Gasperi and encouraged him to push

[37] J. Miller 1986: 132–33, 138.
[38] Miller 1986, 189.
[39] United States, FRUS (1947, vol. 3) 1972, 904–05, 923; J. Miller 1986, xi; Duignan
and Gann 1994, 83.

the Communists out of his coalition. De Gasperi formed a new government that excluded the Communists but, to his embarrassment and that
of the United States, required the support of neofascists.[40] American policy
was not constrained by the Westphalian model, which would have precluded American efforts to alter domestic political conditions in Italy.

Fearing a Communist electoral victory in the 1948 elections, American
leaders increased aid to De Gasperi's government, authorized plans for a
military intervention should a De Gasperi victory touch off a Communist
insurrection, mounted a public relations campaign to convince the Italians
that American aid was critical for Italy's economic success, tried to weaken
Communist control of the labor movement, approved continued military
support for the Italian armed forces, and sought British and French help
in efforts to provide Italy with diplomatic successes that would strengthen
the Christian Democrats. The National Security Council (NSC) authorized the newly established Central Intelligence Agency to launder over $10
million in captured funds that could be covertly provided to the Christian
Democrats and center-left parties. The United States gained support for
a treaty that guaranteed the eventual return of Trieste to Italy. In March
American officials announced that they would terminate Marshall Plan aid
to Italy if the Communists won the election. At least in part because of
American support, anti-Communists forces won a resounding victory in
the April 1948 elections. The Christian Democrats won 48 percent of the
popular vote and increased their parliamentary deputies from 104 to 141.
The Socialists and Social Democrats lost seats. The Communists remained
the largest party on the left.[41]

American efforts to influence domestic political structures and policies
in Italy were contracts with the Christian Democrats. De Gasperi and his
colleagues invited American involvement in Italy's domestic affairs. U.S.
leaders could not dictate their preferences. They recognized the genuine
support enjoyed by the left, including the Communists. Direct military
intervention and occupation might have been precluded by domestic political sentiments and would have been extremely costly. The Americans
needed Italian partners.[42]

After the 1948 Christian Democratic electoral victory, American leaders
hoped to consolidate anti-Communist sentiment through reform programs that would appeal to the working class, but the De Gasperi government did not go along. American suggestions for more expansionist macroeconomic policies were rejected. Keynesian initiatives were never

---

[40] J. Miller 1986, 226–33; Poggiolini 1994, 131; United States, FRUS (1947, vol. 3)
1972, 909–11 (the quotations are from pp. 889 and 909).

[41] J. Miller 1986, 246–48, 249, 255–63; Zegart 1996, chap. 9.

[42] J. Miller 1986, 243–46, 249.

attractive in Italy in part because of an antifascist intellectual tradition that was antipathetic to state manipulation of the economy.[43]

The United States tried but failed to break Communist control over the labor movement in Italy. The CIO and AFL supported dissident groups. Anti-Communist Italian labor leaders visited the United States in April 1949 and met with Truman. The Communist-dominated CGIL, however, remained the largest labor union in Italy. Likewise attempts to develop a more coherent anti-Communist left by supporting dissident groups in the Italian Social Party also failed and the leaders of a weakened Socialist Party continued to be willing to work with the Communists.[44]

De Gasperi cultivated the relationship with the United States to promote his own objectives. Identification with American policies helped to create an ideological rationale for the Christian Democrats. He strengthened the position of the party by having its officials dispense the resources of the state (partly supplied by the Americans) to different constituencies. Fearing capital flight, the Christian Democrats catered to financial interests and large industrialists. De Gasperi and his colleagues were willing to compromise Italy's Westphalian sovereignty so that they could strengthen their domestic position and be integrated into the American dominated international structure.[45]

In sum, American leaders were deeply involved in efforts to influence the development of domestic structures, policies, and personnel in Italy after the Second World War, especially in the critical period beginning with 1947. The Westphalian model did not constrain U.S. rulers, nor their Italian interlocutors. The Americans offered political, financial, military, and ideological resources to the Christian Democrats, who were willing to accept these arrangements largely because they conformed with their own preferences and because they could enhance their chances to rule Italy.

None of the major powers, and certainly neither the United States nor the Soviet Union, was prepared to allow Germans a free hand in developing their own domestic institutional arrangements. The victors all wanted a new Germany, although exactly what that new Germany would be was deeply disputed. Despite, however, the devastation left by the war, the winners were not able to simply impose their preferences. They had to find local allies. This was easier for the Americans and the British than for the Soviets, and it was more attractive, therefore, for the Americans to engage in contracting than it was for Soviet leaders. The Americans pushed to create a Germany in the American image, a project that enjoyed sub-

---

[43] J. Miller 1986, 250–55; Duignan and Gann 1994, 84; P. Hall 1989.
[44] J. Miller 1986, 255–66.
[45] D'Attorre 1981, 79, 81, 87.

stantial although not complete success because it was coincident with the goals of some postwar German leaders, especially Conrad Adenauer and his Christian Democrats. Power, interests, and national values, not the Westphalian model, influenced the behavior of actors.

The costs of direct control led both the Americans and the Soviets to accept international legal sovereignty, that is, to recognize entities—the Germany Democratic Republic and the Federal Republic of Germany—with which they would enter into international agreements, even if they constrained the form these agreements could take. The Soviets used force to preserve Communist control in East Germany. The Americans might also have used force, as they did overtly in Korea and Vietnam and covertly elsewhere, had they been confronted with the threat of a Communist take-over in West Germany.

During the war itself, American plans for postwar policy in Germany were disputed. Secretary of the Treasury Morgenthau advocated deindustrialization, and he received a sympathetic ear from Roosevelt. A policy of deindustrialization would have allowed the Americans to marginalize anyone who had been complicitous with the Nazis. Morgenthau's policies, however, were abandoned in the face of the devastation following the war and the burden of supporting the German population. Moreover, impoverishing Germany might have made communism more attractive. Hence, within a couple of years after the end of the war American attention was focused on rebuilding Germany as a democratic and capitalist country. This inevitably meant relying on existing personnel and structures. The Germans by stalling, resistance, or protest, as well as through legal competence accorded by the occupying powers, always played an active role in the postwar restructuring of their country.[46]

U.S. policy in Germany was based on contractual arrangements with indigenous actors who had domestic support. Despite some disagreements, the Americans were able to find German counterparts who were opposed to communism, supported European integration, and advocated a free-market economy. It was easier to find allies because the Second World War itself had a shattering effect on existing German society. While some German leaders clung to the hope, even after the war, that Germany could assume a neutral position, bridging east and west in terms of both external policies and domestic structures, the cold war, and especially the Berlin blockade, made it evident that this was not a viable option. John J. McCloy, who became the American high commissioner in 1949 believed that he had to support Conrad Adenauer, the leader of the Christian Democrats; he understood that he could not simply dictate to the Germans.

[46] Ermarth 1993, 10–13; Fichter 1981, 106.

American policy could only work if it had the support, or at least the tacit acceptance, of the Germany population.[47]

Under the terms of the occupation statute that created the West German state in 1949, the allied powers retained supreme authority as well as specific authority over foreign trade and exchange, demilitarization, and foreign affairs including international agreements made on behalf of Germany. The German state established in 1949 did not have sovereignty in either the Westphalian or the international legal sense. Germany was not recognized as an independent state until 1955, and even then its situation was ambiguous.[48]

The Americans pursued a variety of objectives in Germany regarding institutional structures, policies, and personnel, all of which were problematic in terms of the Westphalian model. American officials insisted on a federal structure for the new western German state. Many Germans would have preferred a more centralized state. The Americans wanted an industrialized Germany that could participate in an open international economic order. American leaders were antipathetic to state ownership of industry, a policy supported by many inside and outside Germany. Marshall Plan aid made it easier for Ludwig Erhard, who was the director of administration in the American sector and later designated by the Americans to be the first economics minister in Germany, to pursue the free-market policies that he himself believed in. American leaders were also largely successful in their efforts to break up the monopoly structure of German industry. For instance, in the chemical sector I.G. Farben, which had monopolized the German market, was divided up and an oligopolistic structure with Bayer, Hoechst, BASF, and Casella emerged. This change was supported by German actors and was not just forced by the United States.[49]

American leaders wanted German economic integration into Europe, a preference shared by Adenauer and the Christian Democrats, although not by all Germans. The Americans insisted on cooperation in the administration of Marshall Plan aid and created the Organization for European Economic Cooperation. Germany became a member. In 1949 the United States, Britain, France, and the Benelux established an international authority to control the output of the Ruhr industrial region. Germany was given three of fifteen votes, but they were to be cast by the occupying authorities until a government was established. Adenauer supported Ger-

---

[47] Woller 1993, 27–29, 33; Berghahn 1993, 90–100; Schwartz 1993, 37; Jonas 1984, 293–94; Knapp 1981, 46.

[48] Jonas 1984, 86–87, 290–92. For a fuller discussion of West Germany's international legal status from 1955 until reunification, see Chapter 8.

[49] Berghahn 1993, 88–89; Jonas 1984, 285; Knapp 1981, 48.

man participation in the Ruhr authority, as well as German membership in the Council of Europe, policies for which he was chastised by his political opponents for abandoning German sovereignty over the Ruhr and for joining an international organization that might oppose German reunification. Adenauer's position, however, was strengthened by support he received from the United States, including the right to resume consular relations with other countries, to increase shipbuilding capacity, and to sign an economic agreement with the United States.[50]

In other policy areas, however, the Americans were less successful. American efforts to change cultural policies and restructure the educational system were resisted, especially in Bavaria. American rulers wanted a union movement that mirrored that of the United States, and representatives of the American labor movement were active in Germany after the war. The Americans vetoed codetermination, in which labor played an active role in management decisions, during the occupation. These efforts, however, ultimately failed, and the German labor movement emerged as more centralized, more concerned with general economic issues, and more engaged in firm decision making through codetermination than the Americans would have preferred.

Likewise in banking, the Americans attempted to create a structure that mirrored that of the United States with a decentralized *Länder*-based organization of financial institutions. They forced decentralization during the occupation, but were opposed by the British during the immediate postwar years and, more importantly, by the German banks which prevailed in the long run. Recentralization began in 1952 even during the period when the allies still formally retained final authority over German policies. The Korean War had begun and the Americans needed German support. The Americans never succeeded in creating a group of local allies in Germany who were strong enough to maintain the decentralization of the banking system in the long run.[51]

Hence, American policy in Germany during the postwar period was designed to restructure the nature of Germany's domestic polity. The Westphalian principle of autonomy was irrelevant during the occupation period, but, like the minority rights conditions that were set for the recognition of the Balkan states at Berlin in 1878 and all of the smaller states in eastern and central Europe after the First World War, the major powers attempted to configure domestic political structures before they would extend international legal sovereignty. In Germany the Americans operated largely through contracting with indigenous leaders. The success

---

[50] Jonas 1984, 288; E. Peterson 1977, 201.
[51] Ermarth 1993, 10–13; Fichter 1981: 107–12; Eisenberg 1993; Holtfrerich 1995, 420–24, 460.

of American efforts depended on the extent of local support. American policy bolstered the position of Adenauer and the Christian Democrats and their Bavarian allies in the Christian Social Union, who themselves supported European integration, federalism, capitalism, and some industrial restructuring.

The Soviet Union and Eastern Europe

After the Second World War, the basic constitutional structures, policies, and personnel of the eastern European states, with the exception of Yugoslavia and Albania, were determined by the Soviet Union. In the most extreme cases, areas (parts of Poland, Germany, Czechoslovakia, and Romania) and whole countries (Latvia, Estonia, Lithuania) were simply absorbed into the Soviet Union. In the rest of eastern Europe, Stalin imposed Communist regimes. Once these regimes were in place, their leaders remained dependent on Soviet military power, but within substantial constraints they were able to engage in contractual arrangements, especially after 1956. Westphalian sovereignty—the autonomy of domestic constitutional structures, personnel, and policies—was inconsequential. The Westphalian model offers neither an effective analytic starting point, à la realism (the behavior of eastern European rulers was hardly an example of either balancing or bandwagoning), nor an accurate empirical description, à la sociological or English school approaches, of developments in eastern Europe during the cold war. The satellites states were satellites; their institutional paths were not of their own making.

Soviet rulers were motivated by both concerns about national security and the legitimacy of Marxism-Leninism. In both the First and Second World Wars, and the Napoleonic Wars as well, Russia had been invaded from the west. The smaller states of central Europe could provide a buffer but they would only be reliable security allies if they were dominated by Communist regimes. Absent control over their domestic regimes, the strategic logic for the central European states would have been to balance against the Soviet Union provided that they could find an ally in the West.

The relationship between the control of eastern Europe and Soviet security faded, even disappeared, with the development of nuclear weapons and secure second-strike capability. By the 1970s, the territorial and political integrity of the Soviet Union depended on hardened missile sites and nuclear powered submarines. Still, Soviets leaders persisted in maintaining control of eastern European regimes until the Soviet Empire, and the Soviet Union itself, collapsed. Once Communist regimes had been established in eastern Europe, their failure would have jeopardized, and indeed did jeopardize, Soviet political integrity. Soviet rule was legitimated by Marxism-Leninism, a teleological ideology that claimed to provide a scientific understanding of human society and its inevitable evolution from capitalism to socialism to communism. A reversal of this process, the transformation from socialism to capitalism, would suggest that Marxism was wrong, a development that would, and did, affect not just the legitimacy of the regimes of eastern Europe but that of the Soviet Union as well. Once Communist regimes were established, the rulers of the Soviet Union could not let them revert to some other institutional form without jeopardizing their own position.

At the end of the Second World War, Soviet troops occupied much of central and eastern Europe. Stalin had several options. He did not seriously consider alternatives to international legal sovereignty, although one Communist leader in Yugoslavia mused about the possibility of a Union of Soviet Social Republics that would include his own country.[52] Rather, Stalin annexed some areas to the Soviet Union and recognized states whose Westphalian sovereignty was deeply compromised. This strategy provided the Soviets with control over most domestic and foreign policies without burdening them with the direct costs of rule. Over the longer term the Communist rulers of eastern Europe did secure some bargaining power with their Soviet counterparts, but their options were always severely constrained because of their reliance on Soviet military force.

Stalin was at first cautious. Only in Yugoslavia and Albania were Communist regimes in power as a result of indigenous forces. National front governments sponsored by Moscow were formed in other countries. Eastern European Communists did have significant support in some countries, especially Czechoslovakia, which was deeply disillusioned with the West as a result of Munich. Moreover, the war had undermined old political structures. Nevertheless, the Communist participants in these governments were highly dependent on the Soviet Union. Many had spent the war in Moscow and were out of touch with local developments. Without the presence of the Red Army their position would have been precarious.[53]

With the outbreak of the cold war in 1947 Stalin consolidated Communist control in eastern Europe by creating institutional structures and policies that mimicked those of the Soviet Union. The satellite states adopted new constitutions in the period 1947–52 that were modeled on the Soviet Union's. The supremacy of the party was underlined; in every factory, enterprise, town, and village the party committee was the source of authority for all issues. Stalin emphasized the intensification of the class struggle to unmask class enemies, and the use of terror became pervasive

[52] Brzezinski 1967, 39. In fact in the early 1920s the model followed by the Soviets had been to absorb areas that had declared their independence, such as Georgia and Azerbaijan, into the Soviet Union, by conquest if necessary. R. Jones 1990, 2.

[53] Skilling 1966, 36–37; Brzezinski 1967, 20–41.

in eastern Europe including secret trials, forced labor, deportations from major cities, and party purges after 1949. Taxes on peasants were increased and the collectivization of agriculture intensified although with uneven results. (Over 90 percent of the land was collectivized in Bulgaria, but only about 15 percent in Poland.) The educational system was changed to become closer to that of the Soviet Union. Industry was nationalized, and resources were targeted on heavy industry. All of the Communist states adopted multiyear development plans based on the Soviet model. Between 1947 and 1949 the diversity that had characterized the eastern bloc immediately after the war disappeared. Stalin imposed uniformity on the satellite states where he could, Yugoslavia being the obvious exception. As was the case for the United States in the Caribbean and Central America, the Soviet Union had a sphere of influence that made it possible to engage in coercion and imposition to alter the basic constitutional structures of weaker states.[54]

After Stalin's death direct Soviet control over eastern Europe decreased. Leaders in Yugoslavia, Albania, and Romania broke with Soviet foreign policy preferences, although not with communism. Polish rulers had always been able to maintain somewhat greater autonomy—for instance, resisting Soviet pressures for party purges in the late 1940s. In the other eastern European states, Bulgaria, Hungary, Czechoslovakia, and East Germany, Soviet domination became less intrusive. Military intervention was costly because it alienated the local population and raised questions about the reliability of armed forces in eastern Europe.[55] It was more attractive if national Communist rulers could maintain some local support, or at least contain the level of disaffection. The leaders of the five satellite states were able to contract within some limits with the Soviet Union and to move away from simply mimicking the Soviet model. Policies became more diverse. After 1968, for instance, Hungary introduced greater economic decentralization, increased trade with the West, and loosened central planning. Czechoslovakia followed much more orthodox policies, emphasizing large industries and central planning. Poland borrowed heavily from the West in the 1970s in an attempt to secure more modern technologies, and its agricultural sector continued to be dominated by private farmers.

Nevertheless, the autonomy of the rulers of eastern Europe remained constrained throughout the cold war by the threat of Soviet military intervention, and by the Soviet penetration of domestic institutions. As the

---

[54] Brzezinski 1967, 67–103; Paul 1981, 45–46; Koslowski and Kratochwil 1994, 228.

[55] For instance, after the invasion of Hungary in 1956 the Hungarian army was essentially dismantled. Mackintosh 1984, 46.

use of force in East Germany in 1953, Hungary in 1956, and Czechoslovakia in 1968 demonstrated, the leaders of the satellite states could not put at risk the Communist system without inviting military repression. The anticipation of such intervention limited the range of policies that were seriously considered.

The Soviets did not just establish the Communist regimes of eastern Europe; they also penetrated these polities on an ongoing basis. Bilateral consultations with the Soviet leadership were obligatory. Even after the death of Stalin, Soviet leaders insisted on the right to decide who would head the government in the satellite states. Close relations were maintained between the central committee of the Communist Party of the Soviet Union and the party leaders in eastern Europe. Frequently appointments to major party positions in eastern Europe were only given to those individuals with extensive experience in Moscow.[56]

After the war, Stalin dictated many of the economic policies of the eastern European countries. Joint-stock companies owned by the Soviet Union and the east European governments were set up in Romania, Hungary, and Bulgaria. Poland, however resisted such arrangements. The trading patterns of the eastern European countries changed radically from the prewar period, becoming concentrated within the Soviet bloc. For instance, Bulgaria, which had 12 percent of its trade with countries that were to become part of the Soviet bloc in 1937, had 92 percent by 1951; the figures for Hungary went from 13 to 67 percent, for Poland from 7 to 58, for Romania from 18 to 79, and for Czechoslovakia from 11 to 60. Trade with the Soviet Union accounted for 58 percent of Bulgarian trade, 29 percent of Hungarian, 25 percent of Polish, 51 percent of Romanian, and 28 percent of Czech in 1951. Eighty percent of Soviet trade was with eastern Europe. The ruble became the standard currency for international transactions in 1950.[57]

Soviet penetration of the domestic polities of the satellite states was extensive with regard to the secret police and the military. The Soviets often directly controlled the internal security apparatuses of the eastern European states. The Soviet secret police maintained its own autonomous operations in eastern Europe and was empowered to arrest nationals of these countries. The Soviets organized the Polish secret police. The head of the Polish Security Ministry had Soviet officers as his personal guards and was advised by an official of the Soviet Ministry of State Security. At one point, eight out of twenty sections in the Polish Ministry of Internal Security were headed by Soviet officers. The Inspectorate of Party Cadres

---

[56] Brzezinski 1967, 117–20.
[57] Brzezinski 1967, 125–27; Marer 1984, 215–16.

in the Bulgarian Central Committee was staffed with former members of the Soviet secret police. Similar levels of penetration occurred in other countries. In the late 1940s the secret police in the satellite states was subject to orders directly from Moscow.[58]

The Soviets also tightly regulated the militaries of the satellite states. Initially the Soviet Union discouraged armies in eastern Europe, but after 1948 the armed forces of the satellites were built up. The question of loyalty then became critical. Marshal Rokossovsky, a Soviet officer, was appointed as head of the Polish Ministry of Defense in 1949. Soviet officers commanded all of the branches of the Polish armed forces. There were about seventeen Soviet officers with command positions in the Polish army in the late 1940s. In other countries Soviet officers acted as advisors not only to the central command but at the regimental level as well. Soviet practices were adopted. Only in Czechoslovakia, where local party officials were well organized, was Soviet direct control of the military more limited.[59]

After Stalin's death, the level of Soviet penetration, such as appointing officers, declined, but the eastern bloc militaries were organized in such a way to make it very difficult for them to function independent of Soviet forces. The Warsaw Treaty Organization (WTO) was established in 1955. The military doctrines of the Warsaw Pact emphasized the importance of joint military operations among socialist states. In 1961 Marshall Grechko, then the commander in chief of the WTO, introduced a system of joint military exercises that precluded the development of autonomous defense strategies by the members of the pact. Grechko broke up the military forces of the satellite states, placing them in multilateral command structures controlled by Soviet officers. Soviet and satellite country forces were integrated even at small unit levels. The Warsaw Pact headquarters was located in the Soviet Ministry of Defense building in Moscow. The commander in chief of the pact was the first deputy minister of defense of the Soviet Union. The chief of staff of the pact was the head of the directorate of the Soviet General Staff. The leaders of the eastern European militaries were educated at the leading Soviet military academy where promising individuals could be identified, making it easier for Moscow to promote their subsequent careers.[60]

In sum, relations among the states of eastern Europe during the cold war were incomprehensible from the perspective of the Westphalian model. Initially Stalin imposed Communist regimes in eastern Europe, with the exception of Yugoslavia and Albania where indigenous communist rulers exercised effective control. The institutional structures, poli-

---

[58] Brzezinski 1967, 121, 90–94, 119–20.
[59] Brzezinski 1967, 122; Skilling 1966, 175–76.
[60] C. Jones 1984, 91–102; Mackintosh 1984, 44–45, 51–52.

cies, and personnel of the eastern Europe states were often the result of coercion. The threat of Soviet military intervention, should local leaders dismantle communism, was always present. The secret police and military could not act independently of Moscow. The eastern European states were not autonomous.

As has frequently been the case in international relations, the rulers of powerful states enunciated mutually conflicting principles, sovereign equality and the right of intervention, at the same time. After the suppression of the uprising in Hungary in 1956, the Soviet leadership declared that relations among the socialist states should be built on the principle of sovereign equality, but at the same time Bulganin, the Soviet premier, stated that: "Every country should find its own way to socialism, but we cannot permit this to be used to break up the solidarity of the peace camp, and certainly not under the pretext of respecting national peculiarities or extending democracy."[61] The Brezhnev Doctrine articulated by Brezhnev after the repression of Czechoslovakia in 1968 stated that a Communist country had the right of self-determination only to the extent that the interests of the Soviet commonwealth were not jeopardized. "Each of our parties," Brezhnev stated, "is responsible not only to its working class and its people, but also to the international working class, the world Communist movement." The USSR asserted its right to intervene in any Communist state to prevent the success of "counterrevolutionary" elements. At the same time the Soviet rulers endorsed the principle of autonomy and the right of the Soviet Union to intervene to preserve communism.[62] This was not a mutually consistent position.

Nevertheless, the Soviets did not simply annex the eastern European states as they had other areas, nor did they develop some alternative institutional form in which authority structure transcended territory, such as the Europe Economic Community and later the European Union. They accepted the international legal sovereignty of the east European states. International recognition, however, is not a guarantee of autonomy; formal juridical autonomy does not mean de facto autonomy. Rulers in juridically independent states may not have control over their own constitutional structures. While the leaders of eastern Europe during the cold war could not do much (for instance, abandon communism, join NATO, join the European Union), international legal sovereignty made it possible for them to do a little (pursue somewhat different economic policies), more than would have been possible had their states been formally incorporated into the Soviet Union.

---

[61] Quoted in Brzezinski 1967, 249.

[62] Mackintosh 1984, 50; For a discussion of the considerable emphasis which the Soviets gave to the concept of sovereignty during the cold war, see R. Jones 1990.

CONCLUSIONS

The latter part of the twentieth century witnessed a burst of new state creation in the Third World and the reconstitution of existing states in Europe. Autonomy, the basic principle of Westphalian sovereignty, was widely recognized and endorsed. The principle of nonintervention was, for instance, enshrined in the Charter of the United Nations. Nevertheless, it was not uniformly adhered to. In Europe, the Soviet Union and the United States established spheres of influence, demarcated by the lines of occupation at the conclusion of the Second World War. Both superpowers were anxious to establish particular regime types in their respective spheres. For Soviet rulers, this meant the imposition of Communist regimes on most of the states of central Europe. For the United States it meant contracting with local leaders who would support capitalism and democracy, especially in Germany and Italy.

In contrast, the domestic regime structures that emerged out of the European colonial empires in Asia and Africa were largely the result of indigenous decisions. Most colonies had only the most limited economic and strategic value. The colonial powers—France, Britain, Portugal, and the Netherlands—would still have preferred regimes that would have welcomed their influence, but their economic and military resources were limited. The Soviet Union and the United States opposed colonialism. The superpowers were anxious to influence developments in the Third World, but they were not able to establish a condominium, as the Great Powers had in the Balkans in the nineteenth century, nor could they agree on spheres of influence. Direct intervention could be costly, as the Americans and Soviets learned in Vietnam and Afghanistan. Ironically, the rulers of Third World states with limited absolute resources were better able to exercise their Westphalian sovereignty than were the states of central Europe after the cold war. Super power rivalry and limited value preserved the constitutional autonomy of most countries in Asia and Africa.

As was the case in earlier periods, the dominant powers advanced principles that were inconsistent with Westphalian sovereignty. In 1947, President Truman enunciated the Truman Doctrine, asserting the right of the United States to intervene to prevent Communist takeovers. In 1968 Brezhnev elaborated the Brezhnev Doctrine, which stipulated that all Communist parties (read the Communist Party of the Soviet Union) were mutually responsible for each others' fate. These pronouncements were reminiscent of earlier statements, such as Clemenceau's defense of the right of major powers to demand religious and ethnic toleration before recognition in his letter conveying the minority treaty to Poland at Versailles, or Theodore Roosevelt's corollary regarding the right of the

United States to intervene to assure good governance in Central America and the Caribbean.

The variation in outcome in the postwar period between the Third World and Europe was not the result of any difference in the principles held by the relevant actors. The major actors, the leaders of the United States and the Soviet Union, were the same. Rather differences in power and interest led to extensive intervention in Europe and only modest efforts to structure the domestic polities of new Third World states. In Europe the United States and the Soviet Union were able to act with great discretion within their own spheres of influence. In the Third World the low stakes and superpower rivalry usually prevented extensive intervention with regard to basic institutional arrangements.

With the collapse of the Soviet Union the West has been able to act with a freer hand. International financial institutions, for instance, have become more vigorous in insisting on good governance as a condition for international loans. Commitment to democratic practices and principles was written into the Articles of Agreement of the European Bank for Reconstruction and Development founded after the collapse of the Soviet empire. Membership in NATO has been conditioned on appropriate civil military relations.

While the extent to which Westphalian principles have been decoupled from actual practice has varied across geographic regions and over time, international legal sovereignty has been much more consistently adhered to. This has not been the result of some taken-for-granted quality. Alternatives to international legal sovereignty have frequently been on the table. The British attempted to establish the Commonwealth as a distinct political order for their newly independent colonies, but, despite previous success with the white dominions, this initiative had only limited success. In the mid-1940s and late 1950s the French explored but quickly abandoned ideas for a French union that would have created an alternative to international legal sovereignty. For the would-be rulers of new states or newly constituted states, international legal sovereignty was universally more attractive than some innovative institutional form.

CHAPTER 8

Conclusion: Not a Game of Chess

MOST OBSERVERS and analysts of international relations have treated sovereign states as an analytic assumption or a well-institutionalized if not taken-for-granted structure. The bundle of properties associated with sovereignty—territory, recognition, autonomy, and control—have been understood, often implicitly, to characterize states in the international system.[1] In fact, however, only a very few states have possessed all of these attributes. Control over both transborder movements and internal developments has often been problematic. More to the point for this study, the basic principle of Westphalian sovereignty, the autonomy of domestic structures, has frequently been compromised through intervention in the form of coercion or imposition by more powerful states, or through contracts or conventions that have involved invitations for external actors to influence domestic authority structures. While the basic principle of international legal sovereignty, the extension of recognition to juridically autonomous territorial entities, has been more widely honored, it too has been violated. Recognition has been accorded to entities that lack either formal juridical autonomy or territory, and it has been denied to states that possess these attributes. Given the absence of any international authority structures, the asymmetries of power among states, and the diversity of norms espoused by rulers and their constituents, it is impossible for any institutional arrangement at the international level to become embedded. In the international system norms, including those associated with Westphalian sovereignty and international legal sovereignty, have always been characterized by organized hypocrisy. Norms and actions have been decoupled. Logics of consequences have trumped logics of appropriateness.

This study has been concerned with issues of authority rather than control, but a few observations about the latter are in order. States have always operated in an integrated international environment. Even for international capital flows, an area where the contemporary challenge to state control has frequently been emphasized, the degree of change from

[1] I am indebted to Fowler and Bunck 1995, chapter 3 and pp. 93, 124–25, for the notion of sovereignty as a basket or bundle of attributes. The major exception to the generalization that sovereignty has been well ordered is some recent constructivist arguments. These are noted in Chapter 1.

the past and the extent to which global capital markets have become fully integrated have often been overstated. International banking began in Europe in the later Middle Ages. In the early part of the sixteenth century the major financial and trading groups conducted business throughout the world, not just Europe. The Welsers operated in Europe and the Mediterranean and opened a branch in Venezuela in 1528. The Fuggers controlled mines in central Europe and the Alps; had correspondents in Venice; were the dominant firm in Antwerp, the most important financial center of the time; and had branches in Portugal, Spain, Chile, Fiume, and Dubrovnik. They had agents in India and China by the end of the sixteenth century. Braudel suggests that "the empire of this huge firm was vaster than the mighty empire of Charles V and Philip II, on which as we know the sun never set."[2] In the early modern era European rulers were highly dependent on international finance, much more dependent than would be the case for any developed states in the contemporary era. It was only in the nineteenth century that the major European governments developed sophisticated national systems of finance including revenue collection.[3]

Britain, the major source of international capital in the nineteenth century, was much more dependent on global transactions before the First World War than is the case for any country at the end of the twentieth century. By 1914, 10 percent of British income and 6 percent of French income were generated by foreign investments. Nearly a quarter of British wealth was invested overseas. Barings Brothers, the British financial institution that suffered a spectacular collapse in 1995 as a result of speculative dealings by a broker in Singapore, would have ceased to exist in 1890 as a result of questionable loans that had been made to Argentina had it not been for the intervention of the Bank of England, the Bank of France, the British Treasury, and J. P. Morgan.[4]

Moreover, in the contemporary period international capital market integration is far from complete. Real interest rate differentials across countries have remained substantial. Returns to direct investments by foreigners have been lower than the returns to nationals. In a fully integrated global capital market, such disparities would not exist. By some measures the level of integration of capital markets is no higher now than it was in the nineteenth century.[5]

International migration was at its highest levels in the long nineteenth century. Absent immigration after 1870, the U.S. labor force might have

---

[2] Braudel 1982, 186–87 (the quotation is from p. 187).
[3] Tilly 1990a, 53.
[4] Feis 1965, 14, 16, 48, 72; Gilpin 1987, 308; Cohen 1986, 90, 94–95.
[5] Feldstein and Horioka 1980; Obstfeld and Taylor 1997, 8, table 2.1.

been 24 percent smaller in 1910 than it actually was; the Argentine, 86 percent smaller; the Australian, 42 percent; and the Canadian, 44 percent. In contrast, the Irish labor force would have been 45 percent larger; the Italian, 39 percent; and the Norwegian, 24 percent. For Ireland and Sweden emigration rates reached almost 10 percent of the population for some decades during the nineteenth century.[6] International trade flows, measured as a ratio of trade to GNP, increased rapidly during the nineteenth century, fell from the period 1914 through the late 1940s and only attained their earlier levels for some countries in the 1980s. Although the ratio of trade to GNP has grown on average, the rate of growth, even among industrialized countries has been uneven. The ratio of exports to aggregate economic activity did not, for instance, grow at all for Japan between 1970 and 1993.[7]

For international flows other than economic, the claim that the contemporary era represents a qualitative break with the past should be met with some skepticism. Some observers have pointed to AIDS as an example of the way in which the world has become more globalized. A disease, which probably had its origin in nonhuman animals in Africa, spread rapidly throughout the world during the 1980s, causing the death of tens of millions of people. The black death, however, which originated in the Gobi Desert and followed the silk route across central Asia and the Middle East, took the lives of 30–40 percent of Europeans in the fourteenth century. The peoples of the western hemisphere in the sixteenth century were devastated by diseases such as smallpox that were brought by the Europeans. Influenza epidemics killed millions of people during the first half of the twentieth century. AIDS is a great tragedy, but its impact in terms of the proportion of the population affected and the subversion of social, political, and economic institutions is far less than earlier pandemics.

The spread of ideas is not new. Christianity transformed the Roman Empire in the fourth century. The ideas of Mohammed led a group of tribes from the Arabian peninsula to conquer much of the Mediterranean world in the seventh and eighth centuries. The Reformation changed the political map of Europe within a decade after Luther had posted his ninety-five theses on the door of the Schlosskirche in Wittenberg. Indeed, religious ideas, tied to concerns about moral behavior on earth and immortality someplace beyond, were more politically consequential than any of the leading ideas of the late twentieth century, which are so effectively communicated by phone, fax, and the Internet. Grooving with MTV and getting prices right is one thing; burning in hell for all eternity is quite another.

---

[6] J. Williamson 1996, 16, 18, table 2.1.
[7] Derived from figures in World Bank 1995; Thomson and Krasner 1989.

I do not want to claim that globalization has had no impact on state control, but these challenges are not new. Rulers have always operated in a transnational environment; autarky has rarely been an option; regulation and monitoring of transborder flows have always been problematic. The difficulties for states have become more acute in some areas, but less in others. There is no evidence that globalization has systematically undermined state control or led to the homogenization of policies and structures. In fact, globalization and state activity have moved in tandem. The level of government spending for the major countries has, on average increased substantially since 1950 along with increased trade and capital flows. Government policy has not been hamstrung by the openness of international capital markets; there has been no empirical relationship, for instance, between government spending and capital flows. Levels of investment have not been inversely correlated with corporate tax rates. Corporate investment decisions depend on many factors, including the quality of infrastructure—education, telecommunications, transportation—provided by state funds. The organization of firms has varied across countries with regard to financing, governance structures, and suppliers.[8] Social welfare policies and tax policies are not the same across the advanced industrialized states, the entities most affected by globalization.[9] The state has provided collective goods and social safety nets that have made higher levels of trade and capital flows politically tolerable.

In sum, global flows are not new. In some areas, such as migration, movements were higher in the nineteenth century than a hundred years later. Transnational activities have challenged state control in some areas, but these challenges are not manifestly more problematic than in the past.

This study has not, however, been concerned with control. Rather, it has focused on questions of authority associated with international legal and Westphalian sovereignty. Rulers have almost universally sought international legal sovereignty, recognition. Recognition has provided them with resources and opportunities that can enhance their chances of remaining in power. Recognition can pave the way for membership in international organizations, some of which provide financial aid; can facilitate the conclusion of treaties; can increase the chances that their initiatives will not be challenged in other countries' courts because of the act of state doctrine and the principle of sovereign immunity; and can increase domestic political support. Rarely does recognition carry costs and only in a few instances have rulers volunteered to relinquish their international legal sovereignty.

[8] Pauly and Reich 1997.
[9] Garrett 1998.

In contrast, domestic autonomy has frequently been transgressed. Westphalian norms have been decoupled from behavior. While the principle of nonintervention has been widely accepted, it has often been challenged by alternatives such as human rights. Many international documents, including the Charter of the United Nations and the Helsinki Final Act, have endorsed both.

Westphalian sovereignty has been violated through both intervention, which can occur through coercion and imposition, and invitations, which can be included in both conventions and contracts. Coercion and imposition leave the target worse off. The rulers of more powerful states have used their resources to pressure or compel their weaker counterparts to accept unwanted domestic institutional arrangements. In some cases the targets have had no real choice; for the would-be rulers of new states, the threat of nonrecognition has sometimes been the equivalent of "your money or your life." All of the Balkan states that emerged from the Ottoman Empire in the nineteenth century and all of the new states that were created after the First World War had to concede autonomy to secure international legal sovereignty. Without recognition these entities might not have survived as states. In the twentieth century the United States used its military power to dictate domestic political arrangements in Cuba, Haiti, the Dominican Republic, Nicaragua, El Salvador, Panama, Grenada, and Guatemala; likewise the Soviet Union, in Poland, Romania, East Germany, Bulgaria, Hungary, and Czechoslovakia and in the rest of its eastern European sphere of influence. Rulers in stronger states have used economic sanctions to encourage the rulers of target states to alter their domestic political practices; the sanctions imposed against South Africa because of its apartheid practices offer one example. Both coercion and imposition leave the target either worse off than the status quo ante or, in the case of newly created states, with a political structure not of their own choosing. The rulers of weaker states would have preferred some alternative arrangement but they could not secure their desired preferences with regard to their own domestic political structures without being threatened with nonexistence or bearing the costs of sanctions.

Situations in which one state is made worse off are problematic for international legal as well as Westphalian sovereignty. Only voluntary acts are consistent with the norms of international legal sovereignty. Each state is conceived of as a freely willing autonomous entity. Such an entity would not voluntarily reduce its own utility.

Westphalian sovereignty has also been conceded through conventions and contracts that do not involve compulsion. Rulers have invited external actors (states, international financial institutions, international organizations, supranational courts) to become involved in their domestic affairs, including their authority structures. Rulers have, for instance, entered into international human rights agreements, conventions. These have been voluntary acts; the status quo ante remained available. Conventions are not contingent; if one signatory of a human rights agreement violates its terms, this would not necessarily affect the behavior of other parties. Conventions may or may not compromise domestic sovereignty. In some cases conventions have been ineffectual. Rulers have been motivated to sign by a desire to conform with the script of modernity but have had no intention of honoring the terms of these conventions, and the behavior of groups within their own state and civil society has been unaffected. In other cases, human rights agreements have been more consequential. The most telling example is the European Convention on Human Rights, which established both a supranational commission and the European Court of Human Rights. The citizens of signatory states have standing to bring cases to the court, whose decisions are enforceable in national judicial systems. For the rulers of western Europe in the early 1950s the convention was a way to solidify still shaky commitments to a democratic political order.

Contracts as well as conventions can include invitations for external actors to influence domestic authority structures. Rulers sign contracts because they expect to be better off as a result of some action taken by other participants. The terms for religious toleration incorporated in the Peace of Westphalia and other seventeenth- and eighteenth-century treaties were Pareto-improving, mutually contingent arrangements. Rulers adhered to these provisions not because they believed that toleration was desirable in principle, but because violations could lead to retaliation and a spiral of violence that could undermine political stability. Sovereign lending has, in many instances, involved contracts that compromise the domestic autonomy of borrowing states in exchange for the provision of new capital.

Sovereign lending has always involved special risks. If the sovereign reneges, the legal remedies available to the creditor are limited. In the nineteenth and twentieth centuries lenders have sought to assure repayment by making special provision for the collection of certain revenues. In the case of the Ottoman Empire in the last quarter of the nineteenth century, creditors were given the right to establish an organization, the Administration of the Public Debt, which grew to several thousand employees and collected certain state revenues that were committed to the amortization of the empire's loans. Creditor supervision of public finance also took place in Serbia, Egypt, and several Caribbean countries. Since the 1950s the major international financial institutions have attached conditionality requirements to their loans. Here the major objective of the creditor has not been so much to guarantee repayment but rather, for ideological, political, and economic reasons, to promote certain kinds of policies in borrowing countries. Over time the conditions imposed by agencies such as the World Bank and the International Monetary Fund have become more explicitly political—for instance, insisting on the establishment of independent commissions to attack corruption. This trend accelerated after the collapse of the Soviet Union, which left weaker borrowing states with no alternative to the West, something that some of them welcomed, such as the former Communist countries of eastern Europe, and others did not. The last international financial institution to be established, the European Bank for Reconstruction and Development, made commitment to democracy a condition of membership. Borrowers have accepted these terms because they are better off with the money and with some loss of autonomy than without the money and a higher level of autonomy. Finally, the European Union, with its panoply of supranational institutions, is a clear example of a voluntary contractual arrangement that contradicts Westphalian sovereignty.

Contracts and conventions, unlike coercion and imposition, are completely consistent with international legal sovereignty. The utility of rulers is enhanced by inviting the involvement of external actors in their domestic structures. The status quo remains available. Obviously, power can affect the terms of a contract (IMF creditor states would prefer the money without conditionality), but the agreement would not be concluded unless it was Pareto-improving. Contracts and conventions can, however, compromise the domestic autonomy of rulers by opening their domestic authority structures to external influence.

The various elements of sovereignty have not fit together like some organic whole. International legal sovereignty has been the necessary condition for rulers to sometimes violate their Westphalian sovereignty. Westphalian sovereignty does not guarantee domestic control.

Decoupling between principles and practices is an endemic attribute of many aspects of the international environment. International institutions are never embedded. Institutions can become embedded, that is, dictate actual behavior and endure over time or across different environmental conditions, as a result of two mechanisms: one has been elaborated on using the logic of economics, path dependence, and the other the logic of sociology, socialization. Path dependence takes actors as the ontological givens. Institutional structures become locked in because of economies of scale, hardware-software complementarities, network externalities, agglomeration externalities, and other processes that make it instrumentally irrational for an actor to alter a given pattern of behavior once it is initially chosen (often for haphazard and idiosyncratic reasons). None of these processes occurs in the international environment. Perhaps the closest approximation is the emphasis that neoliberal institutional theory places on the importance of initial start-up costs for new organizations. Changes in environmental conditions would, however, lead to the creation of new institutions once the fixed and variable costs of a new arrangement outweigh the variable costs of the existing ones. The proliferation of new international organizations and changes in existing ones (such as the introduction of conditionality to the Articles of Agreement of the International Monetary Fund) suggests that international institutions are not locked in in the way that path dependence would suggest.

Socialization, the second mechanism that can account for embeddedness, takes institutional structures as the ontological givens. Individual entities are generated by societal structures. The norms, interests, and capabilities of these entities, their identities, are a function of their roles and these roles are determined by encompassing institutional arrangements. Socialization can be a powerful mechanism for embedding in stable environments, including domestic polities where values are widely shared and where there are effective authoritative decision-making structures. Socialization has not characterized the international environment. Values have been contested. National political leaders have been responsive to domestic constituencies more than to international ones, and these domestic constituencies have been committed to very different principles—anti-Semitism, religious freedom, religious intolerance, multiethnicity, ethnic cleansing, human rights, Asian values, antirepublicanism, prodemocracy, communism, anticommunism, social welfare, limited government, and so on. These national values have been reflected in foreign-policy preferences. The Soviet Union supported Communist regimes; the United States opposed them. States whose populations are infused with strong social democratic sentiments have given higher levels of foreign aid than states whose citizens believe in a more limited government role.[10] The conservative states of Europe after the Napoleonic Wars formed the Holy Alliance to repress republican governments; more liberal Britain refused to endorse this arrangement. Given the absence of any mechanisms for making institutions durable, resilient, and consequential, it is not surprising that international institutions are not embedded.

Sovereignty is an institutional arrangement associated with a particular bundle of characteristics—recognition, territory, exclusive authority, and effective internal and transborder regulation or control. The analysis presented here suggests that other international arrangements—characterized by other bundles of principles—would, like sovereignty, also not be embedded. Rulers operating in the European feudal system, the Chinese tributary state system, the Islamic system, or the Greek city-state system would like those in the sovereign state system, expound principles that

---

[10] Lumsdaine 1993; Noel and Therien 1995.

they would also violate.[11] The international system is unique. It lacks a hierarchical authority structure; the rulers of specific entities will be confronted with diverse pressures from their constituencies; power is unequally distributed. For any international system, not just the sovereign state one, the upper right quadrant of Figure 2.1, the embedded quadrant, ought to be empty.

ALTERNATIVE STRUCTURES AND INTERNATIONAL LEGAL SOVEREIGNTY

The extent to which particular structures will be institutionalized, rules and norms will be followed, depends on the power and interests of rulers. Westphalian sovereignty has frequently been compromised because autonomy has clashed with competing principles and disparate interests in an environment of asymmetrical power. International legal sovereignty has been more widely honored because interests and rules have been more congruent. But here too, it is incorrect to conceive of the norm that recognition should only be accorded to juridically independent territorial entities as a constitutive rule whose violation would preclude particular kinds of activities. Recognition has been extended to entities with attributes other than those conventionally associated with sovereignty. It has been denied to governments in territories that possessed these attributes.

Alternatives to states have always existed. Some have been short-lived or of limited import, such as the French Community proposed by de Gaulle in the late 1950s or the Commonwealth of Independent States organized by Russia after the collapse of the Soviet Union. Others have been more durable, such as the Holy Roman Empire, which lasted from the ninth century until 1806, and the British Commonwealth. While some older institutions have virtually, although not completely, disappeared, such as protectorates, new ones have appeared, such as the European Union. Some alternatives to sovereignty have endured for hundreds of years, virtually unnoticed, such as Andorra.

These alternatives to sovereignty have different bundles of principles. For the British Commonwealth the bundle of principles has included territory, extraterritorial authority, control, and international recognition. For the European Union the bundle includes territory, recognition (the representatives of the union conduct some international negotiations), supranational authority, and a mixture of territorial and extraterritorial control. For the Order of Malta the bundle of principles includes recognition as a sovereign person but, for many years, no territory.

---

[11] For a discussion of the decoupling between norms and behavior in medieval Europe, see Fischer 1992.

When rulers have confronted new problems they have often invented new rules. The international system is not like the game of chess. It does not have constitutive rules, if such rules are conceived of as making some kinds of action possible and precluding others.[12] The designated moves for each chess piece are the constitutive rules of chess. Moving a bishop in a straight line is a violation of one of these rules; it is not chess if a bishop is not moved along a diagonal. In contrast, alternatives to sovereign statehood have been accommodated in the international system over the past several hundred years. Entities that have lacked one or more of the attributes conventionally associated with sovereignty—territory, recognition, autonomy, and control—have operated perfectly well and have sometimes hardly been noticed, moving bishops in a straight line, as it were, without any of the other players protesting.[13]

Even international legal sovereignty, which is more highly institutionalized, more generally honored than Westphalian sovereignty, has accommodated alternative institutional forms—that is, the recognition of entities that lack either formal autonomy (even if their authority structures are penetrated in practice) or territory. The member states of the Federal State of Germany before the First World War retained the right to send and receive diplomats. The reigning monarchs of these states were still treated as if they were the monarchs of fully independent entities. The cantons of the Swiss Federation retain the formal right to make treaties with other states. France has concluded treaties with certain Canadian provinces.[14]

Andorra, which is a territory nestled in the Pyrenees between France and Spain, has secured international sovereignty even though it is not autonomous. Since the thirteenth century its constitutional structure has provided for coprinceps, initially the bishop of Urgel in Spain and the king of France. In 1993 some nine thousand citizens of Andorra adopted their first formal constitution with the approval of the coprinceps, now the governments of France and Spain. Article 66 gives the coprinceps the right to participate in treaty negotiations involving internal security and

---

[12] Constitutive rules have been conceived of in different ways. Searle, whose formulation is followed here, maintains that constitutive rules make some kinds of activities possible; for instance, the rules of chess make chess playing possible. Dessler 1989, in contrast, defines constitutive rules as those which constrain and enable action. See Searle 1995, 27–29, 43–51, 114–18; Dessler 1989, 453–56. See also Kratochwil 1989, chap. 2.

[13] The number of named alternatives to statehood has declined over time. Areas formally designated as colonies and protectorates, for instance, have disappeared. Moreover, once an entity becomes a state, it has not formally reverted back to something else. Nevertheless, in some cases the functional equivalent continues to exist; for instance, some former American possessions in the Pacific are, in essence, protectorates, although they are called sovereign states. See Strang 1991; Lake 1999.

[14] Oppenheim 1992, 249–53.

defense, diplomatic representation, and judicial cooperation. A treaty cannot be adopted unless it is approved by the representatives of both Andorra and the coprinceps. Each coprinceps can appoint one member to the four-member Constitutional Tribunal. The other two are designated by Andorran authorities. For international lawyers Andorra has usually been categorized as protectorate, but the level of penetration of domestic structures, including the Constitutional Tribunal, extends beyond conventional security arrangements. Andorra became a member of the United Nations in 1993 and the Council of Europe in 1994, despite the fact that its bundle of principles is inconsistent with juridical autonomy because of the formal acceptance of extraterritorial authority.[15]

Rulers have developed new institutional arrangements to meet the needs of a particular situation. In 1967 the United Kingdom created the concept of an associated state, something between a state and a colony, for some its Caribbean possessions. Antigua, Dominica, Grenada, St. Lucia, St. Vincent, St. Christopher, Nevis, and Anguilla became associated states with internal autonomy, but Britain retained control over their foreign affairs. Eventually all of these entities, with the exception of Nevis, which reverted back to being a colony, asserted sovereignty and ended their special relationship with Britain. Nevertheless, while they were associated states they joined multilateral organizations such as the Economic Commission for Latin America. A similar relationship initiated in 1964 exists between the Cook Islands and New Zealand: the islands have formal control over their domestic affairs; New Zealand is in charge of foreign policy. The relationship can be unilaterally terminated, in which case the Cook Islands become independent. The Cook Islands are a member of the World Health Organization, the Food and Agriculture Organization, the International Civil Aviation Organization, and the Asian Development Bank.[16]

The Exclusive Economic Zone (EEZ) for the oceans is another institutional arrangement invented to meet a particular concern of rulers, one that violates the principle that territoriality and authority are coterminous. The EEZ is defined as the area between the territorial sea (twelve nautical miles) and two hundred nautical miles. In this area the littoral state has authority over some activities, the exploitation of resources, but not others, shipping. The provisions of the convention related to the Exclusive Economic Zone were concluded in 1982, although the entire document was not ratified by the major industrialized states until the early 1990s after parts of the text related to the exploitation of deep seabed nodules

[15] Andorra 1993, Article 66; Britannica Online 1994, 1996; Fowler and Bunck 1995, 118–20; Oppenheim 1992, 267–74; Brierly 1963, 136.
[16] Oppenheim 1992, 280–84.

had been modified. The Exclusive Economic Zone was an institutional innovation, and one that is inconsistent with the bundle of attributes associated with sovereignty. Prior to the invention of the EEZ the oceans were divided between the territorial sea, first three miles and then twelve miles wide, over which the coastal state had the same authority and control as it did over its terrestrial territory, and the open oceans, which were not controlled by any state. The initial proponents of expanding the reach of the coastal states were a number of Latin American countries that wanted to enhance exploitation of natural resources, especially fishing. The United States, which was concerned about freedom of movement for its naval forces, freedom that would have been radically curtailed by a substantial expansion of the territorial sea, demurred. The Exclusive Economic Zone was an ideal solution for American leaders: it preserved freedom of navigation while at the same time providing authority over exploitable resources for the country with the longest coastline in the world. Power and interest, not the constitutive rules of sovereignty, led to the invention of a new institutional category. States used their international legal sovereignty to create a form that was consistent with Westphalian sovereignty, since the authority of other states is excluded from the Exclusive Economic Zone, but inconsistent with territoriality, because the littoral state has control over some activities but not others.

Rulers have created a unique status without necessarily providing an appellation. In 1955 the United States, France, and the United Kingdom, recognized the Federal Republic of Germany as having the "full authority of a sovereign State over its international and external affairs," but they did not, in fact, concede full authority. France, Britain, and the United States retained some powers, including the right to declare a state of emergency in all or part of Germany, the retention of full rights with regard to Berlin, and the reservation of full authority with regard to Germany as a whole, unification, and a final peace settlement. These residual rights did not end until the final peace settlement with Germany was concluded in 1990.[17]

Entities have been accorded international legal sovereignty when they have lacked territory. The recognition of governments in exile is a more or less standard practice, but there have been other, more curious violations of the territorial norm. The Knights Hospitaler of St. John of Jerusalem of Rhodes and of Malta, the Order of Malta for short, was originally an order of Crusader knights that was recognized as a sovereign entity when it conquered Rhodes in 1310, an island that was lost to the Ottoman Empire in 1522. In 1530 Emperor Charles V gave the Order the island of Malta for the nominal rent of one falcon per year (the Maltese falcon),

[17] Oppenheim 1992, 137.

as well as a commitment that it garrison Tripoli on the North African coast. In 1798 Napoleon drove the Order from Malta, and it has not had any independent control of territory since. Some observers have argued that it has not had any independent control of territory since it was driven from Rhodes, since Malta could be construed as a fiefdom granted by Charles V.[18] After British control of Malta was affirmed in the Treaty of Paris of 1814, the leaders of the Order made a number of ultimately ineffectual efforts to secure territory. For instance, in 1823 an agreement was signed between the French branch of the Order and the leaders of the Greek rebellion giving the Order immediate control over some small islands in the Peloponnese and promising the return of Rhodes. All of these efforts came to naught. Nevertheless, the Order maintained continuous diplomatic relations with Austria, and with some smaller Italian states as well. By the end of the twentieth century it had been recognized as a sovereign person by many states. In the mid 1990s the Order had embassies in fifty-nine countries and legations in an additional five. It issues diplomatic passports, recognized by other states, to its accredited representatives. The Order is now mainly engaged in charitable work. In a foreword to a study published in 1972 Quintin Jermy Gwyn, the grand chancellor, refers to the Order's "sovereignty dating from the capture of the island of Rhodes in 1310, making it one of the oldest sovereign states in Europe."[19] At the 1998 World Exposition in Lisbon, Portugal, the exhibit of the "Sovereign and Military Order of Malta" was place directly next to that of the United States among the displays of scores of other mostly conventional sovereign states.

When full recognition has been problematic, other categories have been created. The UN General Assembly gave the Palestine Liberation Organization permanent observer status in 1974. Previously, permanent observer status had only been granted to states that were not members of the United Nations and to regional organizations. A number of states recognized the PLO and gave diplomatic status to its local office. When the declaration of Palestine independence was issued in 1988, the United Nations changed the designation to the Palestine observer mission.[20]

The British Commonwealth offers an example of an alternative to sovereignty, which included the recognition of entities that were not formally autonomous, that lasted from the mid-nineteenth century until after the Second World War. The bundle of characteristics that defined the Commonwealth included territory, recognition, and extranational author-

---

[18] The Order does, however, control a building in Rome.
[19] Bradford 1972, 63–67, 117–23, 220, 226. Gwyn is quoted in Sire 1994, 6. Sire 1994, 237–42, 249–50, 271; Oppenheim 1992, 329.
[20] Oppenheim 1992, 163–64, n. 10.

ity. The Commonwealth continued to exist as a juridical entity after the 1950s, but it came to resemble a conventional international organization whose members have had the formal right to exclude external authority, although the Judicial Committee of the Privy Council has continued to be used by some as a court of appeal. The Commonwealth was an institutional system organized by Britain that provided some of its former colonies with a new status, that of a Dominion. Members of the Commonwealth exchanged international representatives, but they were designated as high commissioners rather than ambassadors. The Dominions were recognized by other states and admitted to international organizations even though they were formally subject to British authority in some areas, including foreign affairs, and accepted the British crown as their head of state.

The Commonwealth reflected the desire of British rulers, as well as decision makers and subjects of British descent in overseas possessions, to find an institutional arrangement that would provide for greater autonomy without a complete break with the mother country. Riots in Nova Scotia and New Brunswick in 1839 over the absence of local control of ministers who were appointed by the crown led to an investigation and report by Lord Durham. The Durham report recommended that ministers should command majorities in local assemblies. At the same time Durham suggested that foreign affairs, trade and land policies, and constitutional structures be determined by Britain. In the middle of the nineteenth century British rulers, in consultation with local leaders, established constitutional arrangements through acts of Parliament for Canada, Australia, and New Zealand. These laws, the most well known of which was the British North America Act of 1867, provided for locally elected parliaments and an executive, the governor-general, who was at the same time to represent the will of the local ministers in matters under the purview of the Dominion and of the crown in other issues such as foreign policy.[21]

In practice, rules were persistently contested. The principle of ultimate control by the crown over some questions was in tension with the alternative norm of local governance. The dividing line between British and local authority was frequently disputed. Over time British control of trade, foreign affairs, and constitutional arrangements eroded. Even as early as the middle of the nineteenth century Canada signed commercial treaties with the United States and imposed its own duties. By the 1870s Britain formally acknowledged that Canada, Australia, and New Zealand could decide their own tariff rates, a critical matter for both fiscal and trade policy, since tariffs were the major source of government revenue in the nineteenth century. In 1865, the British Parliament passed the Colonial Laws

---

[21] Mansergh 1969, 51; McIntyre 1977, 25, 49–53.

Validity Act, which stipulated that any colonial or Dominion law that contravened a law of the United Kingdom would be null and void, but in practice this act was ignored. By the latter part of the nineteenth century the Dominions were unilaterally altering their own constitutional arrangements. The right of the Dominions to make their own laws was formally accepted by Britain in the 1931 Statute of Westminster, but until the 1980s certain kinds of legislation in Canada, Australia, and New Zealand, including constitutional amendments, were still subject to approval by the British Parliament.[22]

In foreign affairs more generally and not just with regard to trade, the division of authority between Britain and the Dominions was always problematic. Although Britain still retained formal control over issues of foreign policy in 1914, the support of the Dominions during World War I could not simply be taken for granted. Explicit agreements were reached, for instance, for the transfer of Dominion naval forces to the Admiralty. King George V, on the advice of the British cabinet, declared war for the entire empire, but the actual commitments were made by individual Dominions. The level of cooperation was generally high, but among the Afrikaners in South Africa there was major disaffection and a small rebellion. Conscription was introduced in Canada and New Zealand, but was rejected by a referendum in Australia in 1916. Conscription was a central issue in the 1917 elections in Canada; it was supported by the British population and rejected by the French.

The Dominions, like other entities that have not had formal autonomy, were accorded international recognition. They were admitted to some international organizations, such as the Universal Postal Union, even before the First World War. At the Versailles meeting, the Dominions were part of the British Empire delegation and also represented separately in a status equivalent to that of a small power. India, although still a colony, was also given independent representation as well as being part of the British imperial delegation. The delegates from the Dominions and India signed the peace treaty "for Canada" or "for Australia." At the same time they became members of the League of Nations as signatories of the treaty.[23]

The Commonwealth disappeared de facto if not de jure as an alternative institutional form only after the Second World War. India demanded republican status. No longer would all of the Commonwealth members recognize the crown as the head of state. Nevertheless some members of the Commonwealth continued to accept the Judicial Committee of the Privy

---

[22] McIntyre 1977, 54, 79, 189–93; Mansergh 1969, 49, 182–83; Fowler and Bunck 1995, 52; Oppenheim 1992, 257–66.

[23] Mansergh 1969, 165–80.

Council as a court of appeals, a practice inconsistent with conventional notions of sovereignty.

In sum, from the middle of the nineteenth century until the end of the Second World War, the British Commonwealth offered an alternative institutional form to sovereignty—that is, a different bundle of principles. Westphalian sovereignty was not part of that bundle. Rather, the Dominions accepted, albeit over a decreasing range of activities, the authority of British institutions. Nevertheless, the Dominions and India enjoyed international legal sovereignty.

The European Union offers another example of an alternative bundle of characteristics: it has territory, recognition, control, national authority, extranational authority, and supranational authority. There is no commonly accepted term for the European Union. Is it a state, a commonwealth, a dominion, a confederation of states, a federation of states? Nevertheless, it exists, exists comfortably, in an international environment that is populated primarily by sovereign states, whose characteristic principles do not include supranational or extranational authority, even if rulers have been involved in interventions or invitations that compromise the autonomy of their own polity.

The European Commission and the European Court of Justice are supranational authority structures. National courts accept the rulings of the European Court, an arrangement that was not part of the 1957 Treaty of Rome that created the European Economic Community. Beginning in 1963 the European Court developed four doctrines that made Europe, according to some observers, indistinguishable from the legal structure of a federal state. First, the doctrine of direct effect holds that community legal norms have direct effect in member states with regard to the application of community law. Direct effect applies only to vertical relations between public authorities and individuals. It does not apply to horizontal relationships among individuals. Second, the doctrine of supremacy, which the European Court began to enunciate in 1964, holds that community law, whether in the form of a treaty obligation or an administrative ruling, trumps domestic law whether enacted before or after. Individuals can bring cases in their national courts based on European law. Third, in 1971 the European Court promulgated the doctrine of implied powers which holds that the community has the right to make treaties, because otherwise it could not efficiently carry out its assigned tasks. The Treaty of Rome itself had given the community only very limited treaty-making powers. During the same period the court also ruled that there were certain areas, such as trade, where the community had exclusive powers. Individual states were prohibited from taking any unilateral action in these areas, even actions that did not contradict European Union rules. Finally, the court also asserted that it would review any European Union measures for human rights violations. There were no provisions for human rights in the founding treaties. Granting individuals and the commission the right to bring cases to the court, and the doctrine of direct effect, were departures from conventional international law, which would not give standing to individuals and would expect national enabling legislation before the judgment of any supranational authority could be considered binding in national courts.[24]

In addition to the court, the European Commission and the European Parliament can also exercise supranational authority. Voting arrangements in the European Union are complex. Different issue areas are governed by different rulers. Agenda setting, formal voting, and the right to make the last decision vary among the council, the commission, the European Parliament, and the court. For instance, the Single European Act and the Maastricht treaty provide for majority voting in the council for some issue areas. Since such decisions can be binding in national courts as a result of the doctrines of supremacy and direct effect, a state might find that its partners had legislated policies that it opposed.[25]

The doctrine of mutual recognition, which provides that members of the European Union must recognize the national regulatory measures of other members of the union, creates extraterritorial authority because one member state can enact legislation that, in effect, governs the activities of enterprises in other member states. For instance, an Italian insurance company operating in Germany could be regulated under Italian rather than German law. Unlike national recognition, in which states reciprocally agree to recognize each others' regulating statutes, mutual recognition does not require any such positive act.[26]

The structure of the European Union is hardly settled. It might simply evolve into a conventional federal state. It might become embedded as a distinctly new institutional form, one whose bundle of attributes includes supranational and extranational authority. There is not universal agreement on existing authority structures. For instance, in 1993 the German Constitutional Court stated that the European Union was not a federal state based on a European people but was rather a Confederation of States (Staatenverbund). The German court held that the European Union could only exercise limited power as conferred by the member states. The German court claimed that it had the right to decide whether or not European institutions had exceeded the "sovereign rights accorded to them." Most European lawyers would argue that this is the prerogative

---

[24] Moravcsik 1994, 51; Burley and Mattli 1993; Weiler 1991, 2413–27.

[25] Garrett and Tsebelis 1996; Weiler 1991, 2458–63.

[26] Nicolaidis 1996.

of the European Court. Some have maintained that Europe is, in fact, a federal state, not a confederation of states.[27]

The European Union has also been accorded international status. The European Community has been a participant in many international conferences including the United Nations Conference on the Law of the Seas, and the Conference on Cooperation and Security in Europe. The community has been a signatory to international accords that fall within its purview, including the UN Law of the Seas Convention, various international commodity agreements, the Helsinki Final Act, and several environmental conventions. It is a full member of the Food and Agriculture Organization, although it generally only has observer, nonvoting status in most UN agencies. The community has permanent representation at the OSCE. It also maintains diplomatic representation in a number of countries.[28]

SUMMARY

The international system is not a game of chess. Constitutive rules never exclude alternatives. New entities, with different bundles of formal principles, have been accommodated. Colonies have signed international agreements and been members of international organizations. Entities without territory, such as the Order of Malta, have been accorded international recognition, as have entities whose political structure provides for extranational control of some issues, especially security, such as the Dominions of the British Empire during the first part of the twentieth century, and Andorra at the end of the century.

Most central to the argument of this book, the characteristics that are associated with sovereignty—territory, autonomy, recognition, and control—do not provide an accurate description of the actual practices that have characterized many entities that have been conventionally viewed as sovereign states. Rulers have sometimes had to compromise their Westphalian sovereignty, the exclusion of external authority, to secure recognition, international legal sovereignty. Such was the fate of all of the states that emerged from the Ottoman Empire in the nineteenth century or were created or reconstituted after the First World War. Their rulers or would-be rulers had to accept minority rights provisions, often in their basic constitutional documents, to secure international recognition, a policy that most of them would not have chosen without external pressure. In other cases, rulers have invited external actors to influence their domestic authority structures by entering into contractual relationships or joining

---

[27] Weiler 1991, 2413; Kreile 1996, 18.
[28] For information on the European Union, see http://europa.eu.int/commdg1a/index.html.

conventions. The European Union, the practices of international financial institutions, some minority rights agreements after Versailles, and treaties providing for religious toleration in Europe such as the Peace of Westphalia have all involved invitations to compromise Westphalian sovereignty.

There has never been some ideal time during which all, or even most, political entities conformed with all of the characteristics that have been associated with sovereignty—territory, control, recognition, and autonomy. Alternative principles—notably human and minority rights, fiscal responsibility, and international security—have been used to challenge autonomy. In the absence of any well-established hierarchical structure of authority, coercion and imposition are always options that the strong can deploy against the weak. Other institutional forms have been accorded international recognition, including even entities without territory.

Well-established domestic political institutions can be embedded, be both durable and consequential, because they can be set in a hierarchical structure of authority and underpinned by widely shared values. International institutions operate in a more fluid environment. There are no constitutive rules that preclude rulers from contracting to establish whatever kind of institutional form might serve their needs. Norms can matter, but they can also be mutually contradictory. Logics of consequences can override logics of appropriateness. Rulers, seeking to maintain their own position and promote the interests of their constituents, can choose among competing principles and, if they command adequate resources, engage in coercion or imposition. In a contested environment in which actors, including the rulers of states, embrace different norms, clubs can always be trump.

References

Alcock, Antony. 1979. Three Case Studies. In *The Future of Cultural Minorities*, edited by Antony Alcock, Brian Taylor, and John Welton. London: Macmillan.

Anderson, M. S. 1966. *The Eastern Question, 1774–1923: A Study in International Relations*. London: Macmillan.

Andorra. 1993. Constitution of Andorra. http://www.andora.ad/consell/constituk.htm.

Ansprenger, Franz. 1989. *The Dissolution of the Colonial Empires*. New York: Routledge.

Aoki, Masahiko. Forthcoming. *Towards a Comparative Institutional Analysis*. Cambridge, Mass.: MIT Press.

Arthur, W. B. 1984. Competing Technologies and Economic Prediction. *Options*.

———. 1985. *Competing Technologies and Lock-in by Historical Small Events: The Dynamics of Allocation under Increasing Returns*. CEPR Publication No. 43. Stanford University, Stanford, Calif.: Center for Economic Policy Research.

———. 1986. Industry Location Patterns and the Importance of History. Food Research Institute, Stanford University, Stanford Calif. Mimeograph.

———. 1987. "Self Reinforcing Mechanisms in Economics." Ford Research Institute, Stanford University, Stanford, Calif. Unpublished paper.

Axelrod, Robert M. 1984. *The Evolution of Cooperation*. New York: Basic Books.

Bainton, Roland H. 1951. *The Travail of Religious Liberty: Nine Biographical Studies*. Philadelphia: Westminster Press.

Bartelson, Jens. 1995. *A Genealogy of Sovereignty*. Cambridge: Cambridge University Press.

Bartsch, Sebastian. 1995. *Minderheitenschutz in der internationalen Politik: Völkerbund und KSZE/OSZE in neuer Perspektive*. Oplanden: Westdeutscher Verlag.

Bates, Robert H. 1981. *Markets and States in Tropical Africa: The Political Basis of Agricultural Policies*. Berkeley: University of California Press.

Bates, Robert, Philip Brock, and Jill Tiefenthaler. 1991. Risk and Trade Regimes. *International Organization* 45: 1–18.

Beller, E.A. 1970. The Thirty Years War. In *The New Cambridge Modern History*, vol. 4: *The Decline of Spain and the Thirty Years War, 1609–48/59*, edited by J. P. Cooper, 306–58. Cambridge: Cambridge University Press.

Berghahn, Volker R. 1993. Resisting the Pax Americana? West German Industry and the United States, 1945–55. In *America and the Shaping of German Society, 1945–1955*, edited by Michael Ermarth, 85–100. Providence, R.I.: Berg.

Bethell, Leslie. 1970. *The Abolition of the Brazilian Slave Trade: Britain, Brazil and the Slave Trade Question, 1807–1869*. Cambridge: Cambridge University Press.

Betts, Raymond. 1991. *France and Decolonization, 1900–1960*. New York: St. Martin's Press.

Biersteker, Thomas J., and Cynthia Weber. 1996. The Social Construction of State Soverignty. In *State Sovereignty as a Social Construct*, edited by Thomas J. Biersteker and Cynthia Weber, 1–20. Cambridge: Cambridge University Press.

Bilder, Richard. 1992. Can Minorities Treaties Work? In *The Protection of Minorities and Human Rights*, edited by Yoram Dinstein and Mala Tabory, 59–82. Dordrecht: Martinus Nijhoff.

Blacker, Coit, and Condoleezza Rice. 1998. Belarus: Flight from Sovereignty. Institute for International Studies, Stanford University, Stanford, Calif. Unpublished manuscript.

Blaisdell, Donald C. 1929. *European Financial Control in the Ottoman Empire: A Study of the Establishment, Activities, and Significance of the Administration of the Ottoman Public Debt.* New York: Columbia University Press.

Bloed, Ariel. 1993. The CSCE and the Protection of National Minorities. In *The UN Minority Rights Declaration*, edited by Alan Phillips and Allan Rosas, 95–101. London: Turku/Abo.

Bradford, Ernle. 1972. *The Shield and the Sword: The Knights of St. John.* London: Hodder and Stoughton.

Braudel, Fernand. 1982. *Civilization and Capitalism, 15th–18th Century.* Vol. 2, *The Wheels of Commerce.* Translated by Siân Reynolds. New York: Harper and Row.

Brewer, John. 1989. *The Sinews of Power: War, Money and the English State, 1688–1783.* New York: Knopf.

Brierly, J. L. 1963. *The Law of Nations: An Introduction to the International Law of Peace.* Edited by Humphrey Waldock. 6th ed. New York: Oxford University Press.

Britannica Online. 1994. Book of the Year: World Affairs: ANDORRA. http://www.eb.com:180/cgi-bin/g?DocF=boy/94/H03210.html [accessed 23 November 1998].

———. 1996. Book of the Year: World Affairs: ANDORRA. http://www.eb.com:180/cgi-bin/g?DocF=boy/96/J03660.html [accessed 23 November 1998].

Broad, Robin. 1988. *Unequal Alliance: The World Bank, the International Monetary Fund, and the Philippines.* Berkeley: University of California Press.

Brownlie, Ian, ed. 1992. *Basic Documents on Human Rights.* 3rd ed. Oxford: Clarendon Press.

Broz, J. Lawrence. 1998. The Origins of Central Banking: Solutions to the Free-Rider Problem. *International Organization* 52: 231–68.

Brunsson, Nils. 1989. *The Organization of Hypocrisy: Talk, Decisions and Actions in Organizations.* Chichester: John Wiley and Sons.

Brzezinski, Zbigniew K. 1967. *The Soviet Bloc: Unity and Conflict.* Cambridge, Mass.: Harvard University Press.

Bull, Hedley. 1977. *The Anarchical Society.* New York: Columbia University Press.

———, ed. 1984. *Intervention in World Politics.* New York: Oxford University Press.

Bull, Hedley, and Adam Watson. 1984. *The Expansion of International Society.* Oxford: Oxford University Press.

Burley, Ann Marie, and Walter Mattli. 1993. Europe before the Court: A Political Theory of Legal Integration. *International Organization* 47: 41–76.

Buzan, Barry. 1993. From International Realism to International Society: Structural Realism and Regime Theory Meet the English School. *International Organization* 47: 328–52.

Cardoso, Fernando Henrique, and Enzo Faletto. 1979. *Dependency and Development in Latin America*. Berkeley: University of California Press.

Cerny, Philip G. 1990. *The Changing Architecture of Politics: Structure, Agency, and the Future of the State*. London: Sage.

Chipman, John. 1989. *French Power in Africa*. Oxford: Basil Blackwell.

Claude, Inis L., Jr. 1955. *National Minorities: An International Problem*. Cambridge, Mass.: Harvard University Press.

Clayton, Anthony. 1994. *The Wars of French Decolonization*. London: Longman.

Cohen, Benjamin J. 1986. *In Whose Interest? International Banking and American Foreign Policy*. New Haven: Yale University Press.

Convention on the Elimination of all Forms of Discrimination against Women. In *Basic Documents on Human Rights*, edited by Ian Brownlie. 3rd ed. Oxford: Clarendon Press, 1992.

Cooper, Richard. 1968. *The Economics of Interdependence*. New York: McGraw-Hill.

Crawford, Beverly. 1996. Explaining Defection from International Cooperation: Germany's Unilateral Recognition of Croatia. *World Politics* 48: 482–521.

Croatia, Republic of. 1992. The Constitutional Law of Human Rights and Freedoms and the Rights of National and Ethnic Communities or Minorities in the Republic of Croatia.

Cross, Colin. 1968. *The Fall of the British Empire, 1918–1968*. New York: Coward-McCann.

Croxton, Derek. 1998. The Peace of Westphalia and the Origins of Sovereignty. Mershon Center, Ohio State University, Columbus, Ohio. Unpublished manuscript.

Dakin, Douglas. 1973. *The Greek Struggle for Independence, 1821–1833*. Berkeley: University of California Press.

Damrosch, Lori. 1993. Changing Conceptions of Intervention in International Law. In *Emerging Norms of Justified Intervention: A Collection of Essays from a Project of the American Academy of Arts and Sciences*, edited by Laura W. Reed and Carl Kaysen, 91–110. Cambridge, Mass.: American Academy of Arts and Sciences.

Darwin, John. 1988. *Britain and Decolonisation: The Retreat from Empire in the Post-War World*. Houndmills, Basingstoke: Macmillan.

D'Attorre, Pier Paolo. 1981. The European Recovery Program in Italy: Research Problems. In *The Role of the United States in the Reconstruction of Italy and West Germany, 1943–1949*, edited by Ekkehart Krippendorff. Berlin: John F. Kennedy Institut für Nordamerikastudien, Freie Universität Berlin.

David, Paul A. 1985. Clio and the Economics of QWERTY. *American Economic Review* 75: 332–37.

Dell, Sidney. 1981. *On Being Grandmotherly: The Evolution of IMF Conditionality.* Essays in International Finance No. 144. Princeton, N.J.: International Finance Section, Department of Economics, Princeton University.

Dessler, David. 1989. What's at Stake in the Agent-Structure Debate? *International Organization* 43: 441–73.

Deudney, Daniel H. 1995. The Philadelphian System: Sovereignty, Arms Control, and Balance of Power in the American States-Union, circa 1787–1861. *International Organization* 49: 191–228.

DiMaggio, Paul J., and Walter W. Powell. 1991. Introduction. In *The New Institutionalism in Organizational Analysis,* edited by Paul J. DiMaggio and Walter W. Powell, 1–40. Chicago: University of Chicago Press.

Donnelly, Jack. 1989. *Universal Human Rights in Theory and Practice.* Ithaca, N.Y.: Cornell University Press.

———. 1992. *International Human Rights.* Boulder, Colo.: Westview.

———. 1995. State Sovereignty and International Intervention: The Case of Human Rights. In *Beyond Westphalia?: State Sovereignty and International Intervention,* edited by Gene M. Lyons and Michael Mastanduno, 115–46. Baltimore: Johns Hopkins University Press.

Dontas, Domna N. 1966. *Greece and the Great Powers, 1863–1875.* Thessalonike: Institute for Balkan Studies.

Doty, Roxanne Lynn. 1996. Sovereignty and the Nation: Constructing the Boundaries of National Identity. In *State Sovereignty as a Social Construct,* edited by Thomas Biersteker and Cynthia Weber, 121–47. Cambridge: Cambridge University Press.

Douglas, Mary. 1986. *How Institutions Think.* Syracuse, N.Y.: Syracuse University Press.

Duignan, Peter, and L. H. Gann. 1994. *The USA and the New Europe, 1945–1993.* Oxford: Blackwell.

Eisenberg, Carolyn. 1993. The Limit of Democracy: U.S. Policy and the Rights of German Labor, 1945–1949. In *America and the Shaping of German Society, 1945–1955,* edited by Michael Ermarth, 60–81. Providence, R.I.: Berg.

Ermarth, Michael. 1993. Introduction. In *America and the Shaping of German Society, 1945–1955,* edited by Michael Ermarth, 1–22. Providence, R.I.: Berg.

Esman, Milton. 1995. A Survey of Interventions. In *International Organizations and Ethnic Conflict,* edited by Milton J. Esman and Shibley Telhami, 21–47. Ithaca, N.Y.: Cornell University Press.

European Community. 1991. *Treaty Provisions for the Convention (Carrington Report).* Brussels, 4 November.

Evans, Peter. 1979. *Dependent Development: The Alliance of Multinational, State, and Local Capital in Brazil.* Berkeley: University of California Press.

Farer, Tom J. 1968. Problems of an International Law of Intervention. *Stanford Journal of International Studies* 3: 20–26.

Fearon, James G. 1995. Rationalist Explanations for War. *International Organization* 49: 379–414.

Feis, Herbert. 1965. *Europe, the World's Banker, 1870–1914: An Account of European Foreign Investment and the Connection of World Finance with Diplomacy before World War I.* New York: W. W. Norton.

Feldstein, Martin S., and Charles Horioka. 1980. Domestic Savings and International Capital Flows. *Economic Journal* 90: 314–29.

Fichter, Michael. 1981. U.S. Policy on Trade Unions in Occupied Germany, 1945–48. In *The Role of the United States in the Reconstruction of Italy and West Germany, 1943–1949*, edited by Ekkehart Krippendorff, 105–19. Berlin: John F. Kennedy Institut für Nordamerikastudien, Freie Universität Berlin.

Finnemore, Martha. 1991. Science, the State, and International Society. Ph.D. diss., Department of Political Science, Stanford University.

———. 1996a. *National Interests in International Society.* Ithaca, N.Y.: Cornell University Press.

———. 1996b. Studies of the Modern World-System. *International Organization* 50: 325–47.

Fischer, Markus. 1992. Feudal Europe, 800–1300: Communal Discourse and Conflictual Practices. *International Organization* 46: 427–66.

Forsythe, David P. 1983. *Human Rights and World Politics.* Lincoln: University of Nebraska Press.

———. 1989. *Human Rights and World Politics.*, 2nd ed. Lincoln: University of Nebraska Press.

Fouques-Duparc, Jacques. 1922. *La protection des minorités de race, de langue, et de religion: Étude de droit des gens.* Paris: Librairie Dalloz.

Fowler, Michael Ross, and Julie Marie Bunck. 1995. *Law, Power, and the Sovereign State: The Evolution and Application of the Concept of Sovereignty.* University Park: Pennsylvania State University Press.

Fox, Edward W. 1971. *History in Geographic Perspective: The Other France.* New York: Norton.

Frazer, Jendayi E. 1994. Sustaining Civilian Control: Armed Counterweights in Regime Stability in Africa. Ph.D. diss., Department of Political Science, Stanford University.

Gagliardo, John. 1991. *Germany under the Old Regime, 1600–1790.* London: Longman.

Gallagher, John, and Ronald Edward Robinson, with Alice Denny. 1961. *Africa and the Victorians: The Climax of Imperialism in the Dark Continent.* New York: St. Martin's Press.

Garces, Laura. 1995. The League of Nation's Predicament in Southeastern Europe. Woodrow Wilson and the League of Nations, Part 2. *World Affairs* 158.

Garrett, Geoffrey. 1998. Global Markets and National Politics: Collision Course or Virtuous Cycle. *International Organization* 52: 787–824.

Garrett, Geoffrey, and George Tsebelis. 1996. An Institutional Critique of Intergovernmentalism. *International Organization* 50: 269–99.

Georgescu, Vlad. 1984. *The Romanians: A History.* Columbus: Ohio University Press.

Gilpin, Robert. 1987. *The Political Economy of International Relations.* Princeton, N.J.: Princeton University Press.

Gottlieb, Gideon. 1993. *Nation against State: A New Approach to Ethnic Conflicts and the Decline of Sovereignty.* New York: Council on Foreign Relations Press.

Grieco, Joseph M. 1988. Anarchy and the Limits of Cooperation: A Realist Critique of the Newest Liberal Institutionalism. *International Organization*. 42: 485–507.

———. 1990. *Cooperation among Nations: Europe, America, and Non-Tariff Barriers to Trade*. Ithaca, N.Y.: Cornell University Press.

Group of Lisbon. 1995. *Limits to Competition*. Cambridge: MIT Press.

Gutman, Yisrael, 1989. *The Jews of Poland between Two World Wars*. Hanover, N.H.: University Press of New England for Brandeis University Press.

Hailbronner, Kay. 1992. The Legal Status of Population Groups in a Multinational State under Public International Law. In *The Protection of Minorities and Human Rights*, edited by Yoram Dinstein and Mala Tabory, 117–44. Dordrecht: Martinus Nijhoff.

Hall, Peter A., ed. 1989. *The Political Power of Economic Ideas: Keynesianism across Nations*. Princeton, N.J.: Princeton University Press.

Hall, Rodney Bruce. 1997. Moral Authority as a Power Resource. *International Organization* 51: 591–622.

Hargreaves, John D. 1979. *The End of Colonial Rule in West Africa: Essays in Contemporary History*. London: Macmillan.

———. 1988. *Decolonization in Africa*. London: Longman.

Hartz, Louis. 1955. *The Liberal Tradition in America: An Interpretation of American Political Thought since the Revolution*. New York: Harcourt Brace.

Hehir, J. Brian. 1995. Intervention: From Theories to Cases. *Ethics and International Affairs* 9: 1–14.

Herbst, Jeffrey. 1990. The Structural Adjustment of Politics in Africa. *World Development* 18: 949–58.

Hinsley, F. H. 1986. *Sovereignty*. 2nd ed. Cambridge: Cambridge University Press.

Hoffmann, Stanley. 1984. The Problem of Intervention. In *Intervention in World Politics*, edited by Hedley Bull, 7–28. Oxford: Clarendon Press.

Holborn, Hajo. 1959. *A History of Modern Germany: The Reformation*. New York: Knopf.

Holland, R. F. 1985. *European Decolonization, 1918–1981: An Introductory Survey*. New York: St. Martin's Press.

Holtfrerich, Carl-Ludwig. 1995. The Deutsche Bank, 1945–1957: War, Military Rule and Reconstruction. In *The Deutsche Bank: 1970–1995*, edited by Lothar Gall et al., 357–521. London: Weidenfeld and Nicolson.

Hufbauer, Gary C., Jeffrey J. Schott, and Kimberly A. Elliot. 1990. *Economic Sanctions Reconsidered: History and Current Policy*. 2nd ed. Washington, D.C.: Institute for International Economics.

Hughes, Michael. 1992. *Early Modern Germany, 1477–1806*. London: Macmillan.

International Monetary Fund, Fiscal Affairs Department. 1986. *Fund Supported Programs, Fiscal Policy, and Income Distribution*. Occasional Paper No. 46. Washington, D.C.: International Monetary Fund.

Jackson, Robert H. 1990. *Quasi-States: Sovereignty, International Relations and the Third World*. Cambridge: Cambridge University Press.

Jackson, Robert H., and Alan James. 1993. The Character of Independent Statehood. In *States in a Changing World*, edited by Robert Jackson and Alan James, 3–25. Oxford: Clarendon Press.

Jackson, Robert H., and C. G. Rosberg. 1982. Why Africa's Weak States Persist: The Empirical and the Juridical in Statehood. *World Politics* 35: 1–24.

Janowsky, Oscar Isaiah. 1945. *Nationalities and National Minorities.* New York: Macmillan.

Jelavich, Charles, and Barbara Jelavich. 1977. *The Establishment of the Balkan National States.* Seattle: University of Washington Press.

Jepperson, Ronald L. 1991. Institutions, Institutional Effects, and Institutionalism. In *The New Institutionalism in Organizational Analysis*, edited by Paul J. DiMaggio and Walter W. Powell, 143–63. Chicago: University of Chicago Press.

Jepperson, Ronald L., and John W. Meyer. 1991. The Public Order and the Construction of Formal Organizations. In *The New Institutionalism in Organizational Analysis*, edited by Paul J. DiMaggio and Walter W. Powell, 204–31. Chicago: University of Chicago Press.

Jonas, Manfred. 1984. *The United States and Germany: A Diplomatic History.* Ithaca, N.Y.: Cornell University Press.

Jones, Christopher D. 1984. National Armies and National Sovereignty. In *The Warsaw Pact: Alliance in Transition?*, edited by David Holloway and Jane M. O. Sharp, 87–110. Ithaca, N.Y.: Cornell University Press.

Jones, Dorothy V. 1991. *Code of Peace: Ethics and Security in the World of the Warlord States.* Chicago: University of Chicago Press.

Jones, Robert A. 1990. *The Soviet Concept of "Limited Sovereignty" from Lenin to Gorbachev.* London: Macmillan.

Jordan, Wilbur K. 1932. *The Development of Religious Toleration in England from the Beginning of the English Reformation to the Death of Queen Elizabeth.* London: George Allen and Unwin.

Jouvenel, Bertrand de. 1957. *Sovereignty: An Inquiry into the Political Good.* Translated by J. F. Huntington. Chicago: University of Chicago Press.

Katz, Michael L., and Carl Shapiro. 1994. Systems Competition and Network Effects. *Journal of Economic Perspectives* 8: 93–116.

Katzenstein, Peter J. 1993. Coping with Terrorism: Norms and Internal Security in Germany and Japan. In *Ideas and Foreign Policy*, edited by Judith Goldstein and Robert O. Keohane, 265–95. Ithaca, N.Y.: Cornell University Press.

———. 1996. Introduction: Alternative Perspectives on National Security. In *The Culture of National Security*, edited by Peter J. Katzenstein 1–32. New York: Columbia University Press.

Katzenstein, Peter J., and Nobuo Okawara. 1993. Japan's National Security: Structures, Norms, and Policies. *International Security* 17: 84–119.

Keohane, Robert O. 1984. *After Hegemony: Cooperation and Discord in the World Political Economy.* Princeton: Princeton University Press.

———. 1995. Hobbes's Dilemma and Institutional Change in World Politics: Sovereignty in International Society. In *Whose World Order? Uneven Globalization and the End of the Cold War*, edited by Hans-Henrik Holm and Georg Sorensen, 165–86. Boulder, Colo.: Westview.

Kinsbruner, Jay. 1994. *Independence in Spanish America.* Albuquerque: University of New Mexico Press.

Kissinger, Henry. 1957. *A World Restored: Metternich, Castlereagh and the Problems of Peace, 1812–22.* London: Weidenfeld and Nicholson.

Knapp, Manfred. 1981. U.S. Economic Aid and the Reconstruction of West Germany: Political and Economic Implications of the European Recovery Program. In *The Role of the United States in the Reconstruction of Italy and West Germany, 1943–1949*, edited by Ekkehart Krippendorff, 40–55. Berlin: John F. Kennedy Institut für Nordamerikastudien, Freie Universität Berlin.

Koslowski, Rey, and Friedrich V. Kratochwil, 1994. Understanding Change in International Politics: The Soviet Empire's Demise and the International System. *International Organization* 48: 215–47.

Krasner, Stephen D. 1991. Global Communications and National Power: Life on the Pareto Frontier. *World Politics* 43: 336–66.

Kratochwil, Friedrich V. 1989. *Rules, Norms, and Decisions: On the Conditions of Practical and Legal Reasoning in International Relations and Domestic Affairs.* Cambridge: Cambridge University Press.

Kreile, Michael. 1996. *The Influence of Domestic Political and Economic Actors on Germany's European Policy.* Berlin: Institut für Politikwissenschaft, Humboldt Universität zu Berlin.

Kreps, David. 1990. Corporate Culture. In *Perspectives on Positive Political Economy*, edited by James Alt and Kenneth Shepsle, 90–143. Cambridge: Cambridge University Press.

LaFeber, Walter. 1983. *Inevitable Revolutions: The United States in Central America.* New York: Norton.

Lake, David A. 1996. Anarchy, Hierarchy, and the Variety of International Relations. *International Organization* 50: 1–33.

———. 1999. *Entangling Relations: American Foreign Policy in Its Century.* Princeton, N.J.: Princeton University Press.

Landes, David S. 1979. *Bankers and Pashas: International Finance and Economic Imperialism in Egypt.* Cambridge, Mass.: Harvard University Press.

Langer, William L. 1964. *European Alliances and Alignments, 1871–1890.* 2nd ed. New York: Vintage Books.

Langley, Lester D. 1989. *The United States and the Caribbean in the Twentieth Century.* 4th ed. Athens: University of Georgia Press.

Laponce, J. A. 1960. *The Protection of Minorities.* Berkeley: University of California Press.

Lehmbruch, Gerhard. 1997. From State Authority to Network State: The German State in Developmental Perspective. In *State and Administration in Japan and Germany: A Comparative Perspective on Continuity and Change*, edited by Michio Muramatsu and Frieder Naschold, 39–62. Berlin: Walter de Gruyter.

Lerner, N. 1993. The Evolution of Minority Rights in International Law. In *Peoples and Minorities in International Law*, edited by Catherine Brolmann, Rene Lefeber, and Marjoleine Zieck, 77–102. Dordrecht: Martinus Nijhoff.

Levandis, John A. 1944. *The Greek Foreign Debt and the Great Powers, 1821–1898.* New York: Columbia University Press.

Lewis, Bernard. 1992. Muslims, Christians, and Jews: The Dream of Coexistence. *New York Review of Books* 39 (26 March): 48–52.

———. 1995. *The Middle East: A Brief History of the Last 2,000 Years.* New York: Scribners.

Liebowitz, Stanley, and Stephen E. Margolis. 1990. The Fable of the Keys. *Journal of Law and Economics* 33: 1–25.

———. 1995. Policy and Path Dependence: From QWERTY to Windows 95. *Regulation*, 18: 33–41.

Little, David. 1993. Religion-Catalyst or Impediment to International Law? The Case of Hugo Grotius. *Proceedings of the 87th Annual Meeting of the American Society of International Law*, 322–27. Washington, D.C., 31 March–3 April.

Lindert, Peter H., and Peter J. Morton. 1989. How Sovereign Lending Has Worked. In *Developing Country Debt and Economic Performance*, edited by Jeffrey D. Sachs, 39–106. Chicago: University of Chicago Press.

Lumsdaine, David. 1993. *Moral Vision in International Politics: The Foreign Aid Regime, 1949–89*. Princeton, N.J.: Princeton University Press.

Lynch, John. 1973. *The Spanish American Revolutions, 1808–1826*. New York: Norton.

Macartney, Carlile Aylmer. 1934. *National States and National Minorities*. Oxford: Oxford University Press.

Mackintosh, Malcolm. 1984. The Warsaw Treaty Organization: A History. In *The Warsaw Pact: Alliance in Transition?*, edited by David Holloway and Jane M. O. Sharp, 41–58. Ithaca, N.Y.: Cornell University Press.

Mansergh, Nicholas. 1969. *The Commonwealth Experience*. New York: Praeger.

Mansfield, Peter. 1971. *The British in Egypt*. New York: Holt, Rinehart and Winston.

———. 1991. *A History of the Middle East*. New York: Viking.

March, James, with the assistance of Chip Heath. 1994. *A Primer on Decision Making: How Decisions Happen*. New York: Free Press.

March, James G., and Johan Olsen. 1989. *Rediscovering Institutions: The Organizational Basis of Politics*. New York: Free Press.

———. 1998. The Institutional Dynamics of International Political Orders. *International Organization* 52: 943-969.

Marer, Paul. 1984. Intrabloc Economic Relations and Prospects. In *The Warsaw Pact: Alliance in Transition?*, edited by David Holloway and Jane M. O. Sharp, 215–37. Ithaca, N.Y.: Cornell University Press.

Marichal, Carlos. 1989. *A Century of Debt Crises in Latin America: From Independence to the Great Depression, 1820–1930*. Princeton, N.J.: Princeton University Press.

Marlowe, John. 1975. *Spoiling the Egyptians*. New York, St. Martin's Press.

Martin, Lisa L. 1992. *Coercive Cooperation: Explaining Multilateral Economic Sanctions*. Princeton, N.J.: Princeton University Press.

———. 1995. Democratic Commitments: Legislatures and International Cooperation. Center for International Affairs, Harvard University, Cambridge, Mass. Unpublished manuscript.

Mathews, Jessica Tuchman. 1997. Power Shift. *Foreign Affairs* 76: 50–66.

Mattingly, Garrett. 1955. *Renaissance Diplomacy*. Boston: Houghton-Mifflin.

McIntyre, W. David. 1977. *The Commonwealth of Nations: Origins and Impact, 1869–1971*. Minneapolis: University of Minnesota Press.

McNeill, W. H. 1982. *The Pursuit of Power*. Chicago: University of Chicago Press.

Meyer, John W., John Boli, and George M. Thomas. 1987. Ontology and Rationalization in the Western Cultural Account. In *Institutional Structure: Constituting State, Society, and the Individual*, edited by George M. Thomas, John W. Meyer, Francisco O. Ramirez, and John Boli, 12–37. Newbury Park, Calif.: Sage.

Meyer, John W., John Boli, George M. Thomas, and Francisco O. Ramirez. 1997. World Society and the Nation-State. *American Journal of Sociology*, 103: 144–81.

Meyer, John W., and Brian Rowan. 1991. Institutionalized Organizations: Formal Structure in Myth and Ceremony. In *The New Institutionalism in Organizational Analysis*, edited by Paul J. DiMaggio and Walter W. Powell, 41–62. Chicago: University of Chicago Press.

Miller, James Edward. 1986. *The United States and Italy, 1940–1950: The Politics and Diplomacy of Stabilization*. Chapel Hill: University of North Carolina Press.

Miller, William. 1936. *The Ottoman Empire and Its Successors, 1801–1927*. Cambridge: Cambridge University Press.

Moe, Terry M. 1987. Interests, Institutions, and Positive Theory: The Politics of the NLRB. In *Studies in American Political Development*, vol. 2, edited by Karen Orren and Stephen Skowronek, 236–99. New Haven: Yale University Press.

Moravcsik, Andrew. 1994. Lessons from the European Human Rights Regime. In *Inter-American Dialogue, Advancing Democracy and Human Rights in the Americas: What Role of the OAS?*, 35–58. Washington, D.C.: Inter American Dialogue.

———. 1998. Explaining the Emergence of Human Rights Regimes: Liberal Democracy and Political Uncertainty in Postwar Europe. Weatherhead Center for International Affairs Working Paper. Harvard University, Cambridge, Mass.

Morgenthau, Hans. 1948. *Politics among Nations: The Struggle for Power and Peace*. New York: Knopf.

Munro, Dana Gardner. 1964. *Intervention and Dollar Diplomacy in the Caribbean, 1900–1921*. Princeton, N.J.: Princeton University Press.

Murphy, Alexander B. 1996. The Sovereign State System as Political-Territorial Ideal: Historical and Contemporary Considerations. In *State Sovereignty as a Social Construct*, edited by Thomas Biersteker and Cynthia Weber, 81–120. Cambridge: Cambridge University Press.

Nelson, Richard R., and Sidney G. Winter. 1982. *An Evolutionary Theory of Economic Change*. Cambridge, Mass.: Harvard University Press.

Nevo, Joseph. 1996. *King Abdallah and Palestine: A Territorial Ambition*. London: Macmillan.

Nicolaides, Kalypso. 1996. *Mutual Recognition of Regulatory Regimes: Some Lessons and Prospects, Regulatory Reform and International Market Openness*. Paris: OECD. Reprinted as part of the Jean Monnet Paper Series, Harvard Law School, Fall 1997.

Noel, Alain, and Jean-Philippe Therien. 1995. From Domestic to International Justice: The Welfare State and Foreign Aid. *International Organization* 49: 523–53.

North, Douglass C. 1990. *Institutions, Institutional Change, and Economic Performance*. Cambridge: Cambridge University Press.

North, Douglass C., and Barry R. Weingast. 1989. Constitutions and Commitment: The Evolution of Institutions Governing Public Choice in Seventeenth-Century England. *Journal of Economic History* 49: 803.

Obstfeld, M., and A. M. Taylor. 1997. *The Great Depressions as a Watershed: International Capital Mobility over the Long Run.* Working Paper No. 5960. Cambridge, Mass.: National Bureau of Economic Research.

Onuf, Nicholas Greenwood. 1991. Sovereignty: Outline of a Conceptual History. *Alternatives* 16: 425–46.

Oppenheim, L. 1992. *Oppenheim's International Law.* Edited by Robert Jennings and Arthur Watts. 9th ed. Harlow, Essex: Longman.

Osiander, Andreas. 1994. *The States System of Europe, 1640–1990: Peacemaking and the Conditions of International Stability.* Oxford: Oxford University Press.

Otetea, Andrei, ed. 1985. *A Concise History of Romania.* London: Robert Hale.

Owen, Roger. 1981. *The Middle East in the World Economy, 1800–1914.* Cambridge: Cambridge University Press.

Pamuk, Sevket. 1987. *The Ottoman Empire and European Capitalism, 1820–1913.* Cambridge: Cambridge University Press.

Paul, David W. 1981. *Czechoslovakia: Profile of a Socialist Republic at the Crossroads of Europe.* Boulder, Colo.: Westview.

Pauly, Louis W., and Simon Reich. 1997. National Structures and Multinational Corporate Behavior: Enduring Differences in the Age of Globalization. *International Organization* 51: 1–30.

Pearson, Raymond. 1983. *National Minorities in Eastern Europe, 1848–1945.* New York: St. Martin's Press.

Peterson, Edward N. 1977. *The American Occupation of Germany: Retreat to Victory.* Detroit: Wayne State University Press.

Peterson, M. J. 1982. Political Use of Recognition: The Influence of the International System. *World Politics* 34: 324–352.

———. 1997. *Recognition of Governments: Legal Doctrine and State Practice.* New York: St. Martin's Press.

Platias, Athanassios Georgios. 1986. High Politics in Small Countries: An Inquiry into the Security Policies of Greece, Israel, and Sweden. Ph.D. diss. Department of Government, Cornell University.

Poggiolini, Ilaria. 1994. Italy. In *The Origins of the Cold War in Europe: International Perspectives,* edited by David Reynolds, 121–42. New Haven: Yale University Press.

Powell, Walter W. 1991. Expanding the Scope of Institutional Analysis. In *The New Institutionalism in Organizational Analysis,* edited by Paul J. DiMaggio and Walter W. Powell, 183–203. Chicago: University of Chicago Press.

Ray, James Lee. 1989. The Abolition of Slavery and the End of International War. *International Organization* 43: 405–39.

Rice, Condoleezza. 1984. *The Soviet Union and the Czechoslovak Army, 1948–1983: Uncertain Allegiance.* Princeton, N.J.: Princeton University Press.

Riley, James C. 1980. *International Government Finance and the Amsterdam Capital Market, 1740–1815.* Cambridge: Cambridge University Press.

Robinson, Jacob, Oscar Karbach, Max M. Laserson, Nehemiah Robinson, and Marc Vichniak. 1943. *Were the Minorities Treaties a Failure?* New York: Institute of Jewish Affairs of the American Jewish Congress and the World Jewish Congress.

Rodriguez, Jaime E. 1998. *The Independence of Spanish America*. Cambridge: Cambridge University Press.

Rogers, J. M., and R. M. Ward. 1988. *Süleyman the Magnificent*. London. British Museum.

Rosenau, James 1990. *Turbulence in World Politics: A Theory of Change and Continuity*. Princeton, N.J.: Princeton University Press.

Ruggie, John Gerard. 1993. Territoriality and Beyond: Problematizing Modernity in International Relations. *International Organization* 47: 139–74.

———. 1998. What Makes the World Hang Together? Neo-Utilitarianism and the Social Constructivist Challenge. *International Organization* 52: 855–885.

Ruggie, Mary. 1984. *The State and Working Women: A Comparative Study of Britain and Sweden*. Princeton, N.J.: Princeton University Press.

Schadler, Susan, Franek Rozwadowski, Siddharth Tiwari, and David O. Robinson. 1993. *Economic Adjustment in Low-Income Countries: Experience under the Enhanced Structural Adjustment Facility*. Occasional Paper No. 106. Washington, D.C.: International Monetary Fund.

Schultz, Kenneth A. 1996. Domestic Political Competition and Bargaining in International Crises. Ph.D. diss., Department of Political Science, Stanford University.

Schwartz, Thomas A. 1993. Reeducation and Democracy: The Policies of the United States High Commission in Germany. In *America and the Shaping of German Society, 1945–1955*, edited by Michael Ermarth, 35–46. Providence, R.I.: Berg.

Schwartzberg, Stephen. 1988. The Lion and the Phoenix. *Journal of Middle Eastern Studies* 24: 139–77, 287–311.

Scott, W. Richard. 1995. *Institutions and Organizations*. Thousand Oaks, Calif.: Sage.

Scribner, R. W. 1990. Politics and the Institutionalization of Reform in Germany. In *The New Cambridge Modern History*, vol. 2, The Reformation, 1520–1559, edited by G. R. Elton, 179–98. 2nd ed. Cambridge: Cambridge University Press.

Searle, John R. 1995. *The Construction of Social Reality*. New York: Free Press.

Sharp, Alan. 1979. Britain and the Protection of Minorities at the Paris Peace Conference, 1919. In *Minorities in History*, edited by A. C. Hepburn, 170–88. New York: St. Martin's Press.

———. 1991. *The Versailles Settlement: Peacemaking in Paris, 1919*. New York: St. Martin's Press.

Sharp, Jane M. O. 1984. Security through Detente and Arms Control. In *The Warsaw Pact: Alliance in Transition?*, edited by David Holloway and Jane M. O. Sharp, 161–94. Ithaca, N.Y.: Cornell University Press.

Shepsle, Kenneth A. 1986. Institutional Equilibrium and Equilibrium Institutions. In *Political Science: The Science of Politics*, edited by Herbert F. Weisberg, 51–80. New York: Agathon Press.

Shue, Henry. 1997. Eroding Sovereignty: The Advance of Principle. In *The Morality of Nationalism*, edited by Robert McKim and Jeff McMahan, 340–59. New York: Oxford University Press.

Sigler, Jay A. 1983. *Minority Rights: A Comparative Perspective*. Westport, Conn.: Greenwood Press.

Sikkink, Kathryn. 1993. The Power of Principled Ideas: Human Rights Policies in the United States and Western Europe. In *Ideas and Foreign Policy*, edited by Judith Goldstein and Robert O. Keohane, 139–70. Ithaca, N.Y.: Cornell University Press.

Sire, H.J.A. 1994. *The Knights of Malta*. New Haven: Yale University Press.

Skidmore, Thomas E., and Peter H. Smith. 1989. *Modern Latin America*. New York: Oxford University Press.

Skilling, H. Gordon. 1966. *The Governments of Communist East Europe*. New York: Thomas Y. Crowell.

Skinner, Quentin. 1978. *The Foundations of Modern Political Thought*, vol. 2, *The Age of Reformation*. Cambridge: Cambridge University Press.

Snidal, Duncan. 1991. International Cooperation among Relative Gains Maximizers. *International Studies Quarterly* 35: 387–403.

Soysal, Yasemin Nuhoglu. 1994. *Limits of Citizenship: Migrants and Postnational Membership in Europe*. Chicago: University of Chicago Press.

Spruyt, Hendrik. 1994. *The Sovereign State and Its Competitors*. Princeton, N.J.: Princeton University Press.

St. Clair, William. 1972. *That Greece Might Still Be Free: The Philhellenes in the War of Independence*. London: Oxford University Press.

Stavrianos, Leften Stavros. 1958. *The Balkans since 1453*. New York: Rinehart.

Stein, Arthur A. 1990. *Why Nations Cooperate: Circumstance and Choice in International Relations*. Ithaca, N.Y.: Cornell University Press.

Stone, Julius. 1933. *Regional Guarantees of Minority Rights*. New York: Macmillan.

Strang, David. 1991. Anomaly and Commonplace in European Political Expansion: Realist and Institutional Accounts. *International Organization* 45: 143–62.

——. 1996. Contested Sovereignty: The Social Constuction of Colonial Imperialism. In *State Sovereignty as a Social Construct*, edited by Thomas Biersteker and Cynthia Weber, 22–49. Cambridge: Cambridge University Press.

Strang, David, and Patricia Mei Yin Chang. 1993. The International Labor Organization and the Welfare State: Institutional Effects on National Welfare Spending, 1960–80. *International Organization* 47: 235–62.

Strayer, Joseph R. 1970. *On the Medieval Origins of the Modern State*. Princeton, N.J.: Princeton University Press.

Sugden, Robert. 1989. Spontaneous Order. *Journal of Economic Perspectives* 3: 85–97.

Swidler, Ann. 1986. Culture in Action: Symbols and Strategies. *American Journal of Sociology* 51: 273–286.

Temperley, H. 1966. *The Foreign Policy of Canning, 1822–27*. Hamden, Conn.: Archon Books.

Tetreault, Mary Ann. 1991. Autonomy, Necessity, and the Small State: Ruling Kuwait in the Twentieth Century. *International Organization* 45: 565–91.

Thomas, Ann, and A. J. Thomas. 1956. *Non Intervention: The Law and Its Import in the Americas.* Dallas: Southern Methodist University Press.

Thomas, Daniel C. Forthcoming. *The Power of International Norms: Human Rights, the Helsinki Accords and the Demise of Communism.* Princeton, N.J.: Princeton University Press.

Thomson, Janice E. 1995. State Sovereignty in International Relations: Bridging the Gap between Theory and Empirical Research. *International Studies Quarterly* 39: 213–33.

Thomson, Janice E., and Stephen D. Krasner. 1989. Global Transactions and the Consolidation of Sovereignty. In *Global Changes and Theoretical Challenges: Approaches to World Politics for the 1990s*, edited by E. O. Czempiel and J. N. Rosenau, 195–219. Lexington, Mass.: D.C. Heath.

Thornberry, Patrick. 1993. The UN Declaration on the Rights of Persons Belonging to National or Ethnic, Religious and Linguistic Minorities: Background, Analysis and Observations. In *The UN Minority Rights Declaration*, edited by Alan Phillips and Allan Rosas, 11–72. London: Turku/Abo.

Tilly, Charles. 1990a. *Coercion, Capital, and European States, AD 990–1990.* Cambridge, Mass.: Basil Blackwell.

———. 1990b. *The Comparative Study of State Formation.* Working Paper No. 96. New York: Center for Studies of Social Change, New School for Social Research.

Trachtenberg, Marc. 1993. Intervention in Historical Perspective. In *Emerging Norms of Justified Intervention: A Collection of Essays from a Project of the American Academy of Arts and Sciences*, edited by Laura W. Reed and Carl Kaysen, 15–36. Cambridge, Mass.: American Academy of Arts and Sciences.

Treaty of Berlin. 13 July 1878. In *Major Peace Treaties of Modern History, 1648–1967*, edited by Fred L. Israel, 2:975–97. New York: McGraw Hill, 1967.

Treaty of Münster. 24 October 1648. In *Major Peace Treaties of Modern History, 1648–1967*, edited by Fred L. Israel, 1:7–49. New York: McGraw Hill, 1967.

Treaty of Osnabrück, 1648. In *The Consolidated Treaty Series*, vol. 1, *1648–1649*, edited by Clive Parry, 198–269. Dobbs Ferry, N.Y.: Oceana, 1969.

Treaty of Paris. 30 March 1856. In *Major Peace Treaties of Modern History, 1648–1967*, edited by Fred L. Israel, 2:947–57. New York: McGraw Hill, 1967.

Uganda. 1998. Letter of Intent. October 28. http://www.imf.org/external/np/loi/102898.htm.

United Kingdom, Foreign Office. 1834, 1836. *British and Foreign State Papers.* Vol. 19, *1831–32.* Vol. 20, *1832–33.* London: James Ridgway and Sons.

United Nations. 1945 *Charter of the United Nations.* New York.

United Nations. 1948. Universal Declaration of Human Rights. New York.

———. 1987. *Human Rights: Status of International Instruments as of 1 September 1987.* New York.

———. 1994. *Human Rights: International Instruments: Chart of Ratifications as of 31 December 1993.* New York.

United States, Congress. 1979. Taiwan Relations Act. Public Law 96-8. 96th Congress. Washington, D.C.

United States, Department of State. 1995. *The Bosnia Agreement*, Annex 6, December. Washington, D.C.

———. *Foreign Relations of the United States* [FRUS], various years. Washington, D.C.

Vattel, Emer de. 1852. *The Law of Nations; or, Principles of the Law of Nature, applied to the Conduct and Affairs of Nations and Sovereigns*. From the new edition Translated by Joseph Chitty. Philadelphia: T. & J. W. Johnson, Law Booksellers.

Vincent, R. J. 1986. *Human Rights and International Relations*. New York: Cambridge University Press.

Wallerstein, Immauel. 1974. The Rise and Future Demise of the World Capitalist System: Concepts for Comparative Analysis. *Comparative Studies in Society and History* 16: 387–415.

Waltz, Kenneth. 1979. *Theory of International Politics*. Reading, Mass.: Addison-Wesley.

Watson, Adam. 1992. *The Evolution of International Society: A Comparative Historical Analysis*. London: Routledge.

Watson, J. B., 1971. *Empire to Commonwealth, 1919 to 1970*. London: J. M. Dent and Sons.

Weber, Cynthia and Thomas J. Biersteker. 1996. Reconstructing the Analysis of Sovereignty: Concluding Reflections and Directions for Future Research. In *State Sovereignty as a Social Construct*, edited by Thomas J. Biersteker and Cynthia Weber, 278–86. Cambridge: Cambridge University Press.

Weiler, Joseph H. H. 1991. The Transformation of Europe. *Yale Law Journal* 100: 2403–83.

Weingast, Barry R. 1997. The Political Foundations of Democracy and the Rule of Law. *American Political Science Review* 91: 245–64.

Wendt, Alexander. 1987. The Agent-Structure Problem in International Relations Theory. *International Organization* 41: 336–70.

———. 1992. Anarchy Is What States Make of It: The Social Construction of State Politics. *International Organization* 46: 391–425.

———. 1994. Collective Identity Formation and the International State. *American Political Science Review* 88: 384–97.

Wendt, Alexander, and Daniel Friedheim. 1996. Hierarchy under Anarchy: Informal Empire and the East German State. In *State Sovereignty as a Social Construct*, edited by Thomas J. Biersteker and Cynthia Weber, 240–72. Cambridge: Cambridge University Press.

Wight, Martin. 1968. "Western Values in International Relations." In *Diplomatic Investigations: Essays in the Theory of International Politics*, edited by Herbert Butterfield and Martin Wight, 89–131. Cambridge, Mass.: Harvard University Press.

Williamson, Oliver E. 1975. *Markets and Hierarchies, Analysis and Antitrust Implications*. New York: Free Press.

Williamson, Jeffrey 1996. *Globalization and the Labor Market: Using History to Inform Policy*. Milan: Lezioni Raffaele Mattioli, Banca Commerciale Italiana, Unversita' Commerciale Luigi Bocconi.

Wilson, Mary C. 1987. *King Abdullah, Britain and the Making of Jordan*. Cambridge: Cambridge University Press.

Windsor, Philip. 1984. Superpower Intervention. In *Intervention in World Politics*, edited by Hedley Bull, 45–65. Oxford: Clarendon Press.

Woller, Hans. 1993. Germany in Transition from Stalingrad (1943) to Currency Reform (1948). In *America and the Shaping of German Society, 1945–1955*, edited by Michael Ermarth, 23–34. Providence, R.I.: Berg.

Woodward, Susan L. 1995. *Balkan Tragedy: Chaos and Dissolution after the Cold War*. Washington, D.C.: Brookings Institution.

World Bank. 1995. *World Data*. CD-ROM. Washington, D.C.: World Bank.

———. 1997. *World Development Report, 1997: The State in a Changing World*. Washington, D.C.

Wriston, Walter. 1997. Bits, Bytes, and Diplomacy. *Foreign Affairs*. 76: 172–82.

Zegart, Amy Beth. 1996. In Whose Interest? The Making of American National Security Agencies. Ph.D. diss., Department of Political Science, Stanford University.

Index